❦ ❦ ❦ ❦ ❦ ❦ ❦ ❦ ❦ ❦ ❦ ❦ ❦

# Developing Effective Student Services Programs

*Systematic Approaches for Practitioners*

❦ ❦ ❦ ❦ ❦ ❦ ❦ ❦ ❦ ❦ ❦ ❦

*Margaret J. Barr*
*Lou A. Keating*
*and Associates*

# Developing Effective Student Services Programs

**Jossey-Bass Publishers**

San Francisco • Washington • London • 1985

DEVELOPING EFFECTIVE STUDENT SERVICES PROGRAMS
*Systematic Approaches for Practitioners*
by Margaret J. Barr, Lou A. Keating, and Associates

Copyright © 1985 by: Jossey-Bass Inc., Publishers
433 California Street
San Francisco, California 94104
&
Jossey-Bass Limited
28 Banner Street
London EC1Y 8QE

Library of Congress Cataloging in Publication Data

Barr, Margaret J.
Developing effective student services programs.

(The Jossey-Bass higher education series)
Includes bibliographies and index.
1. Personnel service in higher education—Planning—Ad-
dresses, essays, lectures.  2. College student development
programs—Planning—Addresses, essays, lectures.
I. Keating, Lou Ann. II. Title. III. Series.
LB2343.B32   1985      378'.194      84-47978
ISBN 0-87589-610-3

Manufactured in the United States of America

The paper in this book meets the guidelines for
permanence and durability of the Committee on
Production Guidelines for Book Longevity of the
Council on Library Resources.

JACKET DESIGN BY WILLI BAUM

FIRST EDITION

*Code 8505*

ℐℰ ℐℰ ℐℰ ℐℰ ℐℰ ℐℰ ℐℰ ℐℰ ℐℰ ℐℰ ℐℰ ℐℰ ℐℰ

# The Jossey-Bass Higher Education Series

Consulting Editors
Student Services
and
Counseling Psychology

Ursula Delworth
University of Iowa

Gary R. Hanson
University of Texas, Austin

❦ ❦ ❦ ❦ ❦ ❦ ❦ ❦ ❦ ❦ ❦ ❦ ❦

# Preface

In almost every institution of higher education in the country, student services professionals are at work developing, implementing, and maintaining programs for students—activities designed to facilitate student development or to provide an essential institutional service, such as housing or financial aid. However, little attention is paid to the process of program development. Apparently, student services professionals are expected to know how to conduct programs, or each student services subfunction is considered so unique that staff members must devote themselves only to one—for instance, to housing or orientation or admissions programs. The key elements in program development—elements that can be learned and practiced regardless of the specific responsibility of the professional—are rarely if ever considered.

The three key elements of successful student services programs are the context, the goal, and the plan. The context for student services programs is the specific institution of higher education and the larger sociopolitical environment that affects the institution. The goals are the statement of what will be accomplished through the student services program and the ways the program will facilitate student development. The plan is the blueprint for program development and delineates specific methods, time frames, and resources necessary to meet program goals within the context of the institution.

Successful student services professionals must understand these three key elements and be able to apply that understanding in their specific areas of responsibility. We believe that lack of understanding and knowledge about the context, the goal, or the plan—or about the relationships among these elements—is the major cause of student services program failure. The purpose of this book is to outline those aspects of the context, the goal, and the plan that are present in every effective student services program. Each chapter will provide extensive examples of how these three key elements of program development can be applied in practice and, further, will delineate the core skills and knowledge necessary for effective program implementation.

*Developing Effective Student Services Programs* is directed to student services professionals with responsibility for program design or administration and is geared to the practitioner's question "How can I ensure establishment of effective student services programs?" Every chapter in this book is designed to make accessible to the reader the best thinking in the field on effective program planning techniques. The authors are professionals who were asked to contribute to this volume because of their extensive experience and firsthand knowledge of all levels of program development. Although they do not agree on one single best method of program planning, they share the view that a full understanding of the elements of context, goal, and plan is required to establish effective student services programs.

In the Introduction, we define and illustrate the three key elements of an effective student services program (context, goal, and plan) and describe the relationships among the elements. We then provide specific examples of how these elements apply to the development of effective student services programs. Throughout the book, the terms *student services* and *student affairs* are used interchangeably. In general, *student service* is used to refer to specific activities or groups of activities, such as student union programs or counseling services, and *student affairs* is used when referring to the profession (student affairs profession) or to the organizational structure on a specific campus (the division of student affairs).

Part One discusses four aspects of student services programs' context: an institution's history, mission, politics, and
budget. Chapter One traces the development of the student affairs enterprise within the context of higher education and relates that history to current program planning issues. Chapter
Two discusses a broad institutional view of student services programs from the perspective of a university president. Chapter
Three provides information on the political context that will
assist both the politically naive and the more experienced professional. Chapter Four will be especially helpful to the programmer for whom budgeting procedures and funding formulas
are foreign.

Many program planners in student affairs are doers and
far more comfortable implementing a program than determining appropriate program goals and objectives. Part Two underscores the importance of a systematic approach to goal setting
by examining three aspects of the process. Chapter Five describes a variety of theoretical constructs that can be used in
program planning and proposes an integrative theoretical approach to selecting goals for student services programs. Chapter
Six outlines methods for collecting information necessary to
establish program goals. Chapter Seven highlights several methods for integrating theory and information in the goal setting
process.

In Part Three, on the program plan, Chapter Eight reviews and evaluates major program planning techniques. Chapter Nine illuminates a factor critical to the success or failure of
any program design—that of recruiting and training competent
staff. Chapters Ten and Eleven apply the concepts of context,
goal, and plan to issues raised in the ongoing maintenance or
eventual termination of student services programs. Finally,
Chapter Twelve discusses specific program planning errors that
can occur within and among the three major elements of context, goal, and plan.

Part Four first gives attention to the issues confronting
student affairs in the next decade. Chapter Thirteen, on the
future of student affairs, discusses the changing context for student affairs program planning. The last chapter provides an

overview of the program model presented in the book as well as specific suggestions for applying the model to a variety of program types, program levels, and program problems.

This book represents the efforts of many people. We thank the chapter authors for their time, energy, and patience, and for their willingness to put their ideas to the critical test of reaction from their professional colleagues. We are also indebted to our staff colleagues at Northern Illinois University and the University of Texas at Austin, who supported and helped us through this project. Special thanks go to Dale Parkhouse, Lorene Berger, and Peggy Wimberley, who all worked long and hard to produce the final manuscript, and to Ursula Delworth for her encouragement, guidance, and support. Lou Ann Keating expresses deep appreciation to her husband, William Lasher, and her daughters, Kristin and Claire, for their support and care throughout this project. Finally, we would like to dedicate this book to all our friends and colleagues who labor every day to provide quality services for students. Your vision and dedication are models to all of us.

*November 1984*                                              Margaret J. Barr
                                                             *DeKalb, Illinois*

                                                             Lou A. Keating
                                                             *Austin, Texas*

# Contents

# Contents

❦ ❦ ❦ ❦ ❦ ❦ ❦ ❦ ❦ ❦ ❦ ❦ ❦

# The Authors

Margaret J. Barr is vice-president for student affairs at Northern Illinois University. She received her B.S. degree (1960) from the State University College at Buffalo, her M.S. degree (1964) from Southern Illinois University at Carbondale, and her Ph.D. degree (1980) from the University of Texas at Austin.

Long active in the American College Personnel Association (ACPA), she served as president of the organization in 1983-84. Her previous leadership positions in ACPA include service as president-elect (1982-83); vice-president for commissions (1980-82); chair of Commission II, on Admissions, Orientation and School College Relations (1977-79); and member of the directorate body of Commission III, on Student Residence Programs (1973-76).

Barr has authored, coauthored, or edited over twenty publications in books, monographs, and professional journals including *New Directions for Student Services: Student Affairs and the Law* (1983). Her experience in student services spans more than twenty years, during which time she has held the positions of assistant vice-president for student affairs at Northern Illinois University (1980-82), associate and assistant dean of students at the University of Texas at Austin (1971-80), director of housing and director of the college union at Trenton State College (1967-71), and director and assistant director of

women's residences at the State University College at Bingham-
ton (1964-67).

Lou Ann Keating is assistant dean of students at the University
of Texas at Austin, where she directs project development and
training activities. She received her B.A. degree from Western
Michigan University (1967) and her M.A. degree (1972) and
Ph.D. degree (1975) from Northern Colorado University. She
has coordinated the health information program at the University of Texas at Austin (1978-80), served as a counseling psychologist at Northern Illinois University (1975-77), and was an
area director and hall director in the residence hall system of
Northern Colorado University. She is active in the American
College Personnel Association, has coauthored several articles
on student services program development, and edited (with M. J.
Barr) *New Directions for Student Services: Establishing Effective Student Services Programs* (1979).

John L. Baier is vice-president for student affairs at the University of Alabama. He has more than seventeen years of experience in student services with specific responsibility in student
activities and general administration. He has been active in several professional associations and recently served as president of
the Texas Association of College and University Student Personnel Administrators.

James P. Duncan is executive vice-chancellor for academic affairs of the University of Texas System and professor of higher
education administration at the University of Texas at Austin.
During his seventeen years' experience as a practicing student
services administrator, he supervised housing and the dean of
students office. He has held leadership roles in both the American College Personnel Association and the National Association
of Student Personnel Administrators.

Gary R. Hanson is assistant dean of students at the University
of Texas at Austin, where he conducts research for the division
of student affairs. He has worked at the American College Testing Program and has authored and coauthored many publications

regarding student services programs, including serving as coeditor with Ursula Delworth of *Student Services: A Handbook for the Profession* (1980).

James C. Hurst is chief student affairs officer and professor of psychology at the University of Wyoming. He has served as a counseling center director, psychologist, and dean of students during his twenty years of professional involvement. He is the author of more than forty-five publications, including articles in professional journals, books, and chapters in books. Hurst is a fellow in the American Psychological Association.

Judith K. Jacobson is a doctoral candidate in educational administration at the University of Wyoming. Her professional experience includes work in student activities and college unions.

Sharon H. Justice is associate dean of students at the University of Texas at Austin. She has over ten years' experience in student services with specific responsibility in student activities, housing, orientation, and general administration. She is active in the American College Personnel Association and served as program chair for the 1983 national convention.

Gary Knock is associate dean of the graduate school and professor of educational leadership at Miami University (Ohio). He has been involved in education and training of student services specialists since 1966. From 1978 to 1980 he served as chair of Commission XII of the American College Personnel Association.

William R. Monat is president of Northern Illinois University and professor of political science. He has served as chair of the political science department at Northern Illinois University and provost and academic vice-president at two universities. In September 1984 Monat was named the first chancellor of the Regency System of Illinois.

W. John Pembroke is vice-president for administrative affairs at Northern Illinois University. He has fifteen years' experience in higher education with specific responsibility for budget development, planning, and general academic administration.

John D. Ragle is assistant dean of students at the University of Texas at Austin. His higher education experience is mainly in orientation and transition services for new students. Ragle has been a Danforth fellow and a teacher.

Arthur Sandeen has been vice-president for student affairs at the University of Florida since 1973, where he holds the rank of professor in the College of Education. He is past president of the National Association of Student Personnel Administrators (1977-78). Sandeen has published more than thirty articles on higher education and student affairs and is the author of *Undergraduate Education: Conflict and Change* (1976).

Marvalene H. Styles is the director of counseling services and placement at San Diego State University. She is the immediate past chair of the Association of University and College Counseling and Centers and serves as treasurer of the American College Personnel Association (1983-1985).

Bernard Yancey is a research associate with the student life studies unit at the University of Texas at Austin. He has authored several articles and reports on research and evaluation in student services.

❧ ❧ ❧ ❧ ❧ ❧ ❧ ❧ ❧ ❧ ❧ ❧ ❧

# Developing Effective Student Services Programs

*Systematic Approaches for Practitioners*

Margaret J. Barr
Lou A. Keating

❦ ❦ ❦ ❦ ❦ ❦ ❦ ❦ ❦ ❦ ❦ ❦ ❦

# Introduction:
# Elements
# of Program Development

In recent years student services professionals in colleges and universities have been under increasing pressure to define the role and scope of their programs. Part of the pressure is external and stems from society's requirement that all aspects of higher education be more accountable to their constituents. Some of the pressure comes from within—from a recognition that, as the student services profession matures, it must develop and identify a common body of knowledge, a common approach to its task. Since the entire profession is responsible for one task—that of planning, implementing, or evaluating student services programs —this common task seems a logical starting point in defining our role.

The term *program* is freely used by student services professionals. At conferences and workshops, presenters often describe successful student services programs at their institutions. Descriptive information on specific program efforts is published

1

regularly in the three major student services publications: *Journal of College Student Personnel, National Association of Student Personnel Administrators (NASPA) Journal,* and the *Journal of the National Association of Women Deans, Administrators, and Counselors (NAWDAC).* In addition to descriptive program information, several authors have developed practical and useful models for the program development process (Drum and Figler, 1973; Moore and Delworth, 1976; Morrill and Hurst, 1980). There is not, however, a common definition of the term *program* or a conceptual model for student services programs that relates development, implementation, and maintenance of such programs to theory and practice within the profession.

Some common themes have emerged in previous definitions of student services programs. Wirtz and Magrath (1979, p. 29) define a program as a "planned response toward an identified need for action." Morrill (1980, p. 332) defines a program as a "planned, structured learning experience designed to meet the needs of students." Drum and Figler (1973) approach the definition of program as a descriptive task and attempt to isolate and center on particular developmental needs. Each of these writers emphasizes the need for clear program goals based on appropriate theory, and all advocate systematic planning and assessment processes.

These definitions are useful starting points. However, they contain several limitations. While each of the definitions assumes some assessment of student needs and institutional resources, none explicitly relates programs or program activities to the larger context of higher education. In addition, the previously cited definitions tend to develop programs for one target population at a time rather than taking a more broad-based approach. Finally, the definitions are based primarily on human development theory and give limited attention to relevant aspects of management and organizational theory.

In the future, student services programs must be administratively, fiscally, and politically feasible as well as theoretically sound if support is to be gained or maintained within institutions. Thus, the definitions and models previously cited may not be sufficient. A new definition, a new view of the term *program* is needed. The new model must build on earlier work in the area, be useful to the practitioner involved at any level of program development, account for complex planning variables, and provide a foundation to gain support within an increasingly complex and cautious institutional environment.

The model for program development presented in this volume is based on the following definition of the term *program*: a theoretically based plan, under which action is taken toward a goal within the context of institutions of higher education.

An underlying assumption of this definition is the ability of the student services practitioner to understand and apply a variety of theories to the task of program development. A second assumption of the model and the definition is that there are three equal components of program development: the context, the goal, and the plan or method. A third assumption of the model is that all three program elements must be congruent in order to achieve program success. Student services programs fail when the practitioner does not understand or properly apply one or more of the elements or fails to consider the interdependence and relationships among the program components. Depending on training, work experience, personal talents, and preferences, student services professionals usually focus on only one of these components. For example, the academician or theoretician would perhaps be most interested in clarifying program goals and grounding these program goals in a sound theoretical base. The top-level administrator, of necessity, may deal primarily with contextual issues. The practitioner will often be most interested in the ultimate plan or "blueprint" for program implementation. However, the singularity of these viewpoints often causes errors to occur in the process of developing, implementing, and maintaining programs. Unless attention is given to all three elements, the ultimate program effort will fail. (See Chapter Twelve by Keating for a detailed analysis of programming errors.)

## Context

The general context for student services programs is higher education in the United States. Each institution of higher education must interact with the larger society, in order to garner support for the educational enterprise. Each institution is also affected by the unique characteristics of American higher education, eight of which are cited by Brubacher and Rudy (1958): access and opportunity, public policy, curriculum, integrated philosophies, service, self-regulation, diversity, and governance structures. Each of these characteristics contributes to the context of student services programs.

Public policy—as expressed by statutory enactments, implementing regulations, and the development of a comprehensive high school curriculum—has contributed to the notion that higher education is not limited to the socially or economically elite. The integration of philosophies of higher education from both the German and English traditions has greatly influenced American institutions of higher education. According to Conant (1946), this broadened view of American higher education is based on a fundamental belief in the social equity of all forms of labor and enterprise. The idea of service as a legitimate institutional goal is also uniquely American. In fact, the funding policy of land-grant institutions is based on the concept of providing direct and needed services to society.

Another characteristic of American higher education is its "unsystemized diversity" (Brubacher and Rudy, 1958, p. 406), grounded in a strongly held belief in institutional autonomy and self-regulation. In the United States, standards for higher education are enforced through voluntary cooperation with autonomous accrediting bodies rather than through official regulation.

American higher education is also unique because of the corporate structure of institutional governance—the use of nonresident lay boards to oversee institutions rather than sole reliance on governance by academic faculties. Authority for day-to-day decisions is delegated from the lay boards to the officers of the institution.

Each college or university, no matter how similar to others in typology, has developed a unique response to the larger context of American higher education. Factors that shape the context of a particular institution include size, geographical location, funding sources, the student population, the local community, institutional traditions, internal governance systems, style of the governing board, internal political practices, and the institution's stated mission. Institutions, like people, are constantly in the process of growth, change, and development; it is a mistake to assume that any two institutions are alike on all contextual dimensions.

Within the last decade, student services professionals have responded to the need to consider contextual issues through an increasing interest in the concept of environmental assessment. Huebner (1979), Corazzini (1980), Banning and McKinley (1980), Conyne (1975), and others have developed specific methods to assess the climate of the institution and to use that assessment for the design or redesign of institutional programs. Environmental assessment techniques are useful in understanding the context of student services programs. However, they must be linked with an understanding of the ongoing political and governance processes in the institution, the organizational structure, and the historical context of the institution and its development.

As we have previously noted (Barr and Keating, 1979), the student services professional should not regard "politics" as a negative word. Politics is, instead, an acknowledgment of and respect for the individual factors that influence the decision-making process. Political awareness and the ability to translate that awareness into plans are becoming increasingly important to the survival of student services programs. Fiscal resources are becoming more limited, expectations for accountability are increasing, and the astute practitioner must be able not only to understand these pressures but also to deal with them in effective ways to meet student and institutional needs.

## Goal

All student services programs—whether major administrative units, a series of activities, or a one-time event—attempt to fulfill one or more of three overarching purposes: to provide essential institutional services, to teach life management skills, and to provide links through which students can integrate knowledge gained in both the curricular and cocurricular settings.

*Essential Institutional Services.* The growth of student services programs parallels the historical trend toward specialization in American colleges and universities. The president of a colonial college could simultaneously teach classes, discipline students, serve as librarian and registrar, and preside over the institution. However, with the expansion in size and complexity of institutions of higher education, the president had to delegate some of these functions to others—for instance, to a dean of students, a dean of women, and a registrar (Brubacher and Rudy, 1958; Fenske, 1980).

All colleges and universities need to develop and enforce standards of student conduct and must admit, register, schedule, and advise students at least once a semester. Many colleges and universities also provide minimal health services, job placement services for graduates, financial aid, and full housing and food services. These essential institutional services must be performed efficiently and effectively. To do less denies direct and needed services to students and places the student services organization in a precarious position within the total institutional structure.

*Life Management Skills.* Many student services functions are designed to teach life management skills not acquired or only partially acquired in the formal curriculum. Higher education in the United States has always been organized for "informal education as well as 'formal' instruction" (Brubacher and Rudy, 1958, p. 410)—encompassing curricular, cocurricular, and extracurricular offerings. Although physical skills, communication skills, appreciation of the arts, and values can of course be taught in the formal classroom setting, some skills can best be taught and mastered in a more informal educational environment. To illustrate, interpersonal skills of leadership, group management, and teamwork are often best learned through structured experiences that provide an opportunity to test and fail without the risk of poor grades as an outcome of the process. Skills in judgment, planning, and the assumption of responsibility can sometimes best be mastered by participation in a club, a Greek organization, student government, or committees. Student services professionals have traditionally been charged with the responsibility of planning and developing these informal learning experiences. This instructional goal is central to our emerging role as student development educators (Miller and Prince, 1976; Creamer, 1980). We must, therefore, develop programs that are explicitly directed toward that goal, and we must help others value and understand this legitimate role in the educational process.

*Integration of Knowledge.* The mission of higher education is the creation and transmittal of knowledge. If the collegiate experience is to have value, the individual student must be able to apply the concepts, ideas, and experiences gained in the formal academic setting. Therefore, many student services programs are designed to link with the academic programs of the institution. For example, student services divisions have developed special residence hall floors with an academic emphasis, have provided consultation and support to academic advisers, and have created opportunities for informal interaction with faculty members through coffee hours, group advisement sessions, and special seminar and lecture programs. Some student services units also provide this linkage by offering credit-producing courses. Such courses can be designed to assist specific subpopulations or provide developmental learning opportunities for student paraprofessionals employed in counseling centers, orientation programs, or student housing services (Fried, 1981).

Implementation of the integration of knowledge goal for student services requires the practitioner to understand the formal processes of teaching and learning (Hanson, 1980). Crookston (1976) and Lenning (1977) have broadened the term *teaching* to include all planned program activities that contribute to student learning, in the classroom, outside the classroom, and in the daily management of the institution. A foundation in teaching skills and a knowledge of learning theory and human development theory are prerequisites for successful implementation of the linkage goal of integrating knowledge in student services programs. In addition, the practitioner must understand the institution's organizational structure and have the skills and competencies to manage change within the structure (Christensen, 1980). Finally, in order to link the elements of teaching with the broader institutional mission, student services practitioners must be political in the best sense of the word (Barr and Keating, 1979).

Each student services program must develop specific objectives in order to measure program success. These specific objectives must, however, be congruent with one of these overarching purposes and with the other critical elements of the model.

## Plan

The final component of the program development model is the design of the ultimate program endeavor. Two issues must be considered under this element: the planning techniques employed and the actual end product or program. A program is the end result of a process designed to meet an identifiable goal.

A variety of planning techniques can be used in the process of program development. The choice of planning techniques often depends on the theoretical orientation of the program planner or his or her administrative supervisor. In the 1960s and early 1970s, great reliance was placed on organizational theory and business management accountability models, with the result that management by objectives (MBO) became a popular planning technique (Deegan and Fritz, 1975; Racippo and Foxley, 1980). Unfortunately, planners who used MBO and similar models often became intrigued with the intricacies of the planning process rather than the outcome of a useful, workable plan for program implementation. This is not to say that MBO or similar systems do not have value, but they do have great potential for misuse.

A multistep approach to program planning, developed by Moore and Delworth (1976), makes use of planning teams to design the program and evaluate the effectiveness of the effort. This model has been useful in assisting student services professionals to meet linkage and life management goals. However, planning teams are inherently time-consuming and at times difficult to implement consistently within an institution. Drum and Figler (1973) and Morrill and Hurst (1980) also have presented useful and practical models for the program-planning process. All these approaches draw heavily on developmental and organizational theory as the foundation for the planning process. Because of their emphasis on involvement, these techniques can be frustrating to those who must seek solutions to pressing problems in an efficient and timely manner.

Whatever planning techniques are employed, whatever the size or complexity of the ultimate program endeavor, a systematic, time-delineated program plan must be developed if the student services program is to succeed. The plan must account for all the resources, content, training, and supervision needed to assure that an idea can be implemented. (Specific plans are discussed in greater detail in Chapters Eight, Ten, and Eleven.) Careful plans are detailed, provide for accountability, delineate responsibility, are data based, and require evaluation and assessment (Barr and Cuyjet, 1983). A plan for program implementation is never static and must be sufficiently flexible to account for changing conditions and the emergence of new needs. Thus the plan or the implementation "blueprint" for any specific program is constantly being evaluated and is subject to decisions with regard to program modification or continuation. In our view, the method of choice in planning techniques is less important than the fact that programs are planned in a systematic fashion and that the planning process results in a worthwhile and workable implementation scheme.

### Summary

We have described the three essential elements of successful student services programs: the context, the goal, and the plan. Although the degree of attention to any one element may vary with the complexity of the program development task, all three elements must be attended to in order to ensure program success.

This program development model is generic and applies whether programs are viewed as single events or major administrative units. For the model to be useful and helpful, however, those responsible for program planning must thoroughly understand each element and the interactive nature of the program planning process.

## References

Banning, J. H., and McKinley, D. L. "Conceptions of the Campus Environment." In W. H. Morrill and J. C. Hurst (Eds.), *Dimensions of Intervention for Student Development.* New York: Wiley, 1980.

Barr, M. J., and Cuyjet, M. C. "Program Planning." In R. B. Winston, W. R. Mendenhall, and T. K. Miller (Eds.), *Administration and Leadership in Student Affairs.* Muncie, Ind.: Accelerated Development, 1983.

Barr, M. J., and Keating, L. A. "No Program Is an Island." In M. J. Barr and L. A. Keating (Eds.), *New Directions for Student Services: Establishing Effective Programs,* no. 7. San Francisco: Jossey-Bass, 1979.

Brubacher, J. S., and Rudy, W. *Higher Education in Transition.* New York: Harper & Row, 1958.

Christensen, V. R. "Bringing About Change." In U. Delworth, G. R. Hanson, and Associates, *Student Services: A Handbook for the Profession.* San Francisco: Jossey-Bass, 1980.

Conant, J. B. "America Remakes the University." *Atlantic Monthly,* 1946, *177,* 42.

Conyne, R. K. "Environmental Assessment: Mapping for Counselor Action." *Personnel and Guidance Journal,* 1975, *54,* 151-154.

Corazzini, J. G. "Environmental Redesign." In U. Delworth, G. R. Hanson, and Associates, *Student Services: A Handbook for the Profession.* San Francisco: Jossey-Bass, 1980.

Creamer, D. G. (Ed.). *Student Development In Higher Education: Theories, Practices, and Future Directions.* Washington, D.C.: American College Personnel Association, 1980.

Crookston, B. B. "Student Personnel: All Hail and Farewell." *Personnel and Guidance Journal,* 1976, *55,* 26-29.

Deegan, A. X., and Fritz, R. J. *Management by Objectives*

*(MBO) Goes to College.* Boulder: Division of Continuing Education, University of Colorado, 1975.

Drum, D. J., and Figler, H. E. *Outreach in Counseling.* New York: Intext Educational Publishers, 1973.

Fenske, R. H. "Historical Foundations." In U. Delworth, G. R. Hanson, and Associates, *Student Services: A Handbook for the Profession.* San Francisco: Jossey-Bass, 1980.

Fried, J. (Ed.). *New Directions for Student Services: Education for Student Development,* no. 15. San Francisco: Jossey-Bass, 1981.

Hanson, G. R. "Instruction." In U. Delworth, G. R. Hanson, and Associates, *Student Services: A Handbook for the Profession.* San Francisco: Jossey-Bass, 1980.

Huebner, L. A. "Emergent Issues of Theory and Practice." In L. A. Huebner (Ed.), *New Directions for Student Services: Redesigning Campus Environments,* no. 8. San Francisco: Jossey-Bass, 1979.

Lenning, O. T. "Assessing Student Progress in Academic Achievement." In L. L. Baird (Ed.), *New Directions for Community Colleges: Assessing Student Academic and Social Progress,* no. 18. San Francisco: Jossey-Bass, 1977.

Miller, T. K., and Prince, J. S. *The Future of Student Affairs: A Guide to Student Development for Tomorrow's Higher Education.* San Francisco: Jossey-Bass, 1976.

Moore, M., and Delworth, U. *Training Manual for Student Service Program Development.* Boulder, Colo.: Western Interstate Commission on Higher Education, 1976.

Morrill, W. H. "Program Development." In U. Delworth, G. R. Hanson, and Associates, *Student Services: A Handbook for the Profession.* San Francisco: Jossey-Bass, 1980.

Morrill, W. H., and Hurst, J. C. (Eds.) *Dimensions of Intervention for Student Development.* New York: Wiley, 1980.

Racippo, V. C., and Foxley, C. H. "MIS: A Tool for Planning and Evaluation." In C. H. Foxley (Ed.), *New Directions for Student Services: Applying Management Techniques,* no. 9. San Francisco: Jossey-Bass, 1980.

Williamson, E. G. *Counseling Adolescents.* New York: McGraw-Hill, 1950.

Wirtz, P., and Magrath, D. S. "Creating Quality Programs." In M. J. Barr and L. A. Keating (Eds.), *New Directions for Student Services: Establishing Effective Programs,* no. 7. San Francisco: Jossey-Bass, 1979.

# Part One

❧ ❧ ❧ ❧ ❧ ❧ ❧ ❧ ❧ ❧ ❧ ❧ ❧

# Understanding How the Institution's Context Affects Programs

In the Introduction, we indicated that the context is one of the three key elements in planning and implementing effective student services programs. The context of higher education and student services programs is complex, powerful, and at times confusing. Our shared context includes our history, our philosophical foundations, our current organizations, our political environment both on and off the campus, and the fiscal and human resources necessary to maintain and enhance the educational enterprise. It is essential that student service professionals understand the relationship between student services programs and our larger context. For only through such understanding can the context of higher education be confronted, responded to, and effectively used in establishing quality student services programs.

No student services program exists in a vacuum. Every

13

student services program is embedded in an institution of higher education, and that institution is a part of a larger societal framework. Part One defines the wide variety of contextual issues that must be confronted by the effective student services programmer and provides guidance on how to use the context in the design of quality programs for students.

In Chapter One, Gary Knock provides a comprehensive analysis of the historical and philosophical foundations influencing the current practice of student services professionals. Successful programmers must understand these roots in order to prepare for tomorrow.

Since student services programs are only one part of an institution, effective programmers must learn to examine issues and priorities from an institutional perspective. In Chapter Two, William Monat provides his view from a university president's perspective on the legitimate role and scope of student services programs within the university.

Chapter Three discusses the politics of institutional life. Many student services professionals either fail to recognize or effectively confront the internal and external political environment of higher education. Student services programs must not only survive but also flourish within a politicized environment. Margaret Barr provides concrete suggestions on how to successfully manage that task.

Finally, higher education is a business, and student services professionals need to increase their skill in managing the fiscal portion of programming. In Chapter Four, John Pembroke discusses the fiscal management concerns of higher education in general and student services programs in particular. This final chapter in Part One provides a beginning education for the student services programmer with regard to the dollars and cents issues in programming.

Contextual issues can be difficult to understand, to confront, and to incorporate into successful student services programs. Part One provides guidance for practitioners beginning that process.

1

❧ ❧ ❧ ❧ ❧ ❧ ❧ ❧ ❧ ❧ ❧ ❧ ❧

# Development
# of Student Services
# in Higher Education

From the colonial days to the latter part of the nineteenth
century, responsibility for the development of students was assigned to and assumed by the college president and the members of the faculty, many of whom were clergy. This responsibility went largely unaltered with the establishment of state
universities—in states such as Virginia, North Carolina, Georgia,
and Vermont—until the early decades of the twentieth century.
A thirtyfold expansion of the student population between 1879
and 1930 made it necessary for college and university presidents
to assign direct responsibility for student development to someone (Brubacher and Rudy, 1958, p. 126). The faculty was
charged with the intellectual development of students, and such
specialists as deans of men and women were assigned responsibility for extracurricular student affairs.

    The division of responsibility for intellectual and other
phases of student development has continued and is reflected in

the organizational structure of colleges and universities as divisions of academic affairs and student affairs. (Two additional organizational areas are business and financial affairs, and development and public relations.) By 1975 nearly all collegiate institutions in the United States reflected organizational structures based on operational functions. The area of student affairs has developed not only as an operational area but also as an applied professional field. While the first student affairs specialists were not professionally prepared for their work and usually came from the faculty, a professional field began to evolve early in the twentieth century. In 1899 William Rainey Harper, president of the University of Chicago, stated in an invited lecture at Brown University: "In order that the student may receive the assistance so essential to his highest success, another step in the onward evolution will take place. This step will be the scientific study of the student himself. . . . In the time that is coming, provision must be made, either by the regular instructors or by those appointed especially for the purpose, to study in detail the man or woman to whom instruction is offered. . . . This feature of twentieth-century education will come to be regarded as of greatest importance and fifty years hence will prevail as widely as it is now lacking" (Harper, 1905, p. 320).

A handbook entitled *The Dean of Women* (Rosenberry, 1915) was published several years later. In 1916 the National Association of Deans of Women affiliated, and Paul Monroe offered the first course in college student personnel work at the Columbia University summer school. In 1937 and again in 1949, the Committee on Student Personnel Work of the American Council on Education published documents describing student personnel work at the college level. These statements provided a foundation for professional practice, which was based on three assumptions: (1) Individual differences are anticipated, and every student is recognized as unique. (2) Each individual is to be treated as a functioning whole. (3) The individual's current drives, interests, and needs are to be accepted as the most significant factor in developing a personnel program for any particular campus. These assumptions were and are the underpinnings of the "personnel point of view." While the personnel point of view was conceived to be broader than the services performed by the appointed specialists for student affairs, this philosophical position was primarily adopted by those who provided special programs and services for students.

## Historical Development of American Higher Education

Higher education in the United States is the product of more than twenty-five centuries of evolution and revolution. American higher education is the beneficiary of historical antecedents and developments dating back to the classical period of Greece, the ancient world of Islam, and the Middle Ages of Europe.

*American Colonial Colleges.* The colleges founded before the American Revolution in New England, the Northeast, and the South were established in theocratic colonies and represented efforts to preserve sectarian Protestantism. Harvard College, founded in 1636, was established in the Massachusetts Bay Colony by Congregationalists "dreading to leave an illiterate Ministry to our Churches, when our present Ministers shall lie in the dust" (Morrison, 1935, p. 423). In 1701, as a protest against the religious liberalism that had developed at Harvard, conservative Congregationalist ministers petitioned the Connecticut Colony to establish a collegiate school at New Haven, to be named Yale. The College of William and Mary in Virginia was founded in 1693 by a royal charter that stipulated that one mission of the college was to bring Christianity to Western Indians. The particular interpretation of Christianity to be taught to the Indians of Virginia was that of the Anglican Church of England. The first chancellor of William and Mary was also the bishop of London, and the faculty of the college were required to swear allegiance to the Church of England and the Established Church of Virginia. The other colonial college founded by a royal charter, Dartmouth College in 1769, also was charged with Christianizing Indians.

With few exceptions, only the sons of wealthy and influential colonists were permitted to attend these denominational colleges. The principal responsibility of these institutions was to train students to be religious and moral men. This well-understood mission went largely unchallenged because there was little dissent from the authority of the particular sect that controlled each of the colonies. Moreover, the administration, faculty, and trustees of each institution were members of the founding denomination.

By 1775 nine colleges were in operation in the thirteen colonies. Most of these institutions were small, with enrollments between 100 and 200 and with faculties that seldom numbered more than a half dozen professors and a few tutors. The organizational pattern of each college was dedicated to Christian piety. Prescribed religious behavior was enforced. Compulsory morning and evening prayers and Sunday church services were endemic to the colonial colleges. The daily schedule at the typical college in the early nineteenth century included a long chapel service at 6 A.M. before the start of classes and a shorter service after the last class of the day at 5 P.M.

Certainly an attitude of concern for the student was pervasive in the colonial colleges. The focus of concern, however, was circumscribed to the souls of the young male students and found expression principally in inculcation of religious values and control of behavior. Functions that might be regarded as student services were performed by administrators, faculty, and trustees who were "of the faith" and who acted with the authority of the colony. Students were viewed as immature and in need of guidance and supervision. In the religiously oriented college of colonial America, "student services" were inseparable from the academic program and were performed by all who were viewed as capable of molding young men into Christian gentlemen.

*Establishment of Public Colleges and Universities.* The idea of a state university was nurtured in the nineteenth century by secular, pluralistic, and, after the Civil War, technological developments in American society. The *Dartmouth College* case of 1819 confirmed that henceforth colleges and universities in America would be both private and public. In this landmark case, the U.S. Supreme Court ruled that Dartmouth College could not be taken over or controlled by the state of New

Hampshire because such action would constitute unilateral violation of a contract, in direct contravention of the federal Constitution. The end of the practice of using public funds to support private collegiate institutions was at hand. States were free to establish, support, and control their own public colleges and universities but were not free to take over private colleges at will.

Thomas Jefferson dissented from the decision of the *Dartmouth College* case. Writing to the governor of New Hampshire before the case reached the Supreme Court, Jefferson expressed the view that a state could and should gain control of a collegiate institution when necessary because the institution comprised a public trust no matter what the terms of the institution's charter (Warren, 1922). In 1779 Jefferson had tried unsuccessfully to engineer a takeover of William and Mary by the state of Virginia. The *Dartmouth College* case intensified Jefferson's zeal, and in 1825 he established the first truly state-supported university in the United States, the University of Virginia. The University of Virginia differed from the existing colleges and universities, whether public or private, in that it was secular and nondenominational as well as state supported. In addition, the University of Virginia provided curricular choices for students and the opportunity to undertake advanced levels of instruction. Perhaps the most notable feature of the University of Virginia was an experiment with student self-government. Jefferson believed that students were capable of governing themselves, and he advocated enforcement of university ordinances by a board of student censors selected by the faculty and a university court with student representatives to hear disciplinary cases. The plan failed because the Virginia legislature refused to establish the proposed court and because many of the first students at Charlottesville proved to be young boys of unruly disposition and not the mature, serious type of student whom Jefferson had in mind (Brubacher and Rudy, 1958).

Outside the South, the only section of the nation to fund state universities before the Civil War was the West. The state university idea faced vigorous opposition by various religious and political groups, and a lack of financial support from state legislatures impeded development. At a philosophical level, the Yale Report of 1828 provided for private, church-related colleges a reaffirmation of the value of the narrow, prescribed curriculum they provided and of the virtue of their concern with Christian piety.

The granting of public lands for the establishment of state universities was a significant impetus to the movement toward greater numbers of public colleges and universities. By 1857, the year the Morrill Act was introduced in Congress, the federal government had donated four million acres of public land to fifteen states for the establishment of universities. It was the Morrill Acts of 1862 and 1890, however, that accomplished establishment of "democracy's colleges." In reaction to dissatisfaction with the religiously oriented liberal arts colleges of the land, supporters of "high schools" that would offer instruction in utilitarian areas of study backed a bill introduced by a Vermont congressman, Justin Smith Morrill, in 1857. In 1862 Congress passed the Morrill Act, and President Lincoln signed into law a bill that provided support in every state for at least one college "where the leading object shall be, without excluding other scientific or classical studies, to teach such branches of learning as are related to agriculture and the mechanical arts." Consistent with the provisions of the Morrill Act, each state was given public lands or land script equal to 30,000 acres for each senator and representative under the apportionment of 1860. The new colleges received the proceeds from the sale of more than seventeen million acres of public lands.

The patterns for establishing "democracy's colleges" varied from state to state. Some states assigned the new responsibility for serving agricultural and mechanical interests to existing state universities. Many states established new institutions. Four states created A and M (agricultural and mechanical) colleges out of chartered colleges of agriculture. In some states existing private institutions agreed to offer study in the utilitarian areas specified in the Morrill Act. In both Indiana and New York, combined state and private funds produced the land-grant institution.

Passage of the Hatch Experiment Station Act of 1887

augmented the evolution of the land-grant institutions because it supported the creation of a body of scientific subject matter. This subject matter was then taught and researched in the new A and M colleges. The Morrill Act of 1890 provided for regular federal appropriations for the newly established land-grant institutions.

By the beginning of the twentieth century, the state university was a reality. The idea was nurtured by the two land-grant acts and by citizens' groups, politicians, farmers, and "the common man" as well as by the presidents of state universities. Opposition from private colleges, religious bodies, graduates of private colleges, and a number of academies was effective and continued to be formidable. While the idea of a state university was well established by the turn of the century, more students would enroll in private than in public institutions until mid-century. Because state universities would attract large, heterogeneous student bodies in the latter half of the twentieth century, many of these institutions would establish student services, which would be emulated by other colleges and universities.

*Beginnings of Coeducation.* The American colonial colleges and the new state universities were both intended for young men. A few "academies" or "seminaries" for young women—such as the institution founded by Emma Willard in Troy, New York, in 1921—were established in the early and mid-nineteenth century. These institutions were not generally regarded as colleges and did not attempt to award degrees. Their mission was to provide a type of instruction that would enable a young woman to "fit" into her established "place" in society. Despite the advocacy of feminists Lucinda H. Stone and Sarah Dix Hamlin, lawyer-educator Horace Mann, and a Poughkeepsie, New York, brewer named Matthew Vassar, higher education for women attracted few supporters during the years just before the Civil War. Indeed, the idea provoked deep-seated skepticism and open opposition. It was, however, during this pre-Civil War period that coeducation established a milestone with the admission of women to Oberlin College in 1833. Eight years later, an even more unprecedented event took place when Oberlin awarded the bachelor of arts degree to three female graduates.

During the decades between the Civil War and the turn of the century, women's colleges and the notion of coeducation were established. The pattern in the East was to develop coordinate units of established men's colleges. Also established in this region were a limited number of independent women's colleges, including Bryn Mawr, that offered opportunities for graduate study to women. Women's colleges had been established in the South before the Civil War, and in 1869 another institution for female students resulted from a gift of $100,000 to Tulane University in New Orleans to establish the H. Sophie Newcomb Memorial College for "white girls and young women." Coeducation rather than separate colleges for women was the pattern in the Midwest and the West, especially in the state universities and land-grant institutions. By the early twentieth century, all state universities—except those in Georgia, Louisiana, and Virginia—admitted women.

Opponents of higher education for women were not silenced during the post–Civil War period. Arguments about the propriety and value of higher education for women were voiced as were concerns that coeducation would foster immorality, lower academic standards, and possibly "discredit" American institutions in the eyes of the respected and renowned universities of the world. However, for educational and political reasons, it was clear by 1900 that women students were to be included in American higher education. In that year, more than 70 percent of the colleges and universities of the United States were coeducational.

*Community College Movement.* The concept of a student's following a four-year course of study leading to a bachelor's degree has deep historical roots. While many students who attended America's colonial colleges chose not to remain for four consecutive years of study and many had no intention of earning a bachelor's degree, the number of persons completing college degrees increased during the early twentieth century. This increase resulted from the practical orientation of many state universities; increased enrollments of women students; increases in high school attendance and graduation; and the effects of industrialization, which placed the college graduate in a favored position in the job market.

Whether or not four consecutive years of study were necessary for all students was a question raised by many people. Harvard's president, Charles W. Eliot, injected controversy into this question when in 1888 he expressed misgivings about the steadily advancing age of Harvard's entering freshman (Eliot, 1898). (Actually, most of the students admitted to Harvard at the time were eighteen or nineteen years old.) The rising standards of admission imposed by colleges created a situation demanding more time for preparation in a private or public high school or academy. Columbia University's president, Nicholas Murray Butler, asserted that college standards had been raised so much that, by the first decade of the twentieth century, students were devoting not four but virtually six years to the study of liberal arts and sciences (Butler, 1903).

In 1905 President William Rainey Harper of the University of Chicago proposed a "junior college" based on the model of the German *gymnasium*. Harper believed that a lower-division college offering two years of study would attract students who might otherwise not attend college. Also, Harper expected that his idea would appeal to graduate and professional schools because a more selective student body would be found at the upper division of colleges and universities. It was also Harper's conviction that, since the junior college years constituted secondary and not higher education, in time high schools would expand to include the junior college years.

Many of Harper's ideas were contested, and the notion of four years of study for a bachelor's degree has remained largely unaltered. However, some high schools did expand to include the junior college years; some colleges truncated their offerings to two years and became in fact, if not in name, junior colleges; and some junior colleges were founded as new institutions. For the first two decades of the twentieth century, private junior colleges increased in number more than public junior colleges. From 1920 to the 1960s and 1970s, public junior colleges experienced remarkable growth in both student enrollment and numbers of institutions. With growth and expansion came a broader mission for the junior college. During the second half of the twentieth century, this type of institution became a center of community education and a "community college." These

colleges began to offer not only the first two years of undergraduate study but also programs of education and training of
shorter duration and for specific skill and aptitude development.

The growth and expansion of the community college is
the most dramatic development in American higher education
in the twentieth century. In 1920 fifty-two junior colleges enrolled over 8,000 students. By 1930 the number of two-year
institutions had grown over 400 percent, and approximately
55,000 students attended these schools. By mid-century there
were approximately 500 junior or community colleges enrolling more than a quarter-million students (Horn, 1953). Between
1955 and 1970, the number of two-year institutions increased
by 360, and between 1965 and 1970, student enrollment increased 430 percent (National Center for Education Statistics,
1974). During the decade of the 1980s, the rate of establishment of new two-year institutions has understandably slowed
down, while enrollments in credit and noncredit courses have
reflected a condition of "steady state."

These institutions have "open-door policies" in regard to
admission of students and a mission of community service. It
has been said that the community college seeks to meet educational needs from the "womb to the tomb." Many people are
able to attend college only because there is an accessible, lower-
cost community college within driving distance. The American
community college has even caused a change in nomenclature.
For many individuals and agencies, the two-year community
college is a part of "postsecondary education," which also includes institutions of "higher education."

Despite the undeniable pattern of growth and expansion,
it may be questioned whether the mission of the community
college has been fully realized. The conclusion of the U.S. Office of Education's *Report on Higher Education* (Newman,
1971) was that community colleges have yet to fulfill the promise of their name and that these institutions must develop their
own distinctive mission rather than just absorb students.

*Urban Institutions.* The college or university of the city is
and will remain a cynosure of American higher education for
the final decades of the twentieth century. Many of these urban

schools were founded during the previous century as private, often denominational, institutions. The historical mission of a small ensemble of these schools of the city was scholarship and research. Generally, relationships between host cities and urban institutions were informal or nonexistent until population shifts brought on by industrialization and urbanization created a constituency for these schools.

While many of the colleges and universities founded in the nineteenth century and earlier were located by design away from the "evils" of the city, the urban institutions were located "where the people are" in the twentieth century. "Going away to college" for many city dwellers came to mean taking a bus or subway to class. A number of urban institutions have become partially or fully public supported, and some have been assimilated into state systems of higher education. In an effort to serve students and citizens of urban areas, some public and private colleges and universities also have established branch campuses or extension centers in urban areas.

## Philosophical Foundations and Goals
## of American Higher Education

During the past 350 years, as Henderson and Henderson (1974) note, the nation gradually shifted from a strictly aristocratic philosophy of higher education to a philosophy of meritocracy and then to a philosophy of egalitarianism.

In the early days of the republic, higher education was considered necessary for a small segment of the population. While the early colonial colleges did educate young men who became ministers, lawyers, and business leaders, these institutions did not assume a role of preparing leaders and specialists. Indeed, admission to colonial colleges was limited almost exclusively to the sons of wealthy and socially prominent families. This aristocratic philosophy, which may be traced back to the ancient Greek city-state, posits that education is primarily for the elite. For economic, social, political, and religious reasons, an aristocratic philosophy remained prevalent for more than 300 years.

During the first half of the twentieth century, high school attendance and graduation increased. This development was accompanied by a more gradual increase in college attendance. By 1940, 1.4 million men and women, 15 percent of the traditional college age group, were enrolled in the nation's colleges and universities. The accepted aristocratic philosophy was beginning to give way to a philosophy of meritocracy—the philosophy that all capable people should be educated. In 1947 the President's Commission on Higher Education proclaimed that 49 percent of America's youth had the ability to complete two years of education beyond high school and 32 percent should be encouraged to complete four years. Meritocracy became the prevailing philosophical position by mid-century.

By the mid-1960s, meritocracy faced indomitable challenge from the egalitarian philosophy, which holds that all individuals should have an opportunity to pursue forms of higher education that are consistent with and enhance personal abilities and interests. New institutions, in particular community colleges, and established institutions have adopted practices reflecting their acceptance of a philosophy of egalitarianism. Although the aristocratic philosophy and the philosophy of meritocracy continue to have contemporary advocates, the belief that there should be a "place" for nearly everyone in American higher education has gained wide acceptance and support.

Educational philosophy sets the goals for the higher education enterprise. The historical development of American higher education and the divergence of institutional types and size that has resulted make agreement on overarching goals difficult (see Chapter Seven of this volume). However, certain goals for higher education in the United States have received general support. Heard (1973, p. 16) has observed that "our largest common goal in higher education, indeed in all education, is to create and stimulate the kind of learning that breeds strength and humor and hope within a person, and that helps build a society outside him that stirs his pride and commands his affection." Bowen (1977) has catalogued four additional goals for higher education: preserving, transmitting, and enriching culture; facilitating growth of the whole student; preparing citizens, leaders, and competent workers; and contributing to the betterment of human society.

All or part of Bowen's catalogue of goals has been supported by other scholars. In support of the first goal—preserving, transmitting, and enriching culture—Mueller (1961, p. 5) noted that "the student is not a mere receiver; he is a very active participant in the educative process. The culture can be preserved only [by] the human beings who experience it." The President's Commission on Higher Education (1947, p. 9) stated that "the first goal in education for democracy is the full, rounded, and continuing development of the person."

In regard to Bowen's second goal—facilitating growth of the whole student—the Carnegie Commission on Higher Education (1973) declared that "the college years are an important developmental period, and cognitive and affective activities are closely related to each other" (p. 16).

In support of his goal of preparing citizens, leaders, and competent workers, Bowen (1977) summarized the behavior and performance of college students and graduates on citizenship variables. Freeman (1976) prepared an economic analysis of a potential depression in the college graduate job market.

Bowen's (1977) final goal—contributing to the betterment of society—receives strong though indirect support in the literature. A symbiotic relationship exists between higher education and the society that spawned and supports it. Public and private institutions alike are dependent upon society for sustenance. In return, institutions of higher education not only prepare citizens, leaders, and workers but are also dedicated to discovering new knowledge, applying knowledge in ways that improve the quality of life, and providing public service to public and private agencies and units of society. Federal and state governments, foundations, commercial enterprises, health care units, educational institutions, and social agencies turn to collegiate institutions for assistance and service.

The educational philosophy of the individual institution and the goals of the institution will direct the practical application of these general goals on an individual campus. Higher education is an evolving, changing entity and is a reflection of the greater society (see Chapter Three on politics and Chapter Two on an institutional perspective).

## Higher Education as an Industry

It is certainly reasonable to analyze an enterprise that involves approximately $85 billion annually as an industry. Bowen (1977) explains that, as in other industries, production in higher education uses resources that are transformed into end products called outcomes. Efficiency is measured by comparing the outcomes with the resources used. Accountability is achieved when the outcomes as well as the resources used are identified and measured.

Higher education, according to Bowen (1977), has, over time, acquired well-defined functions, and in performing these functions, higher education is engaged in the production of learning. Higher education's production-producing functions are education, research, and public service. Bowen (1977, p. 8) observes that "education as here defined includes both the curricular and extracurricular influences on students." Learning, the product of higher education, consists primarily of changes in human beings—"changes in their knowledge, their characteristics, and their behavior" (Bowen, 1977, p. 12). "Production in higher education, then," according to Bowen (1977, p. 12), "is not the transformation of resources into tangible products; rather, it is the transformation of resources into desired intangible qualities of human beings."

Individual colleges and universities achieve production or student learning through creation of an environment that is intended, by design, to cause desired changes in people. Bloom (1975, p. 18) refers to environments that are created to produce calculated changes in people as "growth-inducing climates." The environment of a collegiate institution includes both the observable—the buildings and the people—and the unseen elements. The unseen environment, according to Bowen, is a culture. "This culture consists in part of the prevailing technologies (or ways of doing things), such as administrative organization, degree requirements, curricula, methods of instruction and research, work loads, rules, rewards and penalties, extracurricular opportunities, and so on. The culture also includes the common values, expectations, standards, assumptions, traditions, general 'atmosphere,' and behavior patterns of the people involved" (Bowen, 1977, p. 13).

The creation of "growth-inducing climates" is a shared responsibility. Bringing about planned and desired changes in human beings as an accepted "production goal" requires organizational and individual commitment and competence. Administrators, faculty, and student services professionals all have opportunities to contribute both to individual perceptions of an institution's environment and to broader institutional perceptions of environment (Stern, 1970).

The industrial concepts of accountability and efficiency are difficult to achieve in a collegiate environment, but may be preconditions for ultimate institutional survival in a rapidly changing world. Mayhew (1979) indicates that for institutions to prosper changes must occur, but such changes must be sensitive to the role, scope, and tradition of the institution. His recommended areas for improvement include: improving administrative structures and policies, enhancing administrative leadership, developing viable management information systems, establishing long-range plans, increasing faculty performance, and instituting controls on faculty and program costs. Student services programs, as part of the institution, must examine current practices, policies, and procedures to ensure effective use of available resources.

## Evolving Role of Student Services

One of the unique characteristics of American higher education is providing structure for the out-of-class life of college students. In many countries of the world, collegiate institutions assume no responsibility for student development in areas other than intellectual growth. In the United States, the extracurriculum has been organized and requires leadership, management, financial support, and professional staffing.

The development of specialized student services occurred

during the middle decades of the twentieth century. During this period, most graduate-level programs of professional preparation for student services were established. By the mid-1960s, college student personnel work had achieved identity, if not universal acceptance, as a professional field. Student affairs is not an academic discipline. Rather, it is an applied professional field that synthesizes bodies of knowledge and theory from various disciplines. The student affairs profession structures and restructures practice and preparation as a result of knowledge and theory from such disciplines as psychology, sociology, education, organizational development, management, and human development.

As a profession, student affairs must be described as "developing." Wrenn and Darley (1949) conducted a systematic analysis of the field using eight traditional criteria of professions and produced "mixed reviews" for student affairs as a profession. Thirty years later, Stamatakos (1981) applied the same criteria and reported, as had Wrenn and Darley, that student affairs is still en route to professional status. Stamatakos asserted, however, that "student affairs has been in a state of becoming for over a century and has become accepted as a traditional educational/service function of American higher education" (Stamatakos, 1981, p. 204).

*Dean.* The initial "manager" of the extracurriculum was the dean of men or the dean of women. While there is some disagreement on whether he was actually the first dean of men appointed, Le Barron Russell Briggs assumed this position at Harvard in 1890 (Cowley, 1940). Blackburn (1969) reports appointments of deans of women at Swarthmore in 1890 and at the University of Chicago in 1892. Rhatigan (1975) has noted that the work of the early deans developed from the campus up and not from theory down. The dean of men's role provided authority and responsibility for "handling" problems associated with students' adaptation to college life. Statements on the role of the dean of men issued during the early twentieth century suggest that the dean's work with students was rooted in a religious orientation (Appleton, Briggs, and Rhatigan, 1982).

The first deans of women also faced multiple expectations. The dean of women was expected to "deal" with all of the conditions that faced women students in a male-dominated culture and, at the same time, champion the intellectual and personal ambitions of young women. Often these ambitions were not respected, and generally the dean of women's role was viewed by faculty members and other administrators as controlling and limiting the behavior of women students.

The titles of dean of men and dean of women continued into the 1960s and the positions, if not the titles, are still to be found on the campus today. With the demise of the concept of *in loco parentis,* changes in legal definitions of adulthood, and a national shift away from "men's affairs" and "women's affairs" to more androgynous notions, the disciplinary roles of deans of men and women have been altered. The developmental role of the dean of men or dean of women clearly remains even though the administrative titles have largely disappeared.

*Personnel Worker.* A second model of the student services specialist was the personnel worker. Like the dean of men or women and contemporary to the dean model, the personnel worker was a part of the organized extracurriculum. The term *personnel,* which refers to manpower, is a military term borrowed from the French language, as distinguished from *material,* which refers to equipment. The personnel movement of the first half of the twentieth century in the United States affected the military, the labor force, mental health practice, and elementary and secondary education as well as student services in higher education.

In 1919, Walter Dill Scott, who had published the first book on the application of principles of psychology to the selection and training of industrial employees, became president of Northwestern University with the intention of establishing an institutional personnel program. Scott believed that the educational emphasis at Northwestern should be on the individuality of students and on present needs and interests. At a meeting of the Northwestern Board of Trustees, President Scott asserted that a college student should be looked upon as more than a candidate for a degree and must be considered as an individual to be developed and trained for a life of service (Blackburn, 1969).

Vocational guidance became a dominant focus of personnel work in both secondary schools and colleges and universities. Because of this emphasis, the terms *guidance* and *student personnel* were used to describe services provided by personnel workers. These two terms were regarded as nearly synonymous during the years of the personnel movement. By mid-century, the term *guidance* was generally applied to forms of personnel work in secondary schools and *student personnel* was used to reference personnel work with college students.

The model of the personnel worker as the student services specialist overlapped the model of the dean of men or women. The early dean had typically come from the ranks of the faculty and had been selected because he or she was both an academician and a person concerned about student welfare. The personnel worker attempted to be a human service specialist and sought to meet needs and interests of students. These two perspectives are not necessarily divergent or incompatible. During the formative period of the field of student affairs, differences in perspectives, goals, and experiences of deans and personnel workers surfaced. On some campuses the two groups coalesced; however, on other campuses the groups worried about each other and instances of hostility resulted (Appleton, Briggs, and Rhatigan, 1982).

The model of the personnel worker tended to span a wider range of service to students than did the model of the dean of men or women. The responsibility for student discipline that was assigned to and accepted by the dean was a source of separation with the personnel worker. Personnel workers envisioned their professional role as applying the skills of the science of human behavior to the needs of students. Moreover, personnel workers tended to view the deans' disciplining of students as antithetical to their developmental efforts.

It is unfortunate that these two groups became adversaries over the matter of discipline. In truth, discipline implies more than punishment, and many of the early deans of men and women spoke not of "disciplining" students but of "character formation," "citizenship training," and "moral and ethical development." As a sociological or educational concept, discipline implies: (1) virtue that results from the application of one's self to a task or responsibility; (2) a form of rehabilitation or re-education; as well as (3) punishment for illegal or improper human behavior. Personnel workers tended to regard the dean's role as a disciplinarian only in the sense of punishment. This view, of course, separated the "punishing" dean from the "promoting" personnel worker (Appleton, Briggs, and Rhatigan, 1982). The two groups stood united, at least in terms of shared goals, when discipline is considered as a concept of personal responsibility or as a form of rehabilitation or reeducation. In fairness to the deans of men and women, it must be noted that the expansion of higher education engendered by philosophies of meritocracy and egalitarianism altered the homogeneity of student bodies and brought more people to campus. One result of this was an increase in the disciplinary (punishment) role of deans. The personnel worker, in turn, became the specialist in human development.

In 1937 the Committee on Student Personnel Work of the American Council on Education defined the essential nature of student personnel work in higher education in a statement entitled "The Student Personnel Point of View" (American Council on Education, Committee on Student Personnel Work, 1937). This statement imposed on colleges and universities an obligation to consider each student as a whole person and to conceive of education as including attention to physical, social, emotional, and spiritual development as well as intellectual development. The student personnel point of view requires institutional commitment to cultivating mental and physical health, moral values, vocational aptitudes and skills, esthetic appreciations, and social relationships as well as intellectual achievement.

A revised and somewhat altered philosophical statement was published in 1949 and again entitled "The Student Personnel Point of View" (American Council on Education, Committee on Student Personnel Work, 1949). The basic philosophical assumptions underlying both statements are (1) the individual student must be considered as a whole; (2) each student is a unique person and must be treated as such; (3) the total environment of the student is educational and must be used to promote full individual development; and (4) the major and ultimate responsibility for the student's development rests with the student and his or her personal resources. Specific student personnel services were identified in the student personnel point of view to promote comprehensive student development. Also emphasized was the need for coordination of services with authority and responsibility assigned to appropriate persons and agencies. An agenda for the future development of the field was also included.

The student personnel worker emerged as the dominant operational model of the period between 1950 and the mid-1970s. The dean of students' position became the leadership position for the student services (or the student affairs) area. It has been observed that "after losing the battle to the personnel worker, the dean of men frequently won the war by moving up to the dean of students' position" (Appleton, Briggs, and Rhatigan, 1982, p. 30).

*Counselor.* The counselor became the "specialized personnel worker" with the establishment of counseling and testing centers on college and university campuses in the 1930s and 1940s. Services to veterans became the genesis of the counseling centers of today. In some instances, the early counseling centers were established especially to assist veterans of World War II to become acclimated to college life. The Servicemen's Readjustment Act of 1944, more commonly called the G.I. Bill of Rights, provided federal aid for college expenses to thousands of veterans. Counseling centers assisted veterans in maximizing their opportunity to attend college.

E. G. Williamson, former dean of students at the University of Minnesota, is credited with originating the counseling approach to student personnel services. In his 1939 book, *How to Counsel Students,* Williamson asserts that counseling "is the basic type of personnel work with individual students and serves to coordinate and focus the findings and the efforts of other types of workers" (Williamson, 1939, p. 36). In reaction to counseling as a form of advice giving, Williamson regarded counseling as education and stressed that its purpose was to supplement academic work through "a comprehensive program geared to the strategic objective of helping each individual to select and grow toward personal goals, of which one is the full development of each individual member of our democratic society" (Williamson, 1950, p. 4).

As a process, counseling is compatible with the assumptions of the student personnel point of view. Counseling is predicated upon belief in human potential for growth and development and the capacity of human beings to learn more effective and efficient forms of behavior.

Both student affairs practice and professional preparation have been significantly affected by the counseling model. While there has never been complete agreement regarding counseling as a model of professional practice, the expectation that student affairs professionals will possess the kinds of interpersonal skills often regarded as counseling skills has existed for some time. Some observers have expressed concern that as counselors, student services specialists have departed from their mission as educators and have become "therapists," as in a medical model. While expressing agreement with the view that student services professionals must develop skills pertinent to their areas of specialization, Parker (1966) has asserted that counseling training develops major professional skills such as sensitivity to others, skill in interpersonal relationships, interviewing skills, ability to analyze objectively an individual's strengths and weaknesses, awareness of the individual differences between people, the ability to identify people's learning difficulties, and knowledge of how people learn.

That counseling skills are important to the competence of student services professionals has been generally accepted. That every member of a student affairs staff is primarily a counselor has not received the same level of acceptance. Parker's more recent work (Parker, 1978; Parker and Lawson, 1978) evidences a combining of counseling with developmental approaches to working with college students. Whereas Williamson (1939) spoke of counseling as the basic type of personnel work, Gilmore cites counseling as "one of the cornerstone skills in student services" (Gilmore, 1980, p. 296).

*Student Development Educator.* The model of the student development educator accentuates the educative role of the student services professional and opposes the notion that student affairs work is exclusively extracurricular. While the student personnel point of view calls for an institutional response to the education of the whole student, the most visible organizational development at most colleges and universities during the 1950s, 1960s, and 1970s was the creation of a separate student personnel services structure (student affairs division). This structure was unquestionably a part of the organized extracurriculum and was viewed as complementary and supplemental to the academic program. This approach to organizational management provided clear identity for student personnel services but also limited educative efforts to the out-of-class life of students. Despite this reality, attempts to build bridges between the student affairs and academic domains were made (Blaesser, 1949; Brouwer, 1949; Arbuckle, 1953; Hardee, 1955; Barry and Wolf, 1957; and Blaesser and Crookston, 1960).

In 1968 the American College Personnel Association (ACPA) initiated Phase I of the Tomorrow's Higher Education (T.H.E.) Project. ACPA commissioned Robert D. Brown of the University of Nebraska to write the monograph *Student Development in Tomorrow's Higher Education—A Return to the Academy* (Brown, 1972) as a "think piece" for the development of a model of practice that would contribute meaningfully to American higher education into the twenty-first century. The Brown monograph calls for collaboration between student development educators (student services professionals) and the academic faculty in promoting student development. Student development is defined as a responsibility of the total campus and not the exclusive province of the student affairs division. Brown defines and details new roles to be played by student services professionals in promoting cognitive and affective student learning in tandem with the faculty.

Contemporary to the Phase I work of the ACPA Tomorrow's Higher Education Project was revision of the guidelines for student affairs preparation programs by the Professional Development Commission of the Council of Student Personnel Associations in Higher Education (COSPA). In 1972 the commission released a paper entitled "Student Development Services in Higher Education" (Council of Student Personnel Associations in Higher Education, Professional Development Commission, 1972), which underwent review by constituent groups and subsequently was published in 1975 as "Student Development Services in Post Secondary Education" (Council of Student Personnel Associations in Higher Education, Professional Development Commission, 1975).

Both the Brown monograph that focuses upon professional practice and the COSPA statement that addresses professional preparation proposed the model of the student development educator. Moreover, both publications emphasized the need for new conceptualization of the focus and scope of student affairs work in the future. In 1975 the report of a special conference that was Phase II of ACPA's Tomorrow's Higher Education Project outlined a process model for student development and invited submission of exemplary programs (American College Personnel Association, Tomorrow's Higher Education Project, 1975). The Phase II report also underscores that student development is the application of human development concepts in postsecondary institutions; suggests that human development can best be described within two major developmental constructs: life stages and developmental tasks; and urges all members of an academic community to understand human development and to develop competencies necessary to implement the student development model.

In their book *The Future of Student Affairs,* Miller and Prince (1976) describe the processes of helping students learn developmental skills, and they draw attention to theory and research on adult development and college student learning. In addition, the book provides illustrations of programs and projects of student development attempted at specific colleges and universities. Miller and Prince also offer a process model of student development for the implementation of student development philosophy.

*Campus Ecologist.* Implementation of the philosophy of student development has caused some theorists to reconceptualize the role of student services in the campus community. A new view of the campus as the client has emerged (Banning,

1978; Drum, 1980; Morrill, Hurst, and Oetting, 1980). (See Chapter Five and Chapter Eight.) The campus ecologist role provides a framework for the student services professional not only to intervene with the individual student but also to address institutional policies, procedures, and organizational structures that have the potential for interfering with education. Consultation, research, evaluation, and advocacy are added as additional responsibilities for campus student services and require new skills and competencies on the part of the practitioner.

The models of student development and campus ecologist are the latest stage in the evolution of the student services profession. As institutions and the greater society of which they are a part change, new roles for student services will emerge.

## Summary

Since the first appointments of student affairs professionals, the focus of student services has been on the out-of-class life of students, the organized extracurriculum. The expectation continues that the quality of student life outside of the classroom, laboratory, and library will be directly and intentionally enhanced by services designed and performed by student affairs professionals. In addition, a role as a developmental educator has evolved during the past two decades. Recent advances in general knowledge of adult development hold promise that both the student services and the student development educator role will be ameliorated. A current philosophical and operational task for the student affairs profession is to design modes of practice that make effective use of the body of knowledge available.

## References

American College Personnel Association, Tomorrow's Higher Education Project. "A Student Development Model for Student Affairs in Tomorrow's Higher Education." *Journal of College Student Personnel*, 1975, *16*, 334-341.

American Council on Education, Committee on Student Personnel Work. *The Student Personnel Point of View.* American Council on Education Studies, Series 1, Vol. 1, No. 3. Washington, D.C.: American Council on Education, 1937.

American Council on Education, Committee on Student Personnel Work. *The Student Personnel Point of View.* (Rev. ed.) American Council on Education Studies, Series 6, Vol. 1, No. 13. Washington, D.C.: American Council on Education, 1949.

Appleton, J. R., Briggs, C. M., and Rhatigan, J. J. "A Corrective Look Backwards." In H. F. Owens, C. H. Witten, and W. R. Bailey (Eds.), *College Student Personnel Administration.* Springfield, Ill.: Thomas, 1982.

Arbuckle, D. S. *Student Personnel Services in Higher Education.* New York: McGraw-Hill, 1953.

Banning, J. H. (Ed.). *Campus Ecology: A Perspective for Student Affairs.* Portland, Oreg.: National Association of Personnel Administrators, 1978.

Barry, R., and Wolf, B. *Modern Issues in Guidance-Personnel Work.* New York: Teachers College Press, Columbia University, 1957.

Blackburn, J. L. "Perceived Purposes of Student Personnel Programs by Chief Student Personnel Officers as a Function of Academic Preparation and Experience." Unpublished doctoral dissertation, Department of Educational Administration, Florida State University, 1969.

Blaesser, W. W. "The Future of Student Personnel Work in Higher Education." In J. G. Fowlkes (Ed.), *Higher Education for American Society.* Madison: University of Wisconsin Press, 1949.

Blaesser, W. W., and Crookston, B. B. "Student Personnel Work— College and University." In C. W. Harris (Ed.), *Encyclopedia of Educational Research* (3rd ed.). New York: Macmillan, 1960.

Bloom, B. T. (Ed.). *Psychological Stress in the Campus Community.* New York: Behavioral Publications, 1975.

Bowen, H. *Investment in Learning: The Individual and Social Value of American Higher Education.* San Francisco: Jossey-Bass, 1977.

Breneman, D. W. "Conceptual Issues in Modeling the Supply

Side of Higher Education." Paper presented at annual meeting of the Southern Economic Association, Atlanta, November 15, 1974.

Brouwer, P. J. *Student Personnel Services in General Education.* Washington, D.C.: American Council on Education, 1949.

Brown, R. D. *Student Development in Tomorrow's Higher Education—A Return to the Academy.* Washington, D.C.: American College Personnel Association, 1972.

Brown, R. D. "The Student Development Educator Role." In U. Delworth, G. R. Hanson, and Associates, *Student Services: A Handbook for the Profession.* San Francisco: Jossey-Bass, 1980.

Brubacher, J. S., and Rudy, W. *Higher Education in Transition.* New York: Harper & Row, 1958.

Butler, N. M. "The American College." *Educational Review,* 1903, *25,* 10–20.

Carnegie Commission on Higher Education. *The Purposes and Performances of Higher Education in the United States.* New York: McGraw-Hill, 1973.

Cohen, M., and March, J. *Leadership and Ambiguity.* New York: McGraw-Hill, 1974.

Council of Student Personnel Associations in Higher Education, Professional Development Commission. "Student Development Services in Higher Education." Unpublished paper, Council of Student Personnel Associations in Higher Education, Washington, D.C., July 1972.

Council of Student Personnel Associations in Higher Education, Professional Development Commission. "Student Development Services in Post Secondary Education." *Journal of College Student Personnel,* 1975, *16,* 524–528.

Cowley, W. H. "The History and Philosophy of Student Personnel Work." *Journal of the National Association of Deans of Women,* 1940, *3,* 153–162.

Crookston, B. B., and Atykyns, G. C. *A Study of Student Affairs: The Principal Student Affairs Officer, the Functions, the Organization at American Colleges and Universities, 1967-1972. A Preliminary Summary Report.* Storrs, Conn.: University of Connecticut Research Foundation, 1974.

Drum, D. J. "Understanding Student Development." In W. H. Morrill, J. C. Hurst, and E. R. Oetting, *Dimensions of Intervention for Student Development.* New York: Wiley, 1980.

Eliot, C. *Educational Reform.* New York: Century Company, 1898.

Freeman, R. B. *The Overeducated American.* New York: Academic Press, 1976.

Gilmore, S. K. "Counseling." In U. Delworth, G. R. Hanson, and Associates, *Student Services: A Handbook for the Profession.* San Francisco: Jossey-Bass, 1980.

Hardee, M. D. (Ed.). *Counseling and Guidance in General Education.* Yonkers-on-Hudson, N.Y.: World, 1955.

Harper, W. R. *The Trend in Higher Education.* Chicago: University of Chicago Press, 1905.

Heard, A. "The Modern Culture of Higher Education: Many Missions and Nothing Sacred." The Wilson lecture, Board of Higher Education, United Methodist Church, Nashville, 1973.

Henderson, A. D., and Henderson, J. G. *Higher Education in America: Problems, Priorities, and Prospects.* San Francisco: Jossey-Bass, 1974.

Horn, F. H. "The Future of the Junior College." *Educational Forum,* 1953, *17,* 429.

Mayhew, L. B. *Surviving the Eighties: Strategies and Procedures for Solving Fiscal and Enrollment Problems.* San Francisco: Jossey-Bass, 1979.

Miller, T. K., and Prince, J. S. *The Future of Student Affairs: A Guide to Student Development for Tomorrow's Higher Education.* San Francisco: Jossey-Bass, 1976.

Morrill, W. H., Hurst, J. C., and Oetting, E. R. *Dimensions of Intervention for Student Development.* New York: Wiley, 1980.

Morrison, S. E. *Founding of Harvard College.* Cambridge, Mass.: Harvard University Press, 1935.

Mueller, K. H. *Student Personnel Work in Higher Education.* Boston: Houghton Mifflin, 1961.

National Center for Education Statistics. *Digest of Education Statistics.* (1973 ed.) U.S. Department of Health, Education, and Welfare Publication no. (OE) 74-11103. Washington, D.C.: U.S. Government Printing Office, 1974.

Newman, F. *Report on Higher Education.* Washington, D.C.: U.S. Government Printing Office, 1971.

Parker, C. A. "The Place of Counseling in the Preparation of Student Personnel Workers." *Personnel and Guidance Journal,* 1966, *45,* 254-261.

Parker, C. A. *Encouraging Development in College Students.* Minneapolis: University of Minnesota Press, 1978.

Parker, C. A., and Lawson, J. M. "From Theory to Practice to Theory: Consulting with College Faculty." *Personnel and Guidance Journal,* 1978, *56* (7), 425-427.

President's Commission on Higher Education. *Higher Education for American Democracy.* New York: Harper & Row, 1947.

Rhatigan, J. J. "Student Services versus Student Development: Is There a Difference?" *Journal of the National Association for Women Deans, Administrators, and Counselors,* 1975, *38* (2), 51-58.

Rosenberry, L. M. *The Dean of Women.* Boston: Houghton Mifflin, 1915.

Stamatakos, L. C. "Student Affairs Progress Toward Professionalism: Recommendations for Action—Part 2." *Journal of College Student Personnel,* 1981, *22* (3), 197-207.

Stern, G. G. *People in Context.* New York: Wiley, 1970.

Turner, F. J. *The Frontier in American History.* New York: Holt, Rinehart and Winston, 1920.

University of Chicago. *Annual Report of the President, 1898-99.* Chicago: University of Chicago, 1899.

Warren, C. *The Supreme Court in United States History.* Boston: Little, Brown, 1922.

Williamson, E. G. *How to Counsel Students.* New York: McGraw-Hill, 1939.

Williamson, E. G. *Counseling Adolescents.* New York: McGraw-Hill, 1950.

Wrenn, C. G., and Darley, J. G. "An Appraisal of the Professional Status of Personnel Work." In E. G. Williamson (Ed.), *Trends in Student Personnel Work (Parts I and II).* Minneapolis: University of Minnesota Press, 1949.

2         William R. Monat

❦ ❦ ❦ ❦ ❦ ❦ ❦ ❦ ❦ ❦ ❦ ❦ ❦

# Role of Student Services: A President's Perspective

As the president of a large residential state university, I have frequently taken for granted the pervasive presence and contributions of those essential functions of institutional life that convention has termed "student affairs." And yet as those of us serving as chief executive officers survey and identify the discrete functions of our institutional environment, we must come to an inescapable conclusion. The responsibilities of student affairs divisions, be they under the supervision of a dean of students or a vice-president for student affairs, encompass significant facets of both institutional existence and student life.

I find myself taken aback on occasion when I realize that my university manages a residence hall program housing 7,600 students, a health service tending to the needs of potentially 22,000 on-campus students, a student financial aid program overseeing more than $30 million in aid, a placement and career development office that each year arranges over 8,000 student interviews for more than 350 potential employers. In addition, a counseling center last year served more than 4,000 students with personal and academic difficulties, and the university programming office managed, in conjunction with the student government, a host of student activities. Finally, the student judicial office reviewed and adjudicated about 1,400 disciplinary cases. The campus recreation program served more than 150,000 participants in a comprehensive program of recreation and extramural experiences, and a campus childcare center served the needs of our returning students. Clearly, a great number of activities, programs, and services are being provided by our student services division.

What I have described above is fairly typical of the scope and depth of student services responsibilities on most university and college campuses, whether they are residential or commuter. The impact of those responsibilities is probably not fully appreciated by most faculty and staff on any campus and at times is so assumed by students that only when difficulties arise are they even cognizant of the pervasiveness of the range of support services offered on the campus.

Faculty and administrators alike assume, and properly so, that the purposes of a university are instruction, research, and public service. What they often do not acknowledge openly is the necessity for the maintenance of an environment that encourages and reinforces the learning process by creating a culture of support services essential in a community where thousands of young men and women are coming to grips with their own personal journey to self-discovery and maturity.

## National Context of Higher Education

American colleges and universities have played a broader role historically than similar institutions in other parts of the world. Particularly in the twentieth century, American colleges and universities have assumed to varying degrees the missions of instruction, research, and public service (Brubacher and Rudy, 1976). This uniquely American orientation can be found in all types of institutions of higher learning—independent universities that date their origins to the eighteenth century, independent liberal arts colleges, and publicly supported institutions. This is true whether those public institutions evolved from the urban, commuter institutions such as the Free Academy of New York established in 1847, the predecessor of what is now the City University of New York, or the residential state universities established during the nineteenth century, many of which were profoundly influenced in their evolution by the land-grant mission enshrined in the Morrill Act of 1862.

During the twentieth century, except for the post–World War II era, most college and university students entered higher education immediately upon graduation from secondary schools. Although the number of students attending urban, commuter institutions has increased dramatically since World War II, the majority of undergraduate students attend residential campuses. Access to higher education has increasingly become an expectation, and the value of choice has been enhanced both with the advent of federally supported student financial aid and, in many states, with state-supported "scholarship" programs. As a result, since the end of World War II higher education in the United States has become an opportunity open to a larger percentage of the nation's population than in any other country in the world. With access and choice as strong societal values on the one hand and a strong student demand driven career opportunity preference on the other, American higher education occupies a role and pursues a mission unparalleled in human history. These values and forces have created circumstances that each year up to the present have witnessed growing enrollments in institutions of higher education in the United States (see Chapter One).

As we contemplate the twenty-first century, it is increasingly obvious that the forces that have shaped this unique American system of higher education are themselves undergoing perceptible change. There are a number of identifiable trends in the higher education context today.

*Competition for Enrollments.* Despite peak enrollments registered nationwide every year in the recent past, the demographics of population will have a profound influence on higher education during the next decade. That impact may or may not result in significant enrollment reductions depending on the location of institutions, the character of their missions, and the responses they display to a changing educational environment. It is almost trite to observe the reality of declining numbers of high school graduates in most parts of the country with the obvious shrinkage in the pool of potential college and university freshman. Although that decline became apparent several years ago, the full impact has yet to be fully experienced at most American colleges and universities. A smaller pool of potential college and university freshman coupled with a more focused set of academic goals on the part of entering freshmen poses a challenge for most institutions, a challenge that has already begun to introduce increased competition in attracting new "traditional" students to campuses around the country.

That competition in some of the smaller liberal arts colleges has resulted in the introduction of more specific career curricula to the traditional liberal arts mission those institutions have pursued for generations. Another manifestation of the competitive environment can be seen in states with large student financial aid programs. There are increasing pressures being generated by both private and public institutions and systems of higher education to garner a larger share of the available financial aid dollars.

*Quality.* A new "value" was thrust into this environment during 1983 with the increased concern expressed about and attention directed to the quality of elementary, secondary, and higher education. This new concern was most dramatically heralded by the report of the National Commission on Excellence in Education (1983), *A Nation at Risk.* A series of additional reports and recommendations have emerged on the public policy agenda for education generally and higher education specifically. High schools are being admonished to provide more intellectually challenging and academically rigorous graduation requirements, and colleges and universities are being urged to adopt more demanding admissions requirements and to provide a more structured and challenging baccalaureate experience for those students admitted (Boyer and Levine, 1981). Questions are already being raised concerning the impact these new proposals and expectations will have on the underpinning values of access and choice.

*Nontraditional Students.* Many universities, particularly state-supported and land-grant institutions, have for decades served the needs of the adult, place-bound learner and responded to public service opportunities and responsibilities. As the so-called traditional student population declines, institutions that had not previously been attentive to those opportunities have now "discovered" the potential of continuing education and the nontraditional student. In the growing, affluent Chicago suburbs, for example, the educational expectations of the place-bound learner that in the past have largely been attended to by the large state universities, such as Northern Illinois University and the University of Illinois, and a few of the private institutions, such as Roosevelt University, have suddenly been discovered by many small private liberal arts colleges that have proposed and in some cases mounted off-campus programs of a career or vocational character. Consequently, the competition for the traditional student will be matched by increasing competition for the nontraditional student in what can be described in most regions of the United States as a free market environment. How the propensity toward competition will be contained or directed in those states where strong coordinating mechanisms for higher education exist remains to be seen.

*Fiscal Constraints.* Both private and public higher education have increasingly experienced financial difficulties, and this trend is likely to continue unabated in the immediate future. These difficulties represent the classic scissors dilemma. On the one hand, costs have risen sharply during the past decade, driven in part by too many years of double digit inflation and largely uncontrollable increases in energy expenditures (see Chapter Four on fiscal management). At the same time, the financial resources to meet those costs have consistently been less than the increased costs. Significant tuition raises have covered a part of the resource requirements at private institutions but in most instances, if it had not been for federal and state student financial assistance programs, even these responses to increased costs would have been ineffective. Publicly assisted colleges and universities have experienced a relative reduction in financial support measured both in constant dollars and in a proportionate share of overall state expenditures. The responses at these institutions have taken the form of both larger tuition charges to students and severe cost containment and cost reduction measures. Very often expenditures for student services have been deemed more vulnerable to reduction strategies than have been direct commitments to academic programs.

University and college administrators have experienced greater flexibility in containing student services costs and on residential campuses in covering increased costs in residence halls by imposing larger room and board rates. It has been more difficult to contain costs in the academic program area for basically two reasons. Certain necessities such as library materials, instructional equipment and commodities, and instructional staff cannot be significantly reduced in the face of stable or growing enrollments, short of limiting or eliminating specific academic programs. In addition, many academic and professional majors have experienced the full impact of computer and information technology, and if institutions are to continue to provide state-of-the-art instruction, the resources necessary to sustain that technology are absolutely essential.

*Accountability.* General environmental forces affecting many public institutions have had a particular impact upon colleges and universities. A growing force with a number of manifestations has been that of "accountability." All institutions of higher education, particularly publicly assisted colleges and universities, have found it necessary to become more accountable for their performance to students. They have had to account to professional accrediting organizations and to deal with a myriad of external mandates ranging from affirmative action to handicapped accessibility, a growing oversight impulse from state executive and legislative agencies, and a more sophisticated public scrutiny of institutional responsibility.

In summary, therefore, the institutional and environmental context within which student services programming occurs has become increasingly dynamic and constrained at the same time. Eroding fiscal support, demands for accountability, shrinking or changing enrollment patterns, the impact of technology, governmental regulatory mandates, and quality of education issues have made institutional management more complex and more challenging than ever before. Every one of these forces affects the scope, content, and opportunity for student services.

## Institutional Context

There is no single ideal model for effective academic administration. Institutional history, mission, and environment affect profoundly the ways in which colleges and universities are managed and directed. Institutional size can also be a significant variable. Although colleges and universities tend to be more alike than dissimilar, publicly assisted institutions often exhibit organizational structures and management practices different from those prevalent in private, independent institutions.

There is one institutional responsibility, however, that probably has great commonality among all kinds of institutions, and that is student services. The institutional responsibilities encompassed within student services are likely to exist at all colleges and universities, public or private, residential or commuter, large or small. How those responsibilities are perceived and the expectations of accountability will depend on the perspective of the observer. The insight that "where one stands depends upon where one sits" underscores the fragile institutional role of student affairs.

Students, particularly those in student government and student organizations, would like to see the student affairs function, and more specifically the vice-president of student affairs or dean of students, as *the* students' advocate. The faculty very often regard student services as peripheral and, indeed, frequently expendable but would be willing in most instances to acknowledge the necessity for the function as a support service without academic responsibility. Many top university and college administrators, including chief executive officers, often look to the student affairs administrator as a conduit for student opinion on the one hand and as an agent for student discipline on the other but all too often do not acknowledge an organizational status comparable to the academic and financial responsibilities of the institution. Student services administrators and professional personnel regard themselves as professionals performing an essential and critical responsibility and encounter frequent frustrations when their contributions are not accorded the institutional centrality they feel is justified. Given these diverse perceptions of the proper institutional role for student services, it should not be surprising that a common organizational structure does not exist. Since any attempt to describe all or even most organizational patterns would go far beyond the design of this discussion, let me comment on how the student affairs function is organized at one university and how it is perceived by one chief executive officer.

The institution that I serve as president is a large, state-assisted university of some 25,000 students. Over 18,000 of these students are undergraduates and the remainder are enrolled in graduate and professional programs. The student services function is directed primarily to the needs of the on-campus student body. The chief administrator of the student affairs program is a vice-president who serves with three other vice-presidents as part of the top administrative team of the university. The vice-president for student affairs is an integral part of the central management team and interacts equally with both the central administration and the senior deans of the university.

Other organizational patterns may evolve in other institutional contexts. No matter what organizational pattern is in place or what the size of the student services budget, I believe that the importance of the function to an institution is enormous.

The scope of administrative responsibilities of the vice-president for student affairs or dean of students permeates the institution and affects not only students but also faculty and staff in other divisions. The expectations placed upon the vice-president for student affairs by administrative peers at times seem unbounded. It is to the student affairs division that the university administration looks when it comes to the entire web of relationships between the institution and student government and the myriad of student organizations. It is to the student affairs division that the university administration looks for a sensitive and effective student financial aid program. It is to the student affairs division that the university administration looks for a representative and acceptable university programming effort encompassing speakers, concerts, films, and other special activities. It is to the student affairs division the university administration looks for a professionally competent health service and student health insurance program. It is to the student affairs division that the university administration looks for a comprehensive and responsive recreation and intramural program. It is to the student affairs division that the university administration looks for a credible and objective student judicial system. It is to the student affairs division that the university administration looks for a productive and creative career-planning and placement program. It is to the student affairs division that the university administration looks for an unobtrusive but accepted counseling and student development program. And finally, it is to the student affairs division that the university administration looks for a smoothly run and student-accepted residence hall system providing for the housing, feeding, and special programming of students.

Since the core of the institutional mission is the instruction and education of students, the multiple ways in which the student affairs function touches those students has to be and is a major concern of the university administration. While the classroom, studio, laboratory, library, and computer centers are the major instructional vehicles of this and any other institution, the fact is that students spend more time each week outside of these central facilities than they do in them. Although the entire university community must contribute to an institutional environment conducive to learning, it is undeniable that the major part of that support system resides within the student affairs division.

*A Point of View.* At a number of large residential universities, the chief student services officer organizationally reports to the chief academic officer. There well may be unique institutional circumstances supporting that arrangement. If the chief academic officer is in effect the chief campus administrator, as is the case in a number of universities, that organizational pattern would make sense. As the chief executive officer at a large state-assisted university and one who takes seriously his campus management responsibilities, I much prefer an administrative structure that places the chief student affairs administrator in a direct reporting relationship to the president. My experience has led me to the conclusion that there simply are too many potential and occasional actual problems about which the chief executive officer "has a need to know," and that the direct reporting relationship provides the greatest likelihood that that need will be served. For essentially the same reason, I also believe the chief student affairs administrator should be part of the central management team for the campus and a major actor in the decision and information processes involving the chief administrators of other university divisions such as academic affairs, business affairs, administrative affairs, and external affairs. Although research, scholarship, and public service are to a greater or lesser extent significant components of institutional mission, it is the instructional responsibility with the student at its core that continues to be the raison d'être for most American colleges and universities. Organizationally, therefore, my administrative imperatives dictate that the instructional function, encompassing research and scholarship, and the student services function enjoy some degree of structural parity since both serve directly and on a continuing basis our primary clients, the students.

American institutions of higher education have wrestled for decades to define an appropriate role for student organizations, including student government, in overall campus governance. However that role has emerged and is exercised on various campuses, it remains essential, in my judgment, that the chief student affairs administrator be an active participant in overall institutional governance in addition to the administrative roles just portrayed. The student affairs division through its varied responsibilities relates to students, student government, and student organizations on a continuing basis and within a different context than do the faculty and other academic support professionals. That large proportion of students' time not committed to the classroom, laboratory, studio, library, computer, and information-processing facilities and study becomes the major institutional concern for student services professionals. The student affairs perspective, therefore, should have a voice in overall institutional governance.

Although the vice-president for student affairs seldom meets the expectation of any student leaders as *the* advocate for student interests, that officer is more often likely to provide an institutional student perspective that the faculty and other administrators for understandable reasons cannot articulate.

*Institutional Expectations for Student Services.* As colleges and universities move into a much more competitive environment, the chief student affairs administrator should become increasingly involved in advising the university administration on external matters. Indeed, increasingly the external university policy team should provide an active role for the student affairs administrator, because the one university-wide administrator with whom students are more likely to have some contact is the chief student affairs officer. It is reasonable to expect, therefore, that the vice-president for students affairs and other key student affairs administrators become involved in parent and alumni relationships. It is also reasonable to expect that an institution fortunate enough to possess an effective and credible placement service should build upon the continuing relationships that service has developed with employers in fostering mutually advantageous relationships between the university and the industries, corporations, and institutions that employ its graduates. At our university we have found this to be a role with enormous promise.

I have served as either chief academic or chief executive officer at two publicly assisted universities over the past thirteen years. One institution was exclusively a commuter institution and the other one primarily a residential institution. I cannot presume to voice the expectations that other chief executive officers might nurture with respect to the student affairs function but I can express the ones I have developed over the past decade or more. Before enumerating my expectations, let me recapitulate what I have concluded are the major components of the student affairs institutional domain. These will vary from institution to institution and reflect unique institutional development. At some institutions the admissions function, the registration and student records function, and even intercollegiate athletics fall under the aegis of student affairs. Those do not happen to be responsibilities of the student affairs division at our university but certainly can be considered to be legitimate student affairs responsibilities. On some campuses academic counseling and advisement are a part of the student affairs missions although I harbor some strong personal reservations concerning the appropriateness of that assignment. Indeed, several years ago the new student orientation program was transferred from the student affairs division to the academic affairs division because we viewed that important responsibility as more centrally an academic affairs rather than a student services function. But most institutional executives would agree that residence halls, health services, student financial aid offices, student placement and career development, counseling and student development, recreation and intramural programming, student activities and student governance, childcare, student center programming, and student discipline are legitimate, indeed, essential responsibilities for student affairs professionals.

Some of these responsibilities are shared also with the faculty or other administrative divisions of the university. Faculty advisers are usually required for student organizations and clubs. Faculty should serve on committees responsible for lecture and concert series and should play a role in the student discipline process. But even in these activities, it is clear that the administrative responsibility rests with the student affairs division.

As a campus chief executive officer, I expect student services personnel to function as professionals. I expect as professionals they will display at all times a sensitivity and responsiveness to student needs, but maintain an unambiguous posture of institutional responsibility and accountability. I expect as professionals they will voice their assessment and their evaluation of student needs and values. But as officers of the university, they will consistently and unambiguously implement institutional policies and observe institutional procedures. I expect student affairs administrators to understand the environment within which they function, to appreciate the meaning of accountability, and to employ their resources in a manner calculated to achieve effective performance. When these expectations are clearly stated by the university administration, it has been my experience that the student services professional performs professionally and responsibly. Just as I expect to be informed about issues and events where the professional feels "I have a need to know," I also expect the student affairs professional to appreciate institutional perspectives that will at times require accommodations and on occasion interventions. Where there is, for example, an external political sensitivity, I expect the student affairs professional to appreciate that sensitivity in on-the-job performance. Above all else, I expect the student affairs professional to be among the first to appreciate our institutional reality, that is, we are here to provide an institutional environment supportive of education to the students who come to our campus. I expect civility and a genuinely pervasive attitude of serving the student population in a professional and responsible fashion. That does not involve catering to every student whim or fad but it does mean that in those areas of responsibility legitimately within the domain of student affairs, students will be treated with respect and firmness, with understanding and sense of service, and with a clear understanding that the service responsibilities of student services constitute an integral part of the educational mission of the college or university.

The student affairs division at Northern Illinois University has assumed, in concert with responsible student leaders, some significant program initiatives. Three of these have been in many respects pioneering efforts. First, in the early 1970s the student body decided to "tax itself" with a special student fee to provide a bus system that not only provides internal campus transportation but also mass transit for students throughout the larger community so that students living off campus would have regular, scheduled transportation to campus. Since university residence halls provide housing and food services for well under half the students studying on campus, this student-operated bus system has not only developed an essential service but has also greatly enhanced the attractiveness of the university for new students. The student busing committee and the student affairs division worked closely with the city government to make it possible to "piggyback" on the student bus system a mass transit service for the entire city. The second initiative took the form of what now has become a well-established student legal assistance office that employs two full-time attorneys paid from student activity fee income. The student attorneys have limited their service to the extent that they do not represent students against the university but do provide assistance and counsel to all students in most other legal areas. Finally, in 1977, the student government working in concert with the student affairs division developed a comprehensive campus recreation program that has emerged as a national model. That program was most recently capped with authorization by the governing board for a student recreation fee to provide for the construction of a large campus recreation building to meet the continuing, growing recreation needs of a large student body. Strong and aggressive student advisory committees to the campus bus system and the campus recreation program have assured continued student support working with the student affairs division.

The student affairs division has also provided leadership in developing effective consultative processes in three other important student services. The Student Health Center Advisory Committee has worked closely with the Student Health Center, a collaborative effort that gained that center accreditation by the American Association of Ambulatory Care just two years ago. The student affairs division working jointly with the Residence Hall Association and student government has established an effective consultative process producing responsible recommendations each year with respect to room and board rates for the 7,600 students living in university-owned residence halls. Most recently the student affairs division working closely with student government has established a similar consultative process concerning fees to support the university student center. These are achievements and continuing responsibilities of the

student affairs division on our campus that have earned the respect of the entire university community including the student
body.

Beyond those signal achievements, and I am sure every
campus can cite comparable illustrations, I expect from the student affairs division overall sound management of the resources
made available in performing the important tasks assigned to
the division. In addition, however, I look to the student affairs
division to provide the university administration on a continuing basis reliable information with respect to student needs,
problems, and services. Not a week goes by without the necessity for sensitive and effective crisis intervention on the part of
student services professionals. I also expect the student affairs
division to serve as an early warning system in identifying problems and, in most instances, to engage in continuing problem
solving without any top-level direction. Finally, and perhaps
most importantly, I expect the student affairs division to serve
as a responsible advocate on behalf of the student body through
the established decision processes of the university and to function as an "institutional conscience" in sensitizing the entire
university community, faculty, staff, and administration to our
primary mission, that is, educating the students who choose to
attend this university.

I do not expect the student affairs division to "manage"
student behavior. All colleges and universities deal with young
men and women who are in the process not only of gaining an
education but, more important in many respects, are also discovering themselves, identifying personal aspirations, and
maturing as human beings. An effective student affairs professional cadre understands the dynamics and volatility of that
always-changing population and seeks to sustain an institutional
environment that reinforces that personal maturation process.
This responsibility requires that the professional not be reluctant to speak up on behalf of student interests but never speak
down to the student. That responsibility requires patience and
always a professional concern and commitment both to the academic enterprise and to the individual process of personal discovery. That responsibility frequently brings the professional

into events of personal tragedy and conflict. The effective student affairs administrator understands the reality of those responsibilities and represents them to the university administration and the university community.

## Future for Student Affairs

Peering through a cloudy crystal ball is a favorite hobby for academic administrators. I have already suggested certain trends and challenges for higher education as we move toward the twenty-first century. Among the most certain are the need to accommodate to changing student populations; stable or even constricting financial resources; increased accountability for institutional performance; compliance with external public policy mandates affecting all institutions in society, including higher education; increased competition between sectors and among institutions for students, faculty, staff and resources; and the public reassertion of higher expectations with respect to student preparation, student achievement, and institutional performance. These trends and challenges will inevitably touch and shape the mission of student affairs professionals and student services programs.

Student affairs professionals must rethink their service agenda in response to changing student populations. Those changes will take a number of directions but essentially three seem most likely. Most campuses will attract older students, those who are beginning higher education at a later age or who are returning to complete or continue their education. These students, like their more traditional peers, are likely to seek educational experiences more finely tuned to career goals and objectives. Historically, student services programs at most colleges and universities have directed resources and attention to the traditional, on-campus student. The emerging mission of serving adult, place-bound learners certainly poses a challenge and a test of ingenuity to student services programmers. Even on residential campuses, most institutions are mounting vigorous efforts to attract the older and in some instances returning student. Again, this nontraditional campus student population poses both a challenge and a set of opportunities for the student services professional.

The accelerating debate over the "quality of education" will most certainly have an impact, one that is still not clear. New student admissions requirements will become more specific and probably more demanding. The baccalaureate experience in college and university curricula will undoubtedly become more structured and prescriptive. Apart from an abiding concern over student access and choice that these changes generate, the fact is that the net result of this trend will be a somewhat different student population on many college and university campuses. Does this pose a need to reassess the mission of student affairs?

First, the more mature and career-directed student is likely to be very attentive to institutional performance and to insist that the university provide what it promises in the way of curriculum, faculty, facilities, and support services. The current student population on most campuses appears much more selective and discerning in making academic choices and evaluating academic experiences. For that reason alone, colleges and universities are increasingly becoming aware of the need for performance accountability and are taking steps to achieve it. Academic program review has become an established and rigorous process of self-evaluation. On many campuses, including ours, students have insisted on and have received a responsible role in decision processes concerning institutional programs directly affecting students outside the classroom. Not only are students active participants in decision processes with respect to fees but justifiably feel that they have an obligation to assess the performance of those services for which they directly pay. These internally generated accountability processes are likely both to continue and to expand. When coupled with externally mandated accountability policies—whether in affirmative action, handicapped accessibility, Title IX compliance, or civil rights compliance—colleges and universities will need to establish ways to assure institutional performance and accountability. Divisions of student affairs on most campuses have played and will continue to play a crucial role in that process. A challenge to student affairs professionals as well as others on our campuses is that of devising procedures to facilitate institutional accountability.

Second, the emerging competitive environment in higher education and the momentum toward addressing issues of quality will also be at the center of the student services agenda in the years ahead. Working closely with the academic community, student affairs professionals will and must address the "quality of life" issue on college and university campuses and in many ways provide the leadership in that effort. The academic community can and must address concerns over academic quality and academic performance and establish means of assuring both. But the quality of life on a campus extends beyond the classroom, laboratory, and studio. College and university campuses must increasingly be attentive to sustaining an environment conducive to learning. That environment need not and should not mute academic challenges but it must become even more supportive of the differing needs and expectations of a changing student population. As societal life-style changes, such as the emerging concerns for health, exercise, fitness, and individual autonomy, become more enduring, institutional programs and services must be responsive to those styles. It is here that the student affairs function should and must become assertive in its leadership for the entire university community.

Finally, all of these emerging new directions and altered missions for student affairs will most likely occur within the environment of stable or constricting financial support for both colleges and universities and students. Student affairs professionals must work closely with college and university administrations to encourage and support efforts to maintain and indeed increase various forms of student financial assistance. Access to higher education has been one of the great success stories in twentieth-century America, and the financial aid professionals within student affairs must if anything become even more assertive in insisting that the story not end. Student affairs professionals must also work closely with university and college administrations in devising ways to market higher education to an increasingly skeptical public. Colleges and universities will simply have to find ways of conveying the message that publicly supported higher education, whether in state-assisted institutions or private institutions, has been one of the major achievements of American society in our lifetime. It increasingly has become the pervasive foundation for science and technological development, industrial growth and diversification, and general economic well-being. But the overarching contribution of higher education in American society has been its commitment to nurturing an educated population capable of making informed decisions within the framework of democratic government. As professionals in higher education, we should all take some pride in those contributions and accomplishments. Indeed, we must go beyond pride and satisfaction to document what those contributions and achievements have been, continue to be, and will be in the future.

Student affairs professionals will help determine the direction of higher education in the years to come. However, they must recognize that their role is essentially a supportive role. It must be negotiated on each campus and be responsive to the unique circumstances on that campus. The student affairs professional must acknowledge the preeminence of academic leadership, and the academic community, in turn, must recognize the centrality of the student affairs supportive role.

## References

Boyer, E. L., and Levine, A. *A Quest for Common Learning.* Washington, D.C.: The Carnegie Foundation for the Advancement of Teaching, 1981.

Brubacher, J. S., and Rudy, W. *Higher Education in Transition: An American History, 1936–1976.* (Rev. ed.) New York: Harper & Row, 1976.

National Commission on Excellence in Education. *A Nation at Risk: The Imperative for Educational Reform.* Washington, D.C.: U.S. Government Printing Office, 1983.

# 3

Margaret J. Barr

૨ૄ૯ ૨ૄ૯ ૨ૄ૯ ૨ૄ૯ ૨ૄ૯ ૨ૄ૯ ૨ૄ૯ ૨ૄ૯ ૨ૄ૯ ૨ૄ૯ ૨ૄ૯ ૨ૄ૯ ૨ૄ૯

# Internal
# and External Forces
# Influencing Programming

Institutions of higher education are inextricably linked to larger society. These linkages take many forms, including funding support, expectations for student access, governmental regulation, and reactions from specific groups to institutional decisions. These and other linkages weave the fabric of the political environment surrounding and influencing each college or university. This political environment must be accounted for in the decisions, policies, and programs of any college or university. It cannot be ignored.

Consider the following situations faced by two institutions—one a public university, the other a small liberal arts college. In the public institution, uncertainty reigns because of a dispute between the state legislature and the governor over the tax increase introduced by the governor. The campus administration makes plans to respond to the budget reductions that will be necessary if the tax package is not passed. Part of the plan calls for a massive tuition increase. Many students and faculty vehemently oppose the plan and join together in a letter-writing campaign. Parents write both the governor and their legislators expressing outrage over the proposed tuition increase. The same scene is repeated at other public universities throughout the state. The legislature will return to session next spring and half of the current legislators face reelection. Political action and candidate support groups are formed on campuses throughout the state. A tax bill passes but not at the level sought by higher education.

At the private institution, a large donation has just been given to the college to fund a much-needed chemistry laboratory. The student newspaper discovers that the donor made her fortune by investing in South African mining stock and, in fact, the current gift is a block of that stock. Student and faculty groups express outrage that the college would even think of profiting from the exploitation of a Third World people. The administration is convinced that the only way the new laboratory will be built is through this donation. Other corporate and individual donors become uneasy about donating to the campus when protests of this nature could develop. Finally, the donor withdraws her offer of support, the campus quiets down, and the chemistry lab is not built.

Both of these institutions are struggling with the political environment of higher education. These are but two of the many political realities that must be dealt with during the decision-making process on campus. Whether the institution is large or small, public or private, two or four year, there are any number of political forces at work on and in the institution. Simply wishing it was not the case will not make the decisions easier or the forces less potent.

For many student services professionals, there is abstract acceptance of the wider political environment of higher education. Such acceptance and understanding is not, however, often translated to their daily work. The stance often taken by such individuals is that *our* program, *our* activities, *our* policies, and *our* external and internal governance structures are all above politics—a naive view at best. Baldridge (1971), Baldridge and

Tierney (1979), Hines and Hartmark (1980), Richman and Farmer (1974), Saunders (1983), and others have studied the political environment of higher education. Colleges and universities are political bodies and in that sense provide a reflection of the larger society. As Lou Keating and I previously admonished (Barr and Keating, 1979), the astute student services professional should be knowledgeable about the political environment and use that knowledge to develop, maintain, and implement quality student services programs. Unfortunately, the politics of higher education and the relationship of politics to student services program development is not often discussed within the profession.

This chapter is designed to bridge part of that gap by expanding on this earlier work. It is based on our reading, our observations, and those of our colleagues throughout the country, and our experiences as administrators on several campuses. The unique thrust of the chapter is to directly relate the external and internal politics of higher education to program development in student services. Student services professionals must make a choice of the degree of their individual involvement in the political arena. All student services professionals should, however, make that choice deliberately after careful consideration of the issues involved.

## External Political Environment

Although higher education in the United States is over 300 years old, it has never developed a uniform pattern of organization, control, administration, philosophy, or support. Such diversity has developed in part because there is not a state church, there is a deeply ingrained suspicion of centralized power, and all of our colleges and universities are governed by lay boards (Brubacher and Rudy, 1976).

One result of such diversity is lack of uniformity and complexity within higher education. Competition and interest in the enterprise is strong. Kantor and Stein (1979) characterize politicized organizations as those existing under conditions "when environments press or need to be managed, when stockholders are activated, when interests are strong" (p. 303). Their definition of a politicized organization is a fair and accurate description of the current status of American higher education.

*External Environmental Press.* All colleges and universities must confront the external environment and most attempt in some way to manage it. The larger society has a real and direct influence on institutions expressed through a number of avenues. Both private and public institutions are affected by rules, regulations, and statutes emanating from the local, state, and federal government. Lingenfelter (1983) characterizes these governmental influences as micro and macro decisions. "Macro decisions are those which periodically determine higher education's share of state resources and decide fundamental questions of governance, structure, or policy. Micro decisions are those which determine the allocation of resources within higher education and a variety of regulatory issues ranging from program coordination and approval to auditing and accounting procedures" (pp. 68-69). The influence of government on higher education is enormous. Financial aid, research grants, equal opportunity compliance, and the privacy of student records are some of the most obvious influence sources. More subtle but nonetheless powerful are the regulatory issues related to contracts, new construction, and accounting procedures. These latter issues are part of the daily life of most student services programmers.

Environmental press is not only generated through government regulation. Higher education must also be responsive to changing economic conditions, technological advancements, the employment market, and changing societal expectations of education. Managing or responding to a greater environment has become even more complex with the influence of print and electronic media on public opinion. Bennis captures the frustration of a university president when he exclaims after an incident on his campus that "the episode illustrated how the media, particularly TV, make the academic cloister a global village in a goldfish bowl. By focusing on the lurid or superficial they can disrupt a president's proper activities while contributing nothing to the advancement of knowledge" (1979, p. 39). External environmental press can come in many forms and can be activated by many different issues. In a speech more than a decade ago, Clark Kerr stated that the greatest challenge in higher education to be faced in the future was the rise of public power (Kerr, 1982). That statement is even more true today. The external political environment is not an amorphous mass. Instead it is composed of any number of publics or shareholders in the academic enterprise.

*External Shareholders.* Stephen Spurr, former president of the University of Texas at Austin, offers an interesting approach to understanding political pressure groups with an interest in higher education. In his class entitled "Public Policy Issues in Higher Education," he asks students to list all the groups that might have an interest in the institution. Depending on the college or university, such a list might include groups such as students, faculty, staff, parents, alumni, legislators, state and federal agencies, and business or industry. Spurr then focuses the discussion on determining what each of these groups wants or needs from the president of the university and what the president wants or needs from the group. This analysis provides insight into the external and internal forces that bring political pressure on an institution.

A few examples will illustrate the complexity of dealing with external shareholders. New issues of service delivery including remote access, variable admission policies, and child-care have emerged with the demands of adult learners for access to higher education (Keller, 1983). The change of political administrations in Washington has led to a changed emphasis on enforcement of antidiscrimination statutes. New alliances between business and higher education have formed as both attempt to deal effectively with the technological society (Keller, 1983). In the decades ahead, these issues will also shift and change.

External shareholders may be much more difficult to understand and to effectively confront than internal shareholders because new issues constantly arise, agendas frequently change, and new alliances are often formed. The challenge for higher education is to anticipate and respond to the changing agendas of external shareholder groups because even if the groups, the alliances, and the agendas are not stable, each constituency group feels a direct interest in the institution and holds a concurrent expectation that its interest will be accommodated.

Although external shareholder groups may be difficult to define and accommodate, they do provide positive influences on an institution. These influences include serving as sources of material and approval, providing a check on the unilateral exercise of authority, and focusing the institution in the task of defining specific populations where the institution holds a unique responsibility to serve (Kantor and Stein, 1979).

Trustees, regents, or governing boards can be viewed as either external or internal shareholder groups. For most campus-based individuals, the power and authority of governing boards is recognized; however, they are not seen as an integral part of the institution. Governing boards themselves are experiencing a change in their own role definition. Walker (1979) states that "before the 1960s, for example, boards generally accepted as a major responsibility the interpretation and defense of the university to the public. Since then, many boards seem to feel that their function is to represent the interests of the public in the management of the university" (p. 130). Thus even governing boards, with a special relationship to the institution, have changing agendas.

Perspective needs to be maintained when dealing with external shareholder groups for the potential exists for their influence to overcontrol internal policies and procedures. However, Keller warns that "if educational institutions are to reverse, or at least slow down, the trend toward outside interventions in their affairs, they must shape their own destinies in ways that are acceptable to the public and its elected leaders" (1983, p. 25). Thus, external shareholder groups must be approached in positive ways to seek support in meeting sound educational goals.

## Internal Political Environment

Discussions of campus politics and the political environment must focus on both the formal and informal organizational structure of the institution. The formal governance structure and the designated roles of faculty, students, staff, and administrators provide one perspective of the internal political environment. Of equal importance are the informal relationships, coalitions, and significant relationships that emerge within a campus community. In the last two decades these two organizational elements have become even more important as change has been forced on higher education from the external political environment. For "when the environment 'acts up' or change is rapid, nearly everyone's organizational life is touched by and affected by political issues. Indeed, internal and external political issues are intertwined with an organization's life stage" (Kantor and Stein, 1979, p. 303).

*Internal Environmental Press.* Higher education's internal environmental press is a result of a set of conditions unique to American higher education. Control of the organization by lay boards, as previously stated, is one source of press (Keller, 1983). The internal governance structure of the institution is also a contributing factor. Colleges and universities are not simple hierarchies. Instead, they exhibit complex decision processes dominated by committees (Baldridge and Tierney, 1979). At the same time, students are developing into more discriminating consumers of the educational product and are demanding value received for money spent (Chait, 1982). Fiscal resources are constrained and competition within the institution for those scarce resources is intensifying.

The environment of higher education is further complicated by a prevailing idealized view of higher education. Keller (1983) says this belief system views higher education as "an Athenian democracy of professional scholars who know each other and share a bundle of values and aspirations which they practice in their institutional lives" (p. 30). This belief system is confronted on a daily basis on most campuses. Current conditions such as fiscal constraints, external environmental press, sheer size, and organizational complexity provide constant challenges to the idealized view of the educational process. When such challenges occur, stress and political reactions erupt in the environment. A pure, apolitical environment simply does not exist within American higher education. The needs and desires of those who make up the institution combined with issues of money, space, and priorities cause environmental press. The conditions under which such stress will develop may not always be predictable, but that stress and conflict will emerge is inevitable.

*Internal Shareholders.* Four internal shareholder groups can be identified within a college or university: students, faculty, staff, and the administration. Each of these groups has a high degree of interest in the enterprise and can be activated on any number of issues. External forces such as consumer protection, the growth of unionization in education, and the federal response to student financial aid can help shape the responses of these internal shareholder groups. It is a mistake, however, to assume that there will always be agreement by all members of one group on an issue. For example, the elected student government may oppose the new selective service requirements for financial aid while the student newspaper editorializes that they are logical and justifiable. The faculty senate may endorse a proposal to provide contingency contracts depending on the size of classes for the summer session while the women faculty members assigned to the less popular courses that do not make enrollments decry the policy as institutional sexism. Some civil service staff members believe all pay raises should be automatic while others who excel in their work are in favor of merit pay consideration. The list is endless. Thus, debate, disagreement, and conflict can occur within any shareholder group and are almost inevitable between shareholder groups.

Baldridge (1971) states that conflict is a natural phenomenon within higher education. Each shareholder group and subgroup has a set of values and expectations of prime importance to them, but those values and expectations may not be held in common with any other group. Alliances within and between groups shift and change, depending on the vested interest of the constituency group at the time. "We may expect that both students and faculty will challenge administrative authority from time to time and that on occasion the two groups will join forces against the administration and the governing board. But

students and faculty may not always be allies. Administrators
and students may find it advantageous to combine against the
faculty on such matters as attending to undergraduate teaching,
accessibility of faculty members to students, academic requirements, and educational innovations" (Mortimer and McConnell,
1978, p. 163). Thus the astute student of campus politics needs
to be aware of each shareholder group as an entity, recognize the
potential differences within and among groups, and be able to
assess the effects of group reactions on policy and program
decisions.

## Politics and Program Development

Knowledge of and the ability to use campus politics to
meet program goals is an essential skill for the student services
professional. A program, just like an institution, does not exist
in a vacuum and the astute programmer accounts for the changing nature of campus politics as part of the program planning
cycle. Newton and Richardson (1976) found that political skill
is not valued as highly as other skills by the profession. This is a
mistake since it can lead to program errors (see Chapter Twelve
by Keating).

Introduction of a new program idea or suggested modification to an existing program is, by itself, a political act (Baldridge and Tierney, 1979). Those in authority may feel threatened, those with power may feel neglected, and the issue of territory is bound to arise. Careful assessment of both the external
and internal political environment and their respective shareholder groups can help assure that there is at least a fair hearing
for a new idea.

Understanding the subtle differences between authority
and power for decision making is a first step in successful program development or modification. Richman and Farmer (1974)
indicate that legal authority is only the tip of the decision-
making structure within the organization. Knowledge of legal
authority can be gained through study of the formal organization chart. At the very least, study of the formal organization
chart will prevent the error of seeking help from an administra-

tor who no longer has authority over a unit. Step two involves the task of extending the formal organization chart to identify individuals, communication links, and alliances that never appear on paper. This extended organization structure is usually identified through careful observation, informal conversation, and tracking how decisions are actually made. Without knowledge of who can make a specific decision and who can influence that decision through their personal power, programming is a much more difficult task. For true power within the organization may differ in significant ways from what appears on the formal chart. Power within an organization is often vested in the least expected positions. It is gained through referent power (the assistant to), associational influence (the lunching friend), longevity (the twenty-year person), personal initiative, expertise, and access and control of vital information (Richman and Farmer, 1974). Never believe that once the initial assessment of the informal organization chart is made that the task is done. Constant monitoring is needed as agendas change and alliances form and reform. Lack of awareness of such changes can catch the programmer off guard.

Most often the student services programmer will encounter power and authority questions as territorial issues. Territory can either be a perceived sphere of influence by a person or an agency or can be actual physical space. To illustrate, a need is identified to provide additional childcare services for returning adult students. The student services division already has a small childcare center in adjacent space to a child development research laboratory controlled by an academic department. The child development laboratory does not use its space in the afternoon. The director of the childcare center requests permission to use the child development lab space in the afternoon. Not only is the request denied but questions are raised about the legitimacy of the childcare center being located within the division of student affairs. This is clearly a territorial issue: actual space and sphere of influence. Several options are now open to the student service unit: concede and pull back from any proposed service expansion in the afternoon, move the issue to another level within the organizational structure, go to the students with the problem, or refocus the concern on the broader need for expanded childcare services on the campus. Each of these strategies has both short- and long-term consequences for the service unit and the student affairs division. All are political decisions. One issue that should be considered when faced with such a strategy choice is the balance between a short-term gain/loss or a long-term gain. In other words, will the battle be won but the war be lost? Several other questions need to be asked. Will the ultimate goals of childcare on the campus be better served by engaging in the territorial dispute? Will legitimate power and authority for the childcare center be eroded if the territorial issue is not confronted? Can the current territorial dispute actually be used to exert pressure toward resolving the larger institutional problem of providing quality childcare for returning students? The successful programmer will analyze the situation and monitor the issues to assure that attention is focused on the real issue of program goals and student needs rather than the false issue of territory.

Politics and program development are indeed linked. But for many student services professionals, taking a political stance raises questions of ethics and humane values. Is it possible to be political and still be a professional? We feel the answer is a resounding yes. This can only occur, however, under conditions where the practitioner is able to frame an acceptable view and definition of politics.

## Responsible Politics

Although, as Walker (1979) states, a political view is not the only way to observe and interact with the institution, it can provide a useful perspective for the student services professional. To many, the mere thought of becoming political raises questions of ethics and values. The word *politics* brings images of smoke-filled rooms, shady deals, and under-the-table payoffs. Politics *can* be ugly, nonproductive, and unrewarding. But "politics and political behavior are not necessarily corrupt or retrograde" (Walker, 1979, p. 39). Political awareness and concomitant political skills can assist the student services professional in gaining program support. Organizational politics is a reality and political skills provide one method for achieving resolution on issues and managing the inevitable conflict within the institution.

Kantor and Stein (1979) state that "political issues are not the same as interpersonal issues" (p. 306). That view is perhaps the biggest barrier in the effective use of the political system by the student services professional. Our profession is based largely on interpersonal skill development and use of interpersonal skills to help individuals and groups grow and develop. We believe that interpersonal skills can also be responsibly used by the professional in the political arena. However, it cannot be assumed that mere caring and relating are enough. Responsible political behavior for the student services professional involves three additional elements: showing respect, gathering information, and observing and analyzing individual and organizational behavior patterns.

*Respect.* A good politician either on or off the campus exhibits genuine respect for others. Professional politicians view citizens as potential voters with the power to keep or remove them from office. Therefore, the politician tries to assure timely responses to citizen inquiries, extends help in resolving difficulties with government agencies, and provides communication regarding accomplishments on behalf of the citizenry.

The politically astute student services professional should exhibit similar respect for each individual and shareholder group associated with the enterprise. Bases need to be touched, information shared, questions answered, and evidence presented on a regular basis about programs, activities, and services. On a personal level, political respect is expressed by careful attention to issues of professional protocol and personal courtesy. When interacting with a parent, a student, a new staff member, or a powerful member of the academic organization, recognition of that individual's position and feelings is essential. Silently asking the question "How would I feel in his or her place?" often provides that useful perspective.

Political respect is also shown in organizational behaviors. Each agency, department, and division within the institution has a history and tradition. Agencies and departments are usually organized to meet a specific need and are staffed by individuals with expertise in the specified area. This knowledge and experience base must be respectfully acknowledged in interactions although the programmer may not always agree with a specific point of view. There is an implication in the term *political respect* that we recognize and acknowledge the multiple pressures faced by colleagues and students, friends and foes, supporters and opponents. Finally, the respectful political stance is one that embraces the principle that all people, agencies, and groups are owed the courtesy of a respectful hearing of their views.

*Information.* Responsible political behavior involves seeking and analyzing information. It implies a willingness to listen prior to leaping to conclusions. It requires the development of multiple information networks. Responsible political behavior demands "homework" through study of facts, figures, implications, and background material.

There are many sources of information within a college or university. Many individuals on the campus have specialized knowledge that can assist the programmer in filling the information gap. Sometimes information is acquired in casual conversations over coffee or on a cocktail party circuit, although this information usually requires independent verification. Other information emerges through direct inquiry or guided conversations with significant people in the organization. A powerful but little used information source is annual reports and old files on the subject. Some sources of information can only be reached through institutional data files and research reports. Two often overlooked sources of information are the business and institutional research offices. At the very least, a great deal of information must be sought and analyzed prior to making assumptions about individuals or any other part of the organization. Reliance on generalizations or transferring experience from another campus without checking validity within the new organization is a mistake. The responsible campus politician does homework on both a personal and professional level. Remember the well informed are usually the best prepared in any future negotiations.

*Behavioral Patterns.* Most people and organizations develop behavior patterns. The skill lies in recognizing them as patterns and using that knowledge to meet program goals. Most student services professionals account for individual behavior patterns on a daily basis. For example, the knowledge that the vice-president never likes to hear new ideas early in the morning assists in scheduling meetings when action is needed. Understanding that a staff member has difficulty in dealing with conflict helps in developing the team to deal with another agency where conflict may emerge.

Student services professionals, however, usually evidence less skill in recognizing organizational behavior patterns. Institutional tradition, history, and structure all tend to obscure the causes of those behavior patterns. Thus, when we transfer our skill of understanding individual behavior patterns to the organization, we often encounter problems. We expect to understand the antecedents of the organization's behavior. However, it may not be possible or even productive to attempt to reach such a level of understanding. It is more important to recognize that patterns do exist and that elements or issues appearing to be independent are often linked, if only through the history of the organization. To illustrate, the new student life housing officer decides to make a proposal combining the business and student affairs functions. He has done his homework, was noted for his courtesy, and had listened carefully, yet he could not get to first base with his proposal. As he was making his proposal, the following events were in progress. The college business manager told the president she was going to retire at the end of the year. The dean of students was actively seeking a title upgrade to vice-president. The director of campus buildings and grounds had been complaining all over campus about the irresponsibility of the student life staff. The president was dealing with a difficult academic tenure case. No wonder no progress was made on the reorganization. If the housing director makes an assumption that the unified structure was not possible, a strategic political error would have been made. Although the lack of response to the proposal did not appear to be rational, there were reasons. In addition to the changes contemplated in the organization, it may be that resources are limited, the president is essentially neutral about the concept, or other issues have priority. In this illustration, the larger organizational change needed to be resolved prior to making a change in the housing structure. In fact, a negative or nondecision about any issue may only be a signal that the timing is incorrect.

*Ground Rules.* There are a number of ground rules for responsible political behavior by the student services professional. These include but are not limited to the following:

- *Know the goals.* Effective use of the political system requires clarity about what you want to have happen. Vague notions of change usually do not produce success. The student services professional should be able to identify a problem, a needed modification, or an unmet need and then develop a specific plan to resolve the issue. A broad master plan with time lines and resource requirements is essential. The plan, however, should not be rigid but be open to new input and change during the development stage.
- *Set priorities.* Too often we try to do too much and end up not doing anything well. This does not mean that you give up your day-to-day responsibilities in order to pursue a new program thrust. It does mean you do not take on three new programs at the same time. Remember: "The person who sticks to one or two critical issues is most likely to win" (Baldridge and Tierney, 1979, p. 175).
- *Use strategic timing.* The most effective campus politicians have mastered the art of strategic timing. Knowing when to propose a new idea is perhaps the most critical skill in program development. Simple signs are often your most effective guides. Wait for a while if your immediate supervisor is harried or hassled. If a major reorganization plan is in progress, postpone the new idea until the dust settles. Timing issues will vary with each campus. Observe past successes, ask for advice, and pick up clues to hone your timing skills.
- *Build alliances and bridges.* If you find people interested in the idea you are proposing, develop a method to involve them in the program development process. Including

people who have an interest in what you are doing or propose to do helps build a base of support for the new effort.

- *Involve the decision maker.* Be sure that your administrative
  superior is aware of the small steps you are taking to reach
  your goal. Communication with him or her on both a formal
  and informal basis is essential. The knowledge, expertise,
  and political skills of a decision maker can add critical elements to the planning process and eventually assure support
  for the ultimate project.

- *Do not surprise your boss.* This is a corollary to the previous
  rule. No one likes to be surprised, least of all the person who
  must protect you, your agency, and your resources in the
  political arena. Tell your supervisor of both successes and
  failures. An early warning can sometimes avert disaster.

- *Never ignore established committees.* Colleges and universities are filled with committees. Internal shareholders feel
  that their interests are protected through the formal committee structure. If an established committee will have the
  ultimate domain over your plan, test the waters with key
  committee members on an informal basis. You may receive
  valuable help. Another strategy is to volunteer to serve on
  the committee or provide staff assistance to it. Good, solid
  staff work is impressive to most committee members because
  their membership is usually characterized by "fluid participation" (Baldridge and Tierney, 1979, p. 177). By providing
  staff work, you can often give the impetus to see the idea
  through to the conclusion you desire.

- *Identify links and use them.* If you have done your homework, identifying links with other offices, agencies, groups,
  and individuals is much easier. Once you have identified potential linkages, work to improve those ties. Volunteer to
  work with others on projects and assist them in meeting
  their goals. Reciprocity for your ideas is usually then found.

- *Exercise patience.* Good program development requires an
  extraordinary amount of patience. Change is a slow process
  within the academic community and you must be willing for
  some processes to take their natural course, as slow as it may
  be. By exercise of good political skills, you should be able to

keep the concept alive and use the time to discover the real barriers to implementation. This does not mean that you do not prod or question about an issue. It does mean you use strategic timing when you do so.

- *Use the formal system.* There is a highly complex decision-making structure within higher education and it works for the most part. Asking questions of the correct individual can often alleviate a concern without much effort. Attempting to provide good solid staff work at appropriate levels of the organization will avert premature decisions on the program. Usually the formal system of decision making, although cumbersome, does work and you should acquire skill in identifying and using it.

- *Be prepared.* Good programs are developed through fine staff work. You should be prepared for as many questions as possible. If you don't know the answer, admit it and then provide a quick turnaround on the information being sought. Nothing replaces good staff work and a good plan in the process of getting a new idea accepted.

Following the rules does not guarantee success. Despite good planning, a good idea, excellent documentation of a need, or logical organizational issues, a plan or program idea may fail. When that happens, and it will, you must decide whether you want to fight or engage in battle or put off the issue to another day.

*Political Battles.* Many believe you should only fight when victory is assured. At times, however, we do encounter situations where the idea or principle is important and we feel we must fight for adoption. A decision to engage in battle should not be made lightly. There are consequences involved in battles, and those consequences must be evaluated before the decision is made. Prior to making a decision to fight for a principle or idea, ask the question whether the outcome will really make a difference in five years. If the answer is a resounding yes, then preparation should be made to engage in protracted conflict.

One of the preconditions of a successful battle is your

personal and professional integrity within the organization. If you are viewed as a credible individual, a person without the proverbial chip on the shoulder, and a person who does not jump into the fray without all the facts, your success ratio will be improved. A second precondition is that you are very clear about what you want and can live with. Vague battles without a focused outcome generally deteriorate into guerrilla warfare accomplishing very little positive change. Finally, before engaging in battle, a strategy is needed. Your strategy will necessarily vary with the issues, the personalities, and the parts of the organization involved in the conflict. Some issues can and should be confronted directly and others need to be approached more obliquely.

Personal issues with colleagues in your immediate work environments should usually be confronted in a direct, assertive manner. Preparation is required when conflict with individuals in other areas is imminent. Use of your informal communication network can help you understand the position of the person and how that individual might react to a direct confrontation. Within bounds of professional and ethical conduct, you can acquire a great deal of information on how to best resolve a conflict with another individual. Once you design an approach, you can then begin the attempt to resolve the issue.

Agency or department issues require more than an individual strategy—a team effort is required. Use the resources around you to determine the best method of solving the problem. The insights and cooperation of your colleagues may provide new ways to approach the situation or can help you gain perspective regarding the need for battle at this time.

If you decide to engage in a political battle, certain ground rules should be observed. First, let your boss know about the problem and ask for specific help in developing a strategy to resolve the conflict. Second, be professional as you discuss the issue and as you interact with the other individual or agency. Third, be absolutely clear about what you can give up without compromising the principle. Fourth, be pleasant; usually you will have to continue a working relationship during and after the period of conflict. Do not let a disagreement on one issue spill over into all your interactions with the other party. Fifth, actively seek a compromise solution. Your ability to compromise on nonessential elements will enhance your ability to work with the individual or the agency in the future. Finally, if you do win, accept the victory with grace and good humor. Bragging about victories accomplishes nothing but diminution of yourself.

Battles are never easy. They should never be entered into without a just cause. If they are necessary, your strategy should be sound and your conduct above reproach.

### Final Word of Advice

Politics is part of the organization of higher education. Your response to the political environment and your ability to function effectively within it may make the difference in the success of student services programs. There is a danger, however, that you may begin to see all interactions as essentially political. Not all agendas, people, or ideas have political overtones, and it is a mistake to have only a political view of your working environment. It is especially necessary to keep a personal and professional balance when you become involved in campus politics. One way to maintain such a balance is to develop a network or support group both on a personal and professional level. Colleagues and friends, both on and off campus, whose judgment you trust can become invaluable sounding boards and balancing agents. After trust is established, such friends and colleagues can help you maintain perspective, help you do what you do well, and assist you in using the political system toward the positive goal of providing quality student services programs.

### References

Baldridge, J. V. *Power and Conflict in the University.* New York: Wiley, 1971.

Baldridge, J. V., and Tierney, M. L. *New Approaches to Man-*

*agement: Creating Practical Systems of Management Infor-*
*mation and Management by Objectives.* San Francisco: Jossey-Bass, 1979.

Barr, M. J., and Keating, L. A. (Eds.). *New Directions for Stu-*
*dent Services: Establishing Effective Programs,* no. 7. San
Francisco: Jossey-Bass, 1979.

Bennis, W. "Why Leaders Can't Lead." In R. M. Kantor and
B. A. Stein (Eds.), *Life in Organizations.* New York: Basic
Books, 1979.

Brubacher, J. S., and Rudy, W. *Higher Education in Transition.*
(Rev. ed.) New York: Harper & Row, 1976.

Chait, R. P. "An Obituary for Student Affairs: Is There Life
After Death?" Paper presented at national conference of the
National Association of Student Personnel Administrators,
Boston, April 1982.

Hines, E. R. and Hartmark, L. S. *Politics of Higher Education.*
Washington, D.C.: American Association of Higher Education, 1980.

Kantor, R. M., and Stein, B. A. *Life in Organizations.* New
York: Basic Books, 1979.

Keller, G. *Academic Strategy: The Management Revolution in*
*American Higher Education.* Baltimore, Md.: Johns Hopkins
University Press, 1983.

Kerr, C. *The Uses of the University.* (3rd. ed.) Cambridge,
Mass.: Harvard University Press, 1982.

Lingenfelter, P. E. "Institutional Research and State Govern-
ment—A State Agency View." In J. W. Firnberg and W. F.
Lasher (Eds.), *New Directions for Institutional Research: The*
*Politics and Pragmatics of Institutional Research,* no. 38. San
Francisco: Jossey-Bass, 1983.

Mortimer, K. P., and McConnell, T. R. *Sharing Authority Effec-*
*tively: Participation, Interaction, and Discretion.* San Francisco: Jossey-Bass, 1978.

Newton, F., and Richardson, R. "Expected Entry-Level Competencies of Student Personnel Workers." *Journal of College*
*Student Personnel,* 1976, *17* (5), 426-429.

Richman, B. M., and Farmer, R. N. *Leadership, Goals, and Pow-*

er in *Higher Education: A Contingency and Open-Systems Approach to Effective Management.* San Francisco: Jossey-Bass, 1974.

Saunders, L. E. "Politics Within the Institution." In J. W. Firnberg and W. F. Lasher (Eds.), *New Directions for Institutional Research: The Politics and Pragmatics of Institutional Research,* no. 38. San Francisco: Jossey-Bass, 1983.

Walker, D. E. *The Effective Administrator: A Practical Approach to Problem Solving, Decision Making, and Campus Leadership.* San Francisco: Jossey-Bass, 1979.

# 4

W. John Pembroke

❧ ❧ ❧ ❧ ❧ ❧ ❧ ❧ ❧ ❧ ❧ ❧ ❧

# Fiscal Constraints
# on Program Development

Colleges and universities, no matter what the institutional type or size, are facing great fiscal problems in the decade ahead. With general operating costs rising, an eroded base of financial support, the need to provide technological support to enhance learning, potential enrollment declines, and erosion of state and federal support to students and institutions, each college and university is being forced to reexamine how and why resources are used. The current erosion of fiscal support is in stark contrast to the decades of the 1950s and 1960s, when support for higher education was strong and growing. During those decades the philosophy of equal opportunity for access to higher education permeated government policy. With that philosophy came dollars in support of student financial aid, research, program development, and capital construction. As the American economy deteriorated, unemployment rose and inflation grew; one of the consequences was a reduced base of fiscal support for higher education.

Each institution has faced the challenge of reduced fiscal

support in unique ways. Some have increased the direct costs shared to students, some have reduced programs, some have embarked on energy conservation plans, but all institutions have been forced to reexamine institutional goals and priorities in the attempt to provide quality programs and services with a reduced or static fiscal base.

As part of the institution, student services programs have not been immune from the process of goals and priority setting. Unfortunately in many instances, student services professionals have not been prepared to effectively confront the resources battle that inevitably erupts on any college campus during periods of fiscal constraint. Several factors have contributed to the lack of preparedness by professional staff. First, student services professionals often assume management positions without the requisite background in fiscal and organizational management. Although academic administrators are also confronted with this same background deficit, the sometimes perceived nonessential nature of student services programs (Chait, 1982) makes these programs more vulnerable to challenge. Second, student services programs have developed to meet perceived demands and old programs and services are rarely reexamined. Jellema (1972) likens such a development of student services programs to the construction of a New England farmhouse. "As new needs were discovered, new services were added. The result has been a rambling construction attractive and serviceable enough after its fashion but not a very economical model and hardly a structure one would set out to build" (p. 71). Finally, student services professionals have not either by their own volition or by pressure from outside forces examined fiscal procedures and policies. Business practices have often been left to others and only when resources are restricted will staff members begin to pay serious attention to the need to practice sound fiscal management procedures.

Terms such as *budget, cost accounting, maintaining reserves,* and *overhead* have not been part of the student services professionals' vocabulary, let alone reflected in their approach to practice. Ignorance such as this is not bliss, for the sound fiscal management of the institution has become a legitimate concern for all members of the academy. Mayhew (1979) indicates that "budgets are really a statement of educational purpose phrased in fiscal terms" (p. 54). Thus, student services professionals need to be able to clearly articulate the educational purpose of student services programs and practice the principles of sound fiscal management.

## Background of Present Dilemma

The fact that higher education in the United States, both public and private, is entering an era of severe stress is not news to anyone who has been involved in the enterprise during the past several years. The simple fact of the matter is there has been a precipitous erosion in the ability of higher education to cope with new fiscal, societal, and political realities.

To place this recent period in at least a short-term historical perspective, it is interesting to note that the two decades between the mid-1950s and the mid-1970s represented the most prosperous era ever experienced by higher education. It was during this period that students involved in some form of higher education grew from approximately 2.5 million to an almost astounding 8.8 million by 1975 (National Association of College and University Business Officers, 1982, p. 3). This rate of growth was accompanied by a concomitant growth in faculty, expansion of academic and student services programs, and construction of student housing, recreation centers, student unions, and performing arts centers.

Supporting this dramatic explosion were new and expanding commitments of resources from both the state and federal levels of government. The percentage of appropriated tax dollars from the states in support of both public and private education also grew rapidly. At the federal level, a new national commitment was given to provide access to higher education for those who are not in an economic position to afford even modest tuition, fees, and room and board costs. During this two-decade period, financial aid expanded its sense of mission to include minority students in particular. While the growth rate of college and university enrollments more than trebled, the representation of black students, as an example, increased more than eightfold.

Public sector as well as private sector support of faculty research and the essential components of graduate programs also increased. The federal government increased funding for research and development on campuses in the United States by more than tenfold to the point where it represented $3 billion per annum in 1977 (Pusey, 1978). It was precisely during this "golden age" that the seeds of higher education's current dilemma were sown.

Rapid expansion in student populations, building programs, research funding, faculty salaries, and the scope and mission of student financial aid created a crisis in the governance structures in higher education all across the country. Higher education, which was typically organized to have high quality and shared governance structures, simply could not effectively cope with the explosion in growth. The Hydra-like pattern of growth created a situation wherein the only response seemingly available was a precipitous decentralization of decision making. This was not a wholly inappropriate response to the pressures of growth, for many high-quality programs and superior research and development efforts were launched and fostered when decentralization occurred. Under the prevailing conditions of the times, planning and budgeting simply could not proceed in the more traditional hierarchical consultative mode as it had in the past.

However, by the mid-1970s the early signs of "the steady-state environment" or the forecasts of "the end of growth" were becoming pervasive in the literature. Faculty and staff salaries, which had been increased at their greatest rates in history, evidenced annual increments well below the rate of inflation. Student enrollments that had peaked began to taper off and decline modestly. Both private and public sector funding sources began to lose the ability to maintain financial support of higher education.

What had been a positive force in decentralization began to turn into internecine warfare among components of the academy when genuine fiscal contraction began to take place. Student services programs often have been viewed as the first "easy target" during budget reductions. From the faculty perspective, counseling centers, student activities units, and housing programs and staff become attractive locations to capture needed dollars in support of academic programs. Business affairs administrators, looking for new methods to reduce costs, challenge the very existence of many student services operations. The result was that frequently the decentralized governance mechanisms that had evolved over twenty years were found to be cumbersome, created opportunities for "warfare," and were fundamentally incapable of dealing with an era of decline. In addition to inefficient and cumbersome governance mechanisms, institutions also began to feel direct physical problems from trying to do too much with too little.

The National Association of College and University Business Officers began to point out the severity of the deterioration of physical plants all across the country in the early 1980s (Suber, 1982). There have been estimates in the tens of billions of dollars as to the total dollar magnitude of the deferred maintenance problem on campuses across the country. For student services areas, lack of attention to physical facilities has caused particular difficulties. Years of deferred maintenance in residence halls, for example, have resulted in dramatic increases in room and board rates. The housing administrator forced to present budgets requiring rate increases to meet such needs must not only cope with student reaction but also with concern on the part of the rest of the administration that a precipitous rise in room and board rates will reduce enrollments.

The budget problems are not limited to deteriorating physical plants. At the same time, energy costs, which had been reasonably benign, began to increase at annual rates that have had the cumulative effect of nearly quadrupling from 1976 through 1983.

Perhaps the best way to characterize the most recent years is to describe them as a time of increasing decline. The erosion experienced during the late 1970s and early 1980s is clearly just the beginning of a series of crises that will confront American higher education in the future.

The changing population of the United States in and of itself will have a profound influence on the realities facing American higher education. For example, the National Center for Higher Education Statistics has indicated that the decline in the birth rate between the 1960s and mid-1970s was the most precipitous in United States history. Thus, what has been perceived as limitless growth for the past twenty-five years has clearly come to a screeching halt. Budgeting and planning protocols utilized for the past quarter century are simply no longer appropriate. The key challenge confronting higher education is the ability of institutions to radically alter modes of governance, decision making, and planning (Kerr, 1979).

## Current Trends

The admonition that larger is not necessarily better is a notion that must be given greater credence by institutions of higher education in the decade ahead. Clearly our reality is going to be smaller; this does not preclude our ability to make that smaller environment of even greater quality in terms of instruction, scholarly research, and student services than that experienced during the era of growth. Those states that are currently confronted with a deep trough of economic distress, with all of the concomitant social and political pressure, will need to fundamentally redefine the character of their state economic base. This, in turn, will require bold new policy initiatives from governing boards as well as corporate and public sector funding mechanisms for both public and private institutions.

High technology, a much-overused "buzz" word, does represent the wave of the future as the United States moves into a postindustrial technology-based society. It is higher education that plays a quintessential role in sustaining technological innovation and, thereby, promoting economic vigor. Not only must there be a substantial shift in public policy awareness on the part of the legislative and executive branches of government but new modes of linking private sector corporate America in partnership with higher education must be explored and developed.

Student services units must support such initiatives, for as part of the academy their very survival may rely on new ways of doing business.

In addition to this thrust for new sources of support is the need for expanded efforts in the areas of cost containment and productivity. Cost reduction and cost containment methods must be introduced to offset costs that cannot be controlled (such as energy costs). Such cost containment measures will have a real and direct effect on student services programs. For example, justification and support will need to be offered for student/staff ratios in residence halls. Compensation packages will need to be reviewed. New sources of funding for current services will need to be examined. Traditional methods of operation will need to be evaluated.

*Public Institutions.* As the problems and opportunities mentioned previously begin to take on added significance, there has been a trend among public institutions to respond to the need for more adequate levels of revenue by turning to increases in tuition and fees. Double-digit tuition increases have been commonplace all across the country since the late 1970s. It is not atypical to see state taxation increase while at the same time, a smaller portion of state tax revenues are allocated to higher education.

Both private and public higher education is heavily reliant upon state and federal support to students for tuition and fees. Perhaps the most critical issues confronting higher education are the wholesale changes that have been recommended at the federal level to student financial assistance. Additionally, an increasing number of states have adopted public policies of either direct state institutional support or indirect support through state-based scholarships and loan programs for tuition and fees. The entire question of access and opportunity in higher education is increasingly contingent upon the state financial aid dollars; public as well as private higher education has an enormous stake in the adequacy of these allocations. New York State, for example, provides appropriations of public tax dollars directly to private institutions of higher education. Illinois, on the other hand, provides very substantial indirect support for private institutions through the mechanism of the Illinois State Scholarship Commission.

Faced with these realities, public institutions have had to fight "harder for less," a trend that apparently will continue for some time into the future. There are relatively few state governments that have either the force of will or the financial ability to reinvest in higher education in order to protect that which was built during the preceding twenty-five years. Notable exceptions, of course, are several of the Sunbelt states, selected mid-Atlantic states, and parts of the Far West. Nevertheless, it is fair to say that on an aggregate basis, much of the funding that is required to protect the baseline quality of academic programs and the research missions of institutions will have to be borne increasingly out of the tuition and fees charged to students.

*Private Institutions.* Although there are fundamental differences between public and private higher education with respect to the balance among revenue streams, the distinction between public and private tends to blur and become nearly opaque when analyzing the expenditure portion of the operating budget. When one compares institutions that have common characteristics (such as enrollment, size of operating budget, research versus nonresearch) and sense of institutional priorities and mission (such as commitment to basic research, graduate education, regional versus national standing), public and private peer institutions are virtually indistinguishable. Although certainly the processes by which limited financial resources are allocated typically have fewer governance layers in private higher education, it is nevertheless true that the basic approach to budgeting and the attendant concerns have more similarities than differences.

Perhaps the most fundamental distinction between public and private higher education is the disparity on the level of tuition and the extent to which a private institution's general operating budget relies upon those revenues. This simple fact led Baldridge and Tierney to observe: "Private colleges are busy adjusting to the 'new depression' in higher education. The recent depressed era found an increasing number of private institutions running deficits. But as traumatic as this recent period has been, it will appear insignificant when compared with the 'coming depression,' because demographers forecast a significant long-term drop in the student-age population. And the drop will be so large that the current difficulties may pale by comparison" (1979, p. 207). They go on to observe that the only ameliorative measure is proper strategic planning and solid institutional management, both fiscal as well as programmatic.

In addition to the substantial revenue streams from tuition that private institutions depend upon, there are a variety of other sources that are equally important. Several of these are as follows:

- *Endowed funds.* It is not atypical at large private institutions to see large endowments for student scholarships as well as to provide funding to academic programs, either as an augmentation to the operating budget or as an integral part of it. It should be noted that only in extreme situations is the principal of the endowment drawn upon to provide operating budget support. The basic principle of endowed funds is to use only the earnings that derive from investments on an annual basis (Chambers, 1963).
- *Religious or church support.* Nationally there are a substantial number of private colleges and universities that are church related. This affiliation quite typically carries with it direct financial support to the institution's operating and, less frequently, capital budgets.
- *Foundation support.* There are a large number of tax-exempt philanthropic organizations that provide direct institutional funding. Usually grants or allocations from these funds are intended to support either academic program innovation or, equally common, provide enrichment dollars to protect and enhance the quality of existing programs.
- *Institutional foundations and alumni associations.* These organizational entities are usually created to solicit funds from former graduates as well as from private sector corporations where a relationship with the institution has been developed. Although the array of uses to which these funds are put

varies from one institution to another, they are typically distributed among such programs as student scholarships, support of the operating budget, contribution to institutional capital development programs, and ancillary program support not normally contained within the operating budget.

- *Capital development funds.* These funds are used to provide an institution with either new or wholly renovated facilities to house institutional programs. Usually these capital development funds are developed on as broad a contribution base as possible (that is, alumni gifts, contributions from corporations, foundation support, and so on).
- *Research support.* Private institutions that have a primary research and public service mission are extraordinarily dependent upon federal research grants to sustain not only research endeavors but the fundamental building blocks of academic programs. It is not uncommon to look at some of the top-flight private research universities and find as much as 40 percent of their operating budget supported by outside research grants.

Student services programs, whether in public or private institutions, reflect the budgetary conditions of the parent institution. Each student services division, like the institution, will need to examine the base of fiscal support for programs, evaluate the stability of that base, and develop methods to assure adequate support for programs in the future.

### Student Services Budgets

There are two general principles that need to be considered when one talks of budgeting and fiscal management. First, budgeting cannot proceed on any type of a rational basis in the absence of an adequate and sound system of planning. It is the planning process that must necessarily precede and subsequently stay abreast with budgetary developments in order to assure genuinely effective and viable programs. Certainly the planning process must not only be sensitive to program requirements but must also operate within a realistic framework with respect to an appraisal of the range of fiscal resources that are available.

Second, budgeting is not a precise science but rather can be more accurately characterized as an art form. That is not to say that budgets are developed by assembling them in a peculiar Picasso-like abstraction. One simply does not go in and request $100,000 for "the general improvement of life on campus" and expect to get any type of affirmative response either from the administration or an institutional governing body. Certainly any proposal that is advanced should have a sufficient level of specificity to present fiscal decision makers with a complete depiction of the goals and objectives that will be met by the expenditure of dollars. It is in this process where the color, style, texture, and other artlike characteristics can be employed to good effect. For example, the rationale utilized in either defending an existing student services budget or requesting an augmentation of funding should necessarily be fundamentally different in approach than the type of presentation used by an academic department.

*Student Services Budgeting as an Art.* Institutional units and research programs not only share 80 to 85 percent of any senior institutional budget but the decisional processes regarding budgeting for these areas are fundamentally different than those of student services (National Association of College and University Business Officers, 1984). Most of the actors who play critical roles in the budgeting process have a strong academic bent that has an historical connection that can be traced back to Oxford and Cambridge experiences of several centuries ago. When one assesses this factor against the centrality that student services divisions are beginning to attain in many colleges and universities, it is perhaps easier to understand the distance that has yet to be traveled with respect to fully integrating student services programs into overall institutional decision making.

As enrollments decline and resources continue to erode, student services personnel need to effectively make the case for a "fair share" of institutional resources. While it is appropriately the case that the academic program has priority in any good institution, it is equally true that direct ancillary support of students in everything ranging from student financial aid to the quality of campus life to placement services following graduation are essential conditions to what any academic program must have—the students. Simple as it may be, in many institutions across the country these basic causative linkage patterns have yet to be introduced into the budgeting process. Certainly this is an institutional error but more importantly reflects a lack of effective communication on the part of student services professionals. If this situation is not corrected, there is a very real danger that student services budgets, from an institutional perspective, will retrogress to the status of a decade or more ago.

The distinctive and evolving role that a student services division plays within the overall institution needs to be constantly reiterated and refined. Fiscal decision makers, be they university presidents, boards of trustees, legislative committees, or the like constantly need to be reminded of the significance of a student services division and the essential contributions it makes to the fulfillment of the overall mission of the institution. All too frequently student services budgets are treated in an after-the-fact fashion whereby the allocation to student services is made only after all competing interests of the institution have been assessed and funds allocated to them. When this occurs, the typical reason is that professionals responsible for the student services budget have not taken due cognizance of a crisp, clear definition of their divisional mission and goals and have not translated how these goals contribute to and are supportive of the overall mission of the institution. To do these tasks well requires an approach that incorporates tough-minded judgments regarding essential and supportive services within the division. Once the judgments are made, the task for the student services professional is to communicate the requirements necessary to support programs to fiscal decision makers. This should be done at the beginning of the budget development and planning process.

Perhaps the quintessential component in seeking augmentation of funding to a student services division is the ability to clearly rationalize and accurately portray the precise status of all existing components within the division. Much of the budget and planning process revolves around a constant reassessment of "what is." Only after this question is adequately answered do fiscal decision makers typically entertain additional requests of funding for either the expansion of an existing program or the establishment of a new one. This modus operandi is likely to become more prevalent in the decade ahead as the number of people in the traditional college age group declines and institutional funding support mechanisms continue to constrict.

It is axiomatic in the corporate sector that if one does not continue to expand, atrophy begins to set in. This is equally true within higher education and particularly is the case in the area of student services. This does not imply that expansion equates growth in absolute dollars; it does not. Rather what is essential is the constant evolving and fine-tuning of all aspects of a student services program. A continual method of reassessing the development of fiscal resources to meet subtle changes in mission must be developed. Finally, a student services division must possess the ability to respond effectively to new targets of opportunity. For example, one does not have to go back more than two decades to see a radical shift in the mission of student services (see Chapter One). When *in loco parentis* was prevalent on many campuses across the country, budgeting for student services divisions was relatively straightforward and incremental in approach. During the intervening time, assertive notions with respect to the quality of campus life developed in conjunction with a more complete appreciation of the importance of the ancillary activities that are an essential part of the support of sound academic programs. During this evolution, student services very rapidly became a much more complex part of the institution.

Much of what is still wrong with student services budgeting emanates from this extremely rapid era of redefinition of mission without the concomitant sensitizing and educating of those who make the basic fiscal decisions for institutions. Student services budgets are assessed against academic and business affairs operations and must be able to withstand such scrutiny.

*Budgeting Guidelines.* There are at least five considerations that student services professionals might appropriately give attention to in the immediate future. These guidelines may appear to be simple; however, failure to be cognizant of each of them and the way they are interdependent can spell budgetary disaster for a student services division.

- *Know the guidelines.* Virtually every institution has a set of reasonably precise processes and attendant budgetary guidelines that are reexamined each fiscal year. The most merited funding request imaginable will receive short shrift, however, if it is advanced in a fashion that is fundamentally inconsistent with these institutional funding protocols. The student services professional must understand what budgeting guidelines are employed when institutional funding decisions are reached and tailor the student services budget request to fit these guidelines as closely as possible.
- *Know what is possible.* It does very little good to advance even a sound proposal for program enhancement or new program development in the face of an institution-wide budget reduction. Even in a steady-state funding environment, resources continue to be constricted in order to meet existing obligations. Consequently, requests for increases to the student services divisional budget should be predicated on a proposal that documents the precise manner by which the additional funding would either improve the overall funding pattern of the institution or significantly contribute to the overall enrollment, quality, or fiscal state of the institution.
- *Timeliness and deadlines.* Perhaps the most simple yet the most egregious error that academic administrators make is either their carelessness or cavalier attitude in meeting deadlines. Certainly administrative staffs, particularly those in student services divisions, are expected to produce increased amounts of work with fewer staff members. Nevertheless, the best idea or most well-developed concept will simply atrophy and die on the vine if it gets into the decisional process too late. Finally, lack of conformance with established institutional guidelines creates a bad impression that can continue to haunt the division for a number of fiscal

years into the future. Here is an issue of not appearing to be institutionally accountable as are the other components of the institution. As the least senior division of the academy, this is a perception on the part of others that a student services division can ill afford.

- *Forecasting for problems.* Perhaps the most effective way for a student services division to demonstrate the need for integration into the overall governance structure of the institution is by strategic issue identification and planning. It is simply not good enough to recommend expansion of an existing program or the development of a new one without a detailed plan for implementation and a full disclosure of all attendant budget and staff requirements. It is important that budgeting implications be presented for both the short-range and long-term life of the proposed project or program. Another positive aspect of this approach is the potential for the institution to begin to rely on those student services divisions that can not only predict future institutional problems and challenges but also provide a series of alternate solutions that are both policy- and cost-sensitive.
- *Reexamination of mission.* Finally, it is absolutely essential for student services divisions to develop a formalized procedure to consistently reexamine and refine their discrete mission and the unique role of student services in the institution. By doing so, the student services division becomes both responsive and attentive to the changing needs, goals, and priorities of the institution. This will allow student services divisions to constantly monitor their own goals and objectives and assure that they are in tune with those of the institution. Constant updating and reexamination also affords an opportunity to become cognizant of changes in goals and objectives of the institution and to act on them to provide quality services for students.

*Funding Responsibility and Sources.* Typically student services division budgeting at most institutions involves a variety of fund sources. For that reason, although consuming typically less than 5 percent of an institution's overall budget, student services budgeting tends to be one of the more complex and fund source–interdependent divisional budgets. Further complicating the situation is the general pattern of mixed-fund source support within a substantial number of functional areas contained in a typical student services division.

In the broader context of institutional budgeting priorities, the question invariably arises with respect to which components of an institution's budget ought to bear funding responsibility for a specific program area. There are no pat formulas available that can be applied to establish appropriate funding responsibilities for a functional activity; these determinations must, of necessity, be made within the context of each institution's governance structure and sense of mission. For example, many residence hall operations at public universities place the primary burden of revenue bond debt retirement, as well as operating budget costs, directly upon the users or residents of those facilities. Nevertheless, it is also quite common that state-appropriated funds are budgeted for the purpose of providing professional supportive staff in the residence halls. At private institutions the pattern is even more varied and ranges from instances where the rate structure for residence halls is designed to produce a net profit to the general operating budget, to circumstances where a subsidy is provided from the general operating budget that constitutes up to half the budget requirements of a residence hall. A similar range of funding profiles can be found with respect to athletic programs, health services, and student unions.

Strict fund and cost center accounting would suggest that the budget requirements associated with any given functional area should be derived from that fund source. However, this does not take into account fundamental variances among institutional philosophies and environmental characteristics. A commuter- or urban-based college or university may well find it appropriate to use general operating funds to provide a majority of budgetary support necessary to operate campus recreation or student union programs. The rationale for such a decision is the perceived need to provide a focal point for students in order to enhance a sense of genuine academic community. The lack of a residential student population can also lead an institution to appropriately provide subsidy funding for special events such as concerts, lectures, and plays, typically funded by student activity fees. In this instance, the reasons are the same as those of the previous example but also include an added dimension of enhancing town/gown relationships when these events are open to the community and they are actively encouraged to participate.

There are three general criteria that tend to emerge from deliberations regarding fund source responsibility for student services programs. The first and most compelling is a determination of the extent to which any particular programmatic component of a student services division contributes positively to the institution's mission and aspirations. Frequently these deliberations also focus upon contributions to the overall quality of campus life. Second, careful consideration needs to be given between "marketplace" realities and the overall funding profile of the institution. All too frequently, new student program initiatives are suggested without due regard for what the imposition of an additional or increased student fee would have upon the total cost of attending the institution. For new initiatives that seek general operating budget support, care must be exercised not to place this resource configuration in an imbalanced condition. In short, any new program initiatives must necessarily be placed within the broader context of institutional funding requirements on the one hand and marketplace conditions of not pricing the institution out of its natural marketplace. Finally, regardless of the source or balance among funding sources, the enhancement of existing programs or the development of new initiatives tends to be viable only as it addresses central issues regarding the primacy of the academic programs of the institution and therefore directly relates to overall institutional aspirations and sense of mission.

Although a mixed-fund source support for student services is complex, it does have several key advantages over a sole-source funding approach. Principal among these is at least a modicum of protection from sudden disruption in a single-fund source. From a student services perspective, there is very little

to recommend single-source funding for either program maintenance or development. Predominant reliance upon either institutional or user fees leaves a program vulnerable to momentary,
yet nevertheless severe, resource constriction. Whether it be the
volatility of the state appropriations process or that of tuition
income at a private institution, mixed-fund source budgeting affords an opportunity to at least protect the most essential component of a program and, more importantly, buys the time
necessary to readjust to longer term financial realities.

Another advantage of mixed-source funding is that it
allows a student services professional to articulate the role of
student services in an institution-wide context. For example,
health services usually are supported from both institutional as
well as direct user fees. This pattern recognizes the general institutional responsibility for providing health services to students,
while at the same time points out that student users also have a
responsibility to contribute directly to the cost of such services.
Such a joint funding pattern establishes that no single component or constituency group of the institution has exclusive
responsibility or domain over a program or service. Shared funding protocols also document a shared responsibility and obligation for providing student services. It is the student services
division that provides the interconnection or linkage among
funding sources. By doing so, and articulating clearly the notion
of shared responsibilities, a student services professional can
educate the broader institution to the appropriate and necessary
role that a student services division will play increasingly in the
future.

*Problem Areas.* There are two overarching problems that
student services must directly confront in planning and budgeting. First, far too many colleges and universities do not fully
integrate student services into the overall processes of institutional budgeting. Frequently, student services budgets are established on the basis of allocating whatever is left over after the
resource demands of the other divisions have been satisfied.
This "leftover" approach results in a "left out" budgeting sce-
nario. The key ameliorating step is one of educating and sensitizing both the governance structure of the institution and the

policy- and decision-making system to the role that a student services division can, should, and must play in any properly run institution. The articulation of this step is almost the exclusive responsibility of the student services professional; in doing so, he or she must overcome almost 500 years of tradition and bias. Certainly it would be improper to abrogate the primacy of the academic mission and its integrity in any sound institution. The student services professional entering the budgeting fray would be well advised to firmly assert a commitment to the academic mission of the institution. However, there is also a need for an immediate subsequent statement that crisply documents the importance of student services to the overall viability of the institution and its academic programs.

The ability to attract new students and retain those already on campus is heavily dependent upon the overall qualities and ambiance of the campus environment and student life. To a typical parent or prospective student, if indeed there is such, the presence of quality student services such as a health center, recreation program, academic advising, or student orientation is every bit as important as the scholarly reputation of a full professor in English. One does not have to call into question, let alone insult, the notion of scholarly and academic integrity to show how student services are inextricably linked to the academic mission of the institution. Research has suggested that the initial perceptions of prospective students and their parents are most contingent upon student support services than any single institutional characteristic (Noel, 1978). Studies on retention have also documented the importance of student services. It is the student life *outside* the classroom setting that is *more* of a determinant than any other single factor in student-initiated choices with respect to retention (Astin, 1982; Noel, 1978).

The second problem with respect to fiscal management within student services are problems that emanate from within the division itself. It is not uncommon to find a general lack of experience and expertise with respect to financial management among student services professionals. This, in turn, often results in a lack of appreciation of the institution's fiscal management structure and all too frequently leads to either inappropriate or a total lack of effective planning. The remedy for this can be found in a variety of budgeting and fiscal training programs offered by such associations as the American College Personnel Association (ACPA), the National Association of Student Personnel Administrators (NASPA), and the National Association of College and University Business Officers (NACUBO). By sharpening and enhancing budgeting skills and being more attentive to fiscal management, it should be possible to develop new and more appropriate budgeting strategies that are effective, both within a student services division as well as in the broader institutional context.

## A Case Application

By looking at a particular case, the need to apply sound fiscal management procedures during any new program initiative can be demonstrated. Although there are a plethora of examples that could be used, the development of a large number of structured campus recreation programs is recent enough in origin to provide a reasonable, common base for discussion purposes.

During the 1970s, many campuses "backed into" structured recreation programs by incrementally responding to a perceived need for physical fitness. Many of the earlier programs were perceived as an enhancement to campus life through the provision of an additional campus-based amenity. As we move into the eighties, this amenity has increasingly become a mandatory student support service that is simply expected to be present on most campuses. The long-term consequences of responding to this program initiative have had enormous consequences on budgets, staffing patterns, use of facilities, and decisional and governance processes.

There were two immediate impacts that were felt virtually simultaneously as the campus recreation program went from an idea to actual implementation. The first impact was budgetary in nature; what was initially expressed as a desirable additional student service, which could be conducted at virtually little or no cost, caused an almost geometric progression of student demand. Many institutions had to respond by developing formal cost center budgets and providing a steadily increasing professional staff support to meet the program need. At many institutions, the student services professional staff had grossly miscalculated the demand factor for such a program among the student body. By bringing the program on-line without adequate intermediate- and long-range planning, many college and university administrations felt as if they were being "blackmailed" into providing additional funding support as seemingly insatiable demand continued to grow.

Other institutions had a more fortunate experience. In these cases, the professional staff in the student services division did read correctly the latent demand for this type of program. They set about developing a well-documented plan for developing mixed-funding sources among, typically, the general operating budget, general student fees, and a schedule of user charges contingent upon a cost analysis of the precise activities contained within the overall program structure. Programs that evolved utilizing this latter approach clearly benefited, not only in their ability to respond to growing needs in a measured and controlled fashion but, more importantly, because of their position within the broader academic community as responsible, professional administrative components of the institution. Typically, this approach was also attentive to structuring an appropriate system of shared governance, reflecting the mixed-fund source basis upon which the program would be allowed to grow and develop.

At many campuses, what was a $20,000 or $30,000 fund commitment a half dozen or so years ago has evolved into programs with operating budgets well in excess of a quarter of a million dollars. Those institutions that did effective strategic planning in terms of both operating budgets and staffing patterns have been, by and large, rewarded not only with appropriate budgetary increases but with enhanced reputations, and standing across campus as responsible administrators.

A second area of grave concern, where there was inadequate programmatic planning with respect to recreation programs, is in the area of facilities. As student demand grew and participation rates increased dramatically, a great many institutions found that they had an existing space envelope that simply could not come close to meeting the demand. Many institutions found that the campus recreation program created a broad ripple effect and drew into contention the physical education component of the academic affairs division, as well as providing a source of ongoing conflict with intercollegiate athletics. Again, in those institutions where there was a strategic plan developed that took into account the adequacy of facilities, the growth of the program tended to proceed on an orderly and controlled basis. To the extent that there was sound programmatic planning and the presence of an integrated strategic plan that expressed fiscal requirements for operating budgets, staffing plans, as well as facilities requirements, frequently an allocation of capital funds resulted, to either construct a new facility or enhance existing facilities so the program could continue to evolve and mature.

The lesson here is a relatively simple one: Short-sighted budget planning, be it in terms of the operating budget or the capital budget, almost invariably results in contention and conflict among the component parts of an institution. This, in turn, leads to a loss of standing and respect for a student services division—the commodity that can least afford to be lost or inadvertently given away. The integration of short- and long-range strategic planning not only avoids extremely painful pitfalls but also provides the basis for further integration and the recognition of the centrality of the student services division.

## Summary Recommendations

There are several observations and comments contained elsewhere in this chapter that bear repeating as general guidelines or principles with respect to budgeting in a student services division. For the sake of brevity, the following recapitulation may be useful:

1.  Both sound fiscal management and budgetary development require sensitivity to the overall sense of mission and set of

aspirations that an institution possesses. Failure to do so places a student services division in an "odd-man-out" situation with little hope of garnering a broad-gauged, institution-wide support necessary for the division to fulfill its own discrete mission and achieve its aspirations.

2. Cognizance must be given not only to an institution's overall governance system but also to the decision-making processes that provide the framework within which budgetary policies and final funding determinations are made.

3. To the greatest extent appropriate, there needs to be a vastly greater integration and relationship with the academic division of the institution. It is this division that has, appropriately, absolute primacy in terms of an institution's mission; student services professionals need to capitalize on every available opportunity to relate their program to the academic program.

4. Student services professionals need to become a more integral part of the operational management team by being full participants in the institution's administrative management structure; the student services division is then less likely to be overlooked during the intense competition for limited institutional resources that occurs each year.

5. Student services professionals must increasingly take the longer-term view, not only of their programmatic requirements but also of their evolving role within the overall infrastructure of the institution. It is no longer adequate for *any* part of a college or university to sustain budgeting on a year-by-year basis.

6. Finally, and perhaps most importantly, the student services professional must become more effective and assertive in articulating the role, mission, and fundamental integrity of the student services division and its constituent programmatic segments. This articulation needs to occur in a manner that is both fiscally and policy-sensitive. It also should recognize the fundamental ignorance of most other parts of the institution regarding the importance of a student services division to the overall lifeblood of the campus and longer-term viability of the institution.

Student services professionals and the division that house them have come a remarkably long distance in a relatively short time since the days of a "gatekeeper" under *in loco parentis.* Hopefully this growth and professional development will continue to accelerate at the rate we have seen during the past several decades.

## References

Astin, A. W. *Minorities in American Higher Education: Recent Trends, Current Prospects, and Recommendations.* San Francisco: Jossey-Bass, 1982.

Baldridge, J. V., and Tierney, M. L. *New Approaches to Management: Creating Practical Systems of Management Information and Management by Objectives.* San Francisco: Jossey-Bass, 1979.

Chait, R. P. "An Obituary for Student Affairs: Is There Life After Death?" Paper presented at national conference of the National Association of Student Personnel Administrators, Boston, April 1982.

Chambers, M. M. *Financing Higher Education.* Washington, D.C.: Center for Applied Research in Education, 1963.

Jellema, W. W. (Ed.). *Efficient College Management.* San Francisco: Jossey-Bass, 1972.

Kerr, J. C. "Administration of Higher Education in an Era of Change and Conflict: Retrenchment and Reprisal." Paper presented to faculty, University of Illinois, 1979.

Mayhew, L. B. *Surviving the Eighties: Strategies and Procedures for Solving Fiscal and Enrollment Problems.* San Francisco: Jossey-Bass, 1979.

National Association of College and University Business Officers. "15 Percent Enrollment Drop by 90's Predicted." *Business Officer,* November 1982, *16* (5), 13.

National Association of College and University Business Officers. "NACUBO Prepares Comparative Financial Data on Revenues and Expenditures." *Business Officer,* January 1984, *17* (7), 6-7.

Noel, L. "First Steps in Starting a Campus Retention Program." In L. Noel (Ed.), *New Directions for Student Services: Re-*

*ducing the Dropout Rate,* no. 3. San Francisco: Jossey-Bass, 1978.

Pusey, N. *American Higher Education.* Cambridge, Mass.: Harvard University Press, 1978.

Suber, L. T. "Coping with Deferred Maintenance." *Business Officer,* May 1982, *15* (11), 22-24.

# Part Two

❧ ❧ ❧ ❧ ❧ ❧ ❧ ❧ ❧ ❧ ❧ ❧ ❧

# Determining
# Appropriate Goals
# for Student Programs

The first step in establishing successful student services programs is to identify worthwhile and practical goals for our various program endeavors. Student services professionals generally acknowledge the importance of establishing quality program goals; however, in practice we often give this important first step only cursory attention. Questions of *"why* this program?" or *"what* are we trying to accomplish?" are too often quickly supplanted by the practitioner's question of *how* the program will be implemented.

There are several obstacles to effective goal setting in student services. Higher education is characterized by vague goals, and it can be difficult to translate "educating students" into concrete program objectives. Student services professionals have seldom bridged the gap between theory and practice in a satisfactory manner and this failure is especially evident in the goal-setting process. In addition, no one theory guides our program planning efforts; student services program goals are derived from an amalgamation of student development, organization, and management theory. These obstacles contribute to our difficulty in selecting appropriate program goals and in communicating those goals to the publics we serve.

While the profession's problems in setting program goals may be understandable, we cannot afford to ignore this critical link in the program-planning process. In a time when many worthwhile academic, service, and research programs are competing for scarce resources, we must be able to clearly articulate program goals and to outline the negative consequences if the goals are not achieved. The quality and, in some cases, the survival of student services programs are at stake. Therefore, Part Two of this book addresses the question "What are the skills and information needed to select and sell appropriate student services program goals?"

Chapter Five by James Hurst and Judith Jacobson takes us back to the basic problem of bridging theory and practice. The authors propose a conceptual foundation for program development directed to fostering the development of an educated person. They then discuss the values to which a student services division can subscribe and outline a method for translating those values into specific program goals with measurable outcomes. Measurement or evaluation of outcomes implies the use of data in establishing program goals. In Chapter Six, Gary Hanson and Bernard Yancey discuss the role of data in program planning and goal setting. Though these authors review formal data collection methods such as survey research, their emphasis is on expanding the definition of "data" to include a wide variety of factors used to establish goals. Chapter Seven draws the information on theory-to-practice and on data collection together in providing a systematic approach to setting program goals. This chapter identifies barriers to goal setting, discusses a variety of goal-setting techniques and procedures, and outlines critical questions and common errors in the goal-setting process.

Establishing worthwhile program goals is not a simple task; it requires a thorough understanding of theory, of the institutional context, and of specific goal-setting techniques. But the planning and thought demanded during this programming stage can be exciting, for it is through our goals that we state and understand our larger mission and begin the development of quality programs.

5

James C. Hurst
Judith K. Jacobson

❧ ❧ ❧ ❧ ❧ ❧ ❧ ❧ ❧ ❧ ❧ ❧ ❧

# Theories Underlying Students' Needs for Programs

Society's prerogatives are institutional imperatives. As an agent of society, the academy mirrors society's central perennial metaphors: tension between the individual and the group, freedom versus control, inter- and independence (Boyer and Levine, 1981). Societal themes and patterns precede, and in fact cultivate, a set of theories that guide program development in institutions of higher education (Kuhn, 1969; Ferguson, 1980; Barclay, 1983).

The literature documents the nature of societal prerogatives that have been the genesis of perspectives for student services. Aubrey (1977) and Banning (1980) chronicle the emergence of the conceptual and theoretical features that provide the basis of program development for student services.

### Development of Theory

Aubrey (1977) detailed the societal precursors of counseling, but his observations are as relevant for program development in general. He identified the nineteenth-century Industrial Revolution as the major factor in the emergence of counseling. The transition from an agrarian society, with its relative self-sufficiency of individuals and families in typically simple pastoral settings, to a more complex interdependent nation characterized by mass production and specialization of goods and services was an imperative for counseling in particular and program development in general. Industrialization at the turn of the century introduced a dramatic new complexity in higher education and the vocational configuration of the country, and that, in turn, created a climate in which programming to support students emerged as a function of educational institutions (see Chapter One by Knock). These early movements were, however, pragmatic and functional activities reactive to powerful environmental and societal influences. They were not developed on a philosophical or theoretical base.

Changing emphases in American society continue to have an impact. Aubrey identifies the 1950s as the period during which theoretical formulations and pretheory conceptualizations were developed. Essentially, the initial impact of the Industrial Revolution was the emergence of pragmatic and usable principles with half a century passing before a foundation in theory was constructed.

Banning (1980) has proposed another historical chronology of the conceptual features for the profession that further illustrates the interconnectedness of society and the institution. An unenlightened, atheoretical perspective was generated from the agrarian society when the earliest institutions of higher learning were devised to inculcate piety, train character, and instill moral discipline (Mueller, 1961; Rudolph, 1962; Handlin and Handlin, 1970). The unenlightened perspective can be characterized by control, rigid mandates, serious consequences for abuses of rules, and nonnegotiable parameters. Institutions during the agrarian period had incongruously joined the degree-granting academic function with quasi-parental functions. In essence, then, the roots of student services and, therefore, program development can be traced to the beginning of formalized higher education. Initially, volunteer or designated faculty members, usually clergy, served as surrogate parents invoking heavily moralistic discipline and frequent mandatory programming based on orthodox religion. Appeals to piety sought to bring religious sanction to bear upon the young. Devoid of formal theory, services were rendered at the discretion of these designated "student services" faculty.

Faculty members and administrative officials began to abandon the rigors of this type of ministering as societal interest in intense religious indoctrination waned. By the mid-nineteenth century, the prototypes of deans of men and women were established to directly work with the affairs of students. With expansion in size and complexity in higher education, new emerging social orders, and congressional legislation such as the Morrill Act of 1862, institutions sought new ways to respond to societal prerogatives. The activities and programs that developed under these circumstances were still neither theoretical nor even conceptual in nature, but rather pragmatic and practical. They were programs and services developed for young people, most of whom were beyond the influence of their parents for the first time in their lives. *In loco parentis* prevailed as the structuring principle, the perspective of the day, illustrating the practical and atheoretical configuration of student affairs. Inasmuch as the primary responsibility of parents involves provision for financial support, housing, food, discipline, and counsel, the types of services that emerged through the *in loco parentis* rationale duplicated parental responsibility. Decade by decade, changing societal expectations regarding the development of new knowledge (research), the changing roles of faculty, and the resultant decrease in direct faculty involvement with extracurricular lives of students provided an institutional imperative for the emergence of the student services profession.

The adjustive perspective (Banning, 1980) for student services had its beginning during the early 1900s and extended through the first half of the century. The parochial *in loco parentis* notion of delimiting behaviors was expanded to incorporate an emphasis on serving students while helping them adjust to college life. By mid-century, treatment strategies such as counseling or psychotherapy were invoked to help those ill or deficient students function properly on campus. Thus, the emphasis was on adjusting students to produce an appropriate fit to institutional constraints by help-oriented services.

Development became the hallmark of the profession during the third quarter of the twentieth century. In the 1950s and 1960s, the significant foundations for counseling theory were developed. In the 1970s the theoretical foundations for student affairs were generated. During this decade the most significant progress in the discovery, creation, and investigation of student development theory occurred (Widick, Knefelkamp, and Parker, 1980; Huebner, 1980; Knefelkamp, 1980; Rodgers, 1980; DeCoster and Mable, 1981; Fried, 1981; Hanson, 1982; Kitchener, 1982; Miller, Winston, and Mendenhall, 1983). These theories enabled the profession to create program interventions based on human development constructs, rather than on pragmatic concerns to have students "adjust." Instead of treating students and ensuring their adjustment, the focus turned toward developing student skills and competencies. Teaching students to become active agents in shaping their environments became one of the goals of student services. Banning (1978) describes this period as transitional, leading to the conceptualization of campus ecology.

Campus ecology is a perspective for student services programming that addresses the intentional design of educational environments for the purpose of promoting student development. The ecological perspective (Banning, 1980) represents a viewpoint for student services that shares the long-standing concern for individual change but incorporates in a systematic manner the importance of the environment in such change. The conceptual notions of person-environment interaction, organizational/management theory, and student development theory together compose campus ecology. The one-sidedness of the other perspectives is overcome by acknowledging that the institutional environment is also subject to adjustment and development. The ecological perspective acknowledges that institutional settings are reflective of, and responsive to, the societal context in which they are lodged. Student services units also must be responsive both to the context of society and the institution.

## Nontheoretical Program Development

The student affairs profession went through a long period during which it had no theoretical or conceptual foundation. The rationale for its existence during this period was *in loco parentis*. That rationale was both nontheoretical and nonconceptual. Program development that occurs in the absence of theory or conceptualization may or may not relate to the education and development of students. The tradition and heritage of student services work has supported program development reflective of such variables as:

- *The personal interests of professional staff.* During the late 1960s, the development of human sexuality workshops was a common practice among student affairs professionals. It is likely that in many instances these workshops were developed as a result of the interests of professional staff members rather than a priority need that was identified among students. Often such programs were devoid of needs assessment and/or evaluative features and merely reflected staff interests.
- *The skill or knowledge of professional staff.* Professional staff members carry with them a repertoire of acquired skills, often reflecting the uniqueness and special interests of the institution and program from which a staff member graduated. Examples include paraprofessional training, systematic desensitization, minority student programming, leadership training, and attending behavior training. Although program development that reflects the manifest skills of a professional staff may be of good quality, it may have little or no relationship to the needs of a student population.
- *Emerging crises.* Program development that is the result of a series of crises all too often is designed at the remedial level; that is, designed to deal with the wreckage caused by the crises. In general, program development at an institutional level that is reactive to crises leaves broad areas of student development needs unaddressed.
- *Professional fads.* There was a time when sensitivity sessions, T groups, and encounter groups were major activities of stu-

dent services professionals. Few of the professionals involved in those activities seemed prepared to explain how they fit into a comprehensive, systematic program of student development in a student services division.

- *Political expediency.* Although institutional political considerations are a legitimate ingredient in program identification and development, if they receive too high a priority, student needs may go unmet. Although the interest and desires of the president, vice-presidents, or deans need to be responded to if continuing resources are to be expected, they practically never reflect a theoretical, conceptual, or systematic basis for program development.

- *Special interest groups.* The legitimacy of investing resources to fill the needs or demands of special interest groups demands careful and continuing scrutiny. On one campus, a president was seriously contemplating the termination of the Reserve Officers Training Corps program in response to what appeared to be campus-wide support for such a move. A rigorously planned and implemented survey research project revealed, however, that the president was being unduly influenced by a small group of dissidents who were carefully orchestrating a campaign designed to reflect campus-wide support when, in fact, very little existed (Hurst and Hubbell, 1971). On many campuses, however, ethnic minorities, handicapped students, women, and older returning students are special interest groups that have a legitimate claim to special program development and investment of resources.

- *Tradition.* Continuing a student service or implementing a program simply because it occurred last year and the year before continues to be one of the most pernicious rationales for a program intervention. Although tradition may play a powerful role in preserving societal continuity, the flux and change of student populations eventually renders most programs obsolete. Balance between tradition that generates a debilitating mind set, and one that preserves continuity, must be achieved.

The traditional organizational structure of the typical division of student services also inadvertently encourages program development outside the realms of theoretical and conceptual guidance. Although some variation of organizational structure in divisions of student services exists across the country, there is much more similarity than divergence. A typical organizational configuration includes a counseling center, housing, a student union, career planning and placement, a minority student services program, financial aid, student activities, and international student programming. Other student activity programming frequently included as part of the organizational configuration includes a center for academic advising, admissions, and registration and records. These administrative elements within the traditional organizational structure have emerged throughout the years for good reason. They serve well the manifest needs of student populations. A major disadvantage, however, is the compartmentalization of effort that is likely to occur within this organizational structure. Programs that emerge from within each administrative component are very likely to reflect a rather narrow perception of program development. For example, programs based on counseling intervention may well improve and enhance the counseling available to students. What must be remembered, however, is that counseling is not an end in itself. Counseling is a vehicle by which certain human development processes are likely to occur, and so it is with academic advising, discipline activities, placement, financial aid, and so on. None of them are ends in themselves, but they are instead procedures hopefully reflecting a commitment to the larger process of education and student development to reconstitute the traditional mind set.

A number of generic student development functions can be identified that are fundamental in nature and cut through the artificial boundaries that typically appear within the administrative unit of a division of student services. For example, recruitment and enrollment of new students involves admissions, registration, new student orientation, housing, and financial aid, as well as a number of academic areas outside a student services division. The transitions attendant to successfully entering a university also involve diverse areas such as registration, academic advising, career counseling, new student orientation, student activities, and housing. Efforts designed to enhance the extracurricular richness of the institution and thus the retention of students also cross traditional organizational lines. Typically, student unions, activities offices, judicial offices, housing, campus recreation, counseling and career services, leadership development programs, quality student employment programs, and health service units all strive to contribute to this goal. Finally, a number of units focus on the transitions attendant to leaving the institution either prior to or at graduation. A commitment to these superordinate concepts of program development will ordinarily enhance the more narrow "in-house" program development that occurs within the confines of the units in a traditional organizational structure.

## Education, Development, and the Campus Community

It is essential that student services professionals relate the theory and constructs of student development and campus ecology to the main mission of our educational institutions. Part of that relationship involves the development of effective program interventions. Current events have again raised the question "What is an educated person?" Historically this question has been entertained by scholars whose answers are framed within the contexts of their academic disciplines. Traditionally, student services have contributed to this endeavor most notably through management and organization, leaving the academicians to articulate answers to the questions of the essence of education.

Student services have served well in this capacity. Auxiliary and/or subsidiary functions should not be abandoned but complemented with a new vision of how we might contribute to the educational enterprise. This is to suggest that through program development and implementation we actively address the questions: "What is the nature of the educated person?" "How can we document the learning we promote?" "How can student services respond to the national agenda of the academy as both servant and critic of society?" (Boyer and Hechinger, 1981). Contingent upon contemporary societal prerogatives, what conceptual/theoretical tenets shall be employed in our response?

Naisbitt (1982) contends that we are living in the time of the "parenthesis," that this time between eras, during a shift in dominant structuring principles, is one of extraordinary leverage. The much-heralded transformation from industrial order to an information-specific society is no longer future tense. Current institutional imperatives will reconstitute traditional student services. It is a time of questioning, of possibilities, a time of great capacity for change. The destiny of student services may be fashioned by those who venture to engage in the asking of the questions: "What repertoire of skills and competencies constitute the educated person?" and "How can we intentionally design environments that will foster the educational process?" The substance of program development in student services emerges from the answers to such questions. In developing programs within the student services unit, attention must be given to the broader campus community. To assume that intellectual development is the province of the faculty and to assume that the maintenance, control, judicial, and custodial features of student life are the province of student services is a limiting dichotomy (Blake, 1979; Knefelkamp, 1980; Barr and Fried, 1981). In order to allay this dichotomy, overtures to the faculty must be made by student services. Currently student services professionals have access to the conceptual tools of student development and campus ecology that will help increase dialogue, understanding, and cooperation on the campus. Barr and Fried (1981) contend that the campus may be perceived as having two separate and distinct subcultures, each with its own values, loyalties, customs, and language. The belief that faculty and student affairs are polar opposites perpetuates one of the perennial vexations of higher education: its inability to formalize a commitment to student development.

The presence of student services on campus should be justified by an understanding of and commitment to student development and the intentional design of environments that promote development commensurate with the intellectual sophistication acquired within the confines of the formal classroom. Or, with the educated person as the intended outcome, student affairs and faculty could together devise strategies that would encourage the investment of all campus constituents in the educational enterprise.

*Common Learning.* *A Quest for Common Learning* (Boyer and Levine, 1981), a Carnegie Foundation essay, suggests six themes that should be of proper concern to institutions of higher learning. These themes are derived from societal prerogatives that have been cast as institutional imperatives. The six areas considered indispensable if students are to adequately understand themselves, their society, and the world in which they live are (1) shared use of symbols, (2) shared membership in groups and institutions, (3) shared producing and consuming, (4) shared relationship with nature, (5) shared sense of time, and (6) shared values and beliefs. Curiously, the Carnegie Council essay pays no tribute to the body of literature of student development to which we as a profession subscribe. These six intentions are proposed within the academic context, yet are equally applicable if translated to the province of student services. Furthermore, the translation could provide the sought-after bridge between academic and student services. Scholars from both academic and student services are contributing literature that could, if acknowledged and applied, foster a common language and endorse common values and loyalties.

*Reconstituted Campus Community.* The myth that student development, campus ecology, and the tenets of common learning are mutually exclusive must be dispelled. The essence of the educated person is contained in elements of common development distilled from the student development literature and common learning emerging from formal academic instruction. The educated person integrates both knowledge gained from formal instruction and skills acquired through developmental growth. From this perspective both campus agents, student services professionals, and the academic faculty are indispensable to the process of educating students.

Given this view, student development emerges as the content variable and the campus environment as the process variable—the vehicle through which programs and interventions may be derived that will facilitate the characteristics of the educated person. The theory base of student development/campus ecology can serve then as a management premise that provides for common learning and common development in the quest for producing the educated person.

The identification of and commitment to this shared theoretical/conceptual approach to program development is essential to student services as a profession. The programs offered by student services are, after all, the clearest statement of the substance and vitality of the profession.

## A Theoretical/Conceptual Approach
## to Program Development

Morrill, Oetting, and Hurst (1974) have devised a three-dimensional conceptual format for defining, describing, and interrelating the purpose, target, and method of intervention for student development, as outlined in *Dimensions of Intervention for Student Development* (Morrill, Hurst, and Oetting, 1980). Inasmuch as theory-based program development is ultimately a vehicle by which individual students may grow and develop, a modification and reapplication of the Morrill, Oetting, and Hurst "cube" holds promise for defining, describing, and interrelating the purpose, target, and method dimensions specifically for program development (see Figure 1).

*Purpose of Intervention.* The most important element in any effort to incorporate theory in program development is the determination of the purpose of the program. It is in the determination of the purpose that the actual activity of the intervention strategy correlates with the theoretical formulation. In essence, the purpose of the program intervention must contain fundamental derivatives of a theoretical formulation. Ultimately, all student services programs are directed toward eliciting a change in how students think, feel, or behave. Therefore, the ultimate purpose of a program intervention must be composed of a theoretical formulation of individual student development.

Drum (1980) reviewed a wide variety of human development theories and classified them into categories of behavioral, structural, adaptive, psychological, and descriptive theories of human development. He then proposed a seven-dimensional

Figure 1. Theoretical/Conceptual Foundation for Program Development.

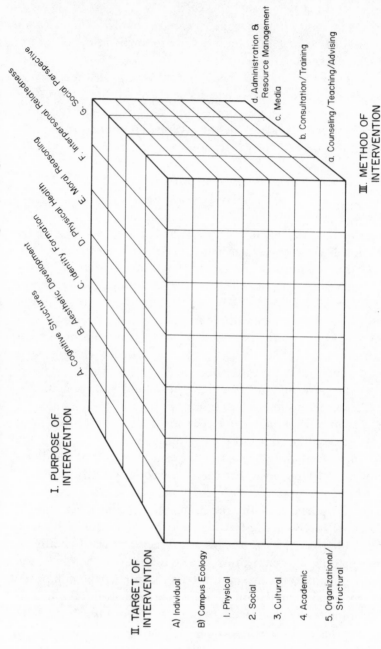

I. PURPOSE OF INTERVENTION

A. Cognitive Structures
B. Aesthetic Development
C. Identity Formation
D. Physical Health
E. Moral Reasoning
F. Interpersonal Relatedness
G. Social perspective

II. TARGET OF INTERVENTION

A) Individual
B) Campus Ecology
1. Physical
2. Social
3. Cultural
4. Academic
5. Organizational/ Structural

III. METHOD OF INTERVENTION

a. Counseling/Teaching/Advising
b. Consultation/Training
c. Media
d. Administration & Resource Management

Hurst, J.C. & Jacobson, J.K.
1984

model of student development that contained the following assumptions:

1.  Human development is characterized by growth toward more complexity, internal integration, and finer discrimination. Development proceeds most favorably when sufficient demands, challenges, and threats are perceived by the individual and when fear of being overwhelmed by them is minimized by both external support and inner coherence.
2.  As development proceeds, there is less tendency to anchor beliefs, values, and judgments external to the self and more to utilize internalized personal beliefs in negotiating life. In short, as development increases, less emphasis is placed on the form of a response and more attention is focused on the substance of one's beliefs and actions.
3.  Developmental change is a continuous process. Student development seems to be characterized by a gradual blending of one stage into the next, with small units of growth and change fusing to provide the supportive base for transformation to a higher degree.
4.  Even though developmental change is a continuous process, it is not uniformly one-dimensional. Developmental advancements, as well as regressions and stabilizations, are important factors in the change process. It appears that following the attainment of a higher stage of development, a period of stabilization and integration occurs as the individual develops more coherence within the stage.
5.  Quantitative changes, such as (1) shift in the valence of an existing value or quality, (2) addition of a new response mode, (3) utilization of more data in decision making, and (4) development of slightly different tests and preferences, are the important building blocks on which the more qualitative (stage) changes are built. Therefore, movement from one stage to another is likely to be based on a host of more quantitative shifts in beliefs, values, attitudes, and so on, which occur as a person attempts to adapt to the increasingly complex demands of living.

The seven dimensions of student development that Drum formulates are cognitive structures, esthetic development, identity formation, physical health, moral reasoning, interpersonal relatedness, and social perspective. An inspection of Figure 1 will reveal that the seven elements contained within the horizontal axis entitled "Purpose of Intervention" are those proposed by Drum as the fundamental categories of student development. The following examples illustrate this application.

- *Cognitive structures dimension.* This dimension is designed to describe and define how an individual cognitively processes and interprets information, ideas, concepts, and knowledge. After reviewing the work of Harvey, Hunt, and Schroder (1961), Perry (1970), Piaget (1950), Chickering (1969), and Heath (1977), Drum concludes that cognitive development during the college years is characterized by increased complexity of thought in problem solving, reduction and utilization of biased data, finer differentiation and integration of conflicting stimuli, and better ability to distill, analyze, and synthesize data. The descriptors used to describe the continuum for the most basic cognitive style through the refined level of development are simplistic, realistic, and reflective.

- *Esthetic development dimension.* The recognition and appreciation of all varieties of beauty in art, music, drama, literature, and dance is a commonly described goal for higher education. Drum describes the most basic level of development as governed by instilled preferences; that is, preferences the individual has acquired from those around him/her. The continuum of development moves from instilled preferences through a broadened appreciation. Other preferences are still taken into consideration, but the individual is able to draw personal esthetic conclusions. The person capable of enhanced sensitivity, the most refined level of development, is capable of sensitivity to beauty and of articulating the personal meaning of that beauty.

- *Identity formation dimension.* Identity is defined as a coherent self-image that remains stable through a variety of circumstances and demands. It is an internal sameness. The most elementary level of development along the identity formation dimension is the conforming individual who provides self-identity in response to external rules and regulations. This dimension of student development extends through the experimental position wherein external rules and expectancies are modified according to internal locus of control. The intentional person is at the highest level of development and is the person who is able to respond to the fundamental questions of "Who am I?" and "Who am I becoming?"

- *Physical health dimension.* The inextricable connection between physical, mental, and emotional well-being is well documented. The acquisition and maintenance of physical health is described by Drum with three levels of development. The first is described as unintentional practice. Essentially, the student at this level simply does not attend overtly to physical health. The middle level of development, selective management, describes an increased sense of internal management of healthful behaviors. The highest developmental level, personal responsibility, describes a person who displays an advanced understanding of the physical body and its interfacing with thoughts, feelings, and the external world.

- *Moral reasoning dimension.* The developmental level for this dimension begins with an externalized locus wherein an individual is governed by the moral reasoning of others. The middle development position is an internalized locus that provides some balance of an internalized nature to the external position. An integrated locus wherein the individual is able to achieve and sustain a balance between externalized demands and internalized wishes is the refined level.

- *Interpersonal relatedness dimension.* This scale attempts to account for college students' interactions with others. The most basic level of development is described as self-centered wherein the individual is bound by concern for self. The middle position or role-dominated position describes a higher level of development but one that is still heavily impacted by external role expectations. The highest or intimate level is reached when a student comes to appreciate and implement the interdependence and reciprocity of relationships.

• *Social perspective dimension*. This scale attempts to describe how students perceive, conceptualize, and deal with a complex, multiethnic world. The three-position developmental scale begins with ethnocentric, which describes the individual unable to move beyond the personal social environment. Relativism is the middle position on this scale. The anthropocentric position, wherein the student recognizes that culture is an expression of regional or localized creations of the human aggregate, is the refined level.

Program development begins with either implicitly or explicitly stated values. It must be recognized that Drum's (1980) five assumptions mentioned earlier in this section are value-laden statements. Essentially, a theoretical foundation for program development provides the framework within which a consistent set of value statements may be articulated. For example, the Purpose of Intervention dimensions displayed in Figure 1 propose inherent values related to moving from basic to refined levels of development within each of the seven dimensions proposed by Drum. An initial step, then, that is fundamental in systematic program development is determining the dimension the programmer wishes to impact, followed by the derivation of a goal statement that reflects the movement from a basic to a refined level within the dimension. It is a contention that these seven developmental dimensions are part and parcel of the common learning variable described as critical to the essence of the educated person. Although Drum's formulations are used in Figure 1, the formulations of Chickering (1969), Harvey, Hunt, and Schroder (1961), Loevinger (1976), Kohlberg (1971), Perry (1970), and other conceptualizers could just as easily be inserted in the Purpose of Intervention dimension of Figure 1.

*Target of Intervention*. One of the most significant observations by Morrill, Oetting, and Hurst (1974) in their conceptual formulation was the variety of targets or foci that an intervention may address. Although they recognized that the ultimate intent was to affect the way that an individual thinks, feels, or behaves, they recognized that the immediate target of a program intervention did not have to be limited to the individual. One-on-one counseling and advising, or classroom teaching, are examples of the individual as a target of intervention.

All other targets of program intervention may be categorized as elements of the environment. Banning (1980) proposes that the concept of campus ecology provides the most productive framework within which to conceptualize environmental targets of intervention. He proposes that the campus may also be considered the "client" or the "patient" and therefore a legitimate target. Campus ecology infers both the identification of the important elements in student/environment interaction as well as the possibility of intentionally modifying person/environment interactions for the purposes of enhancing individual education and development. Campus ecology is made up of five dimensions in the student's environment, as shown in Figure 1:

- *Physical dimension.* Buildings, trees, light, temperature, climate, architecture, and geographical distance are all examples of physical environment. They also represent elements that can be utilized within an ecological context. The acoustics, colors, and temperature in a classroom may well impact cognitive development. The existence and placement of statuary and works of art may affect esthetic development. The existence of swimming pools, tennis courts, and jogging trails relate to physical development. The proximity of living units to classrooms and locations designed to attract groups of students to relate together informally affect interpersonal relatedness and perhaps social perspective.
- *Social dimension.* The sum total of a student's expectations, inclinations, preferences, and actual activities with groups of other students comprises the social dimension of campus ecology. These are reflected in values, norms, behaviors, demographics, and opinions. Intentional efforts to bring students together to investigate themes such as honor codes, sexism, racism, and the future can enhance cognitive development. Student committees to recommend esthetic improve-

ments to the campus may relate to the esthetic realm. Topical discussion groups can relate to identity formation. Intramural programs may relate to the physical development. The existence of student disciplinary boards and boards for student appeals may relate to the moral development of students in a social setting. Finally, the creation of challenges and opportunities to encounter differences in life-styles, religious orientations, and economic and political preferences may impact interpersonal relatedness and social perspectives.

- *Cultural dimension.* Cultural sterility or richness may have a profound impact on each of the seven elements proposed by Drum (1980) and listed under Purposes of Intervention in the model in Figure 1. Multicultural and multilingual movies and theater may enhance cognitive development as well as appreciation for the varieties of esthetic beauty and social responsiveness. Ethnic banquets in residence halls, cultural celebrations, and sundries in the bookstore contribute to awareness of differences to be celebrated. First-person exposure to individuals from a variety of cultures may impact identity formation. Participation in sporting events that reflect cultures different from our own may also relate to identity formation and expose students to the moral, judicial, and legal systems reflected in other cultures.

- *Academic dimension.* The academic dimension relates primarily to the curriculum. The education of students is typically attributed to this feature of the campus community and might foster common learning as proposed by the Carnegie Foundation. Student affairs can contribute in a myriad of ways to the academic mission by the deliberate management of opportunities that foster development commensurate with the intellectual sophistication derived in formal classrooms.

- *Organizational/structural dimension.* The organizational/ structural component of a campus defines clearly the degree to which a student or, for that matter, faculty and staff may become involved in the shaping or creating of the campus community. Organizational structure reflects the implicit and explicit rules that govern the institution, its laws, policies, procedures, and codes. The nonexistence, for example, of a student appeal process may directly impact opportunities for moral development. Also, a decentralized series of committees functioning independently of each other will, in all likelihood, provide a nonsystematic and nonintentional program of cultural or esthetic programming from which a student may have difficulty choosing.

*Method of Intervention.* The actual methods by which program interventions occur seem endless in variety. They may, however, be classified within four broad categories: direct, indirect, media, and management. The first of these is a direct type of intervention wherein an individual interacts directly with the target in a counseling/advising/teaching capacity. Inasmuch as counseling, advising, and teaching have long been accepted methods of intervention, there is an ample body of literature related to them (Gilmore, 1980; Duson, King, and Murphy, 1978; Holahan, 1977; Grites, 1979; Winston, Ender, and Miller, 1982; Fried, 1981; Hanson, 1980).

It is also possible to impact targets of intervention in an indirect way such as consulting with or training others to prepare them to work directly with the student. Consultation and training emerged in recognition of this method as a procedure by which legitimate program interventions can occur (Gallessich, 1982; Hamilton and Meade, 1979; Delworth, 1978; Brown, 1972).

Whereas media interventions originally emphasized the printed page, programmed manuals, videotapes, films and slide shows, perhaps the greatest potential now lies in the adaptation and utilization of computer technology. Horizons have been expanded and visions created that program development professionals can explore.

Finally, using administrative/organizational development procedures and resource management to impact targets for the purpose of student development continues to be an established and powerful mode of intervention. The administrative creation of a faculty/staff council to jointly deal with student services problems and solutions is an example of an administrative intervention. Others include the modification of policies, the coordination of previously uncoordinated student development committees, and the preparation of institutional plans that address how all campus constituents contribute to the essence of an educated person.

## Summary

Earlier in this chapter the elements of the educated person were described as identified by the Carnegie Foundation in *A Quest for Common Learning* (Boyer and Levine, 1981). Although the publication does not acknowledge the correlative body of student development literature, it features common goals reminiscent of those we subscribe to in program development. Reconciliation of the academic curriculum and student services interventions can be fostered by discovering and articulating the common values that preside over the educational enterprise. The concept of the educated person generates the substance for these common values. The legitimacy of student services at institutions of higher learning may be contingent upon a collective ability to contribute through program development new and meaningful ways to create the educated person.

The three-dimensional model described in Figure 1 provides the substance for understanding the importance of creating a theoretical/conceptual foundation for program development. Program development based on the theories of student development, utilizing the vehicle of campus ecology, has the greatest potential for responding to the challenge of incorporation into the academic mainstream.

## References

Aubrey, R. F. "Historical Development of Guidance and Counseling and Implications for the Future." *Personnel and Guidance Journal,* 1977, *10,* 288-295.

Banning, J. H. (Ed.). *Campus Ecology: A Perspective for Student Affairs.* Portland, Oreg.: National Association of Student Personnel Administrators, 1978.

Banning, J. H. "The Campus Ecology Manager Role." In U. Delworth, G. R. Hanson, and Associates, *Student Services: A Handbook for the Profession.* San Francisco: Jossey-Bass, 1980.

Barclay, J. R. "Searching for a New Paradigm in Counseling." *Personnel and Guidance Journal,* 1983, *62* (1), 2.

Barr, M. J., and Fried, J. "Facts, Feelings, and Academic Credit." In J. Fried (Ed.), *New Directions for Student Services: Education for Student Development,* no. 15. San Francisco: Jossey-Bass, 1981.

Blake, E. S. "Classroom and Context: An Educational Dialectic." *Academe,* 1979, *65,* 280-292.

Boyer, E. L., and Hechinger, F. M. *Higher Learning in the Nation's Service.* Washington, D.C.: The Carnegie Foundation for the Advancement of Teaching, 1981.

Boyer, E. L., and Levine, A. *A Quest for Common Learning.* Washington, D.C.: The Carnegie Foundation for the Advancement of Teaching, 1981.

Brown, R. D. *Student Development in Tomorrow's Education: A Return to the Academy.* Student Personnel Series, no. 16. Washington, D.C.: American College Personnel Association, 1972.

Chickering, A. W. *Education and Identity.* San Francisco: Jossey-Bass, 1969.

DeCoster, D., and Mable, P. (Eds.). *New Directions for Student Services: Understanding Today's Students,* no. 16. San Francisco: Jossey-Bass, 1981.

Delworth, U. (Ed.). *New Directions for Student Services: Training Competent Staff,* no. 2. San Francisco: Jossey-Bass, 1978.

Drum, D. J. "Understanding Student Development." In W. H. Morrill, J. C. Hurst, and E. R. Oetting (Eds.), *Dimensions of Intervention for Student Development.* New York: Wiley, 1980.

Duson, B. M., King, M. R., and Murphy, B. "Building Blocks for a Campus Helping Network." *Journal of College Student Personnel,* 1978, *19,* 76-84.

Ferguson, M. *The Aquarian Conspiracy: Personal and Social Transformation in the 1980s.* Los Angeles: Tarcher, 1980.

Fried, J. (Ed.). *New Directions for Student Services: Education for Student Development,* no. 15. San Francisco: Jossey-Bass, 1981.

Gallessich, J. *The Profession and Practice of Consultation: A Handbook for Consultants, Trainers of Consultants, and Consumers of Consultation Services.* San Francisco: Jossey-Bass, 1982.

Gilmore, S. K. "Counseling." In U. Delworth, G. R. Hanson, and Associates, *Student Services: A Handbook for the Profession.* San Francisco: Jossey-Bass, 1980.

Grites, T. J. *Academic Advising: Getting Us Through the Eighties.* Washington, D.C.: American Association for Higher Education/Educational Resources Information Center, 1979.

Hamilton, M. K., and Meade, C. J. (Eds.). *New Directions for Student Services: Consulting on Campus,* no. 5. San Francisco: Jossey-Bass, 1979.

Handlin, O., and Handlin, M. F. *The American College and American Culture.* The Carnegie Commission on Higher Education. New York: McGraw-Hill, 1970.

Hanson, G. R. "Instruction." In U. Delworth, G. R. Hanson, and Associates, *Student Services: A Handbook for the Profession.* San Francisco: Jossey-Bass, 1980.

Hanson, G. R. (Ed.). *New Directions for Student Services: Measuring Student Development,* no. 20. San Francisco: Jossey-Bass, 1982.

Harvey, D. J., Hunt, D. E., and Schroder, H. M. *Conceptual Systems and Personality Organization.* New York: Wiley, 1961.

Heath, D. H. *Maturity and Competence.* New York: Gardner Press, 1977.

Holahan, C. J. "Consultation in Environmental Psychology: A Case Study of a New Counseling Role." *Journal of Counseling Psychology,* 1977, *24* (3), 251-254.

Huebner, L. A. "Interaction of Student and Campus." In U. Delworth, G. R. Hanson, and Associates, *Student Services: A Handbook for the Profession.* San Francisco: Jossey-Bass, 1980.

Hurst, J. C., and Hubbell, R. N. "Does Vociferation = Validity?" *National Association of Student Personnel Administrators Journal,* 1971, *9,* 270-275.

Kitchener, K. S. "Human Development and the College Campus: Sequences and Tasks." In G. R. Hanson (Ed.), *New Directions for Student Services: Measuring Student Development*, no. 20. San Francisco: Jossey-Bass, 1982.

Knefelkamp, L. L. "Faculty and Student Development in the 80s: Renewing the Community of Scholars." In *Integrating Adult Development Theory with Higher Education Practice*. Washington, D.C.: American Association for Higher Education/Educational Resources Information Center, 1980.

Kohlberg, L. "Stages of Moral Development." In C. M. Beck, B. S. Crittenden, and E. V. Sullivan (Eds.), *Moral Education*. Toronto, Canada: University of Toronto Press, 1971.

Kuhn, T. S. *The Structure of Scientific Revolutions*. Chicago: University of Chicago Press, 1969.

Loevinger, J. *Ego Development: Conceptions and Theories*. San Francisco: Jossey-Bass, 1976.

Miller, T. K., Winston, R. B., and Mendenhall, W. R. "Human Development and Higher Education." In T. K. Miller, R. B. Winston, and W. R. Mendenhall (Eds.), *Administration and Leadership in Student Affairs*. Muncie, Ind.: Accelerated Development, 1983.

Morrill, W. H., Hurst, J. C., and Oetting, E. R. *Dimensions of Intervention for Student Development*. New York: Wiley, 1980.

Morrill, W. H., Oetting, E. R., and Hurst, J. C. "Dimensions of Counselor Functioning." *Personnel and Guidance Journal*, 1974, *52* (6), 354-359.

Mueller, K. H. *Student Personnel Work in Higher Education*. Boston: Houghton Mifflin, 1961.

Naisbitt, J. *Megatrends: Ten New Directions Transforming Our Lives*. New York: Warner Books, 1982.

Perry, W. *Forms of Intellectual and Ethical Development in the College Years*. New York: Holt, Reinhart and Winston, 1970.

Piaget, J. *The Psychology of Intelligence*. New York: Harcourt Brace Jovanovich, 1950.

Rodgers, R. R. "Theories Underlying Student Development." In D. G. Creamer (Ed.), *Student Development in Higher Educa-*

*tion.* Cincinnati, Ohio: American College Personnel Association (ACPA) Media, 1980.

Rudolph, F. *The American College and University.* New York: Knopf, 1962.

Widick, C., Knefelkamp, L. L., and Parker, C. A. "Student Development." In U. Delworth, G. R. Hanson, and Associates, *Student Services: A Handbook for the Profession.* San Francisco: Jossey-Bass, 1980.

Winston, R. B., Jr., Ender, S. C., and Miller, T. K. (Eds.). *New Directions for Student Services: Developmental Approaches to Academic Advising,* no. 17. San Francisco: Jossey-Bass, 1982.

6

Gary R. Hanson
Bernard D. Yancey

❧ ❧ ❧ ❧ ❧ ❧ ❧ ❧ ❧ ❧ ❧ ❧ ❧

# Gathering Information
# to Determine Program Needs

Everyone uses data in planning student services programs, but
not everyone knows how, or when, or why they use them. Most
program ideas begin with some form of data that suggest why
the program should be developed. For example, a colleague may
mention that she will scream the next time a student comes in
and complains about poor academic advising, or a recent needs
assessment survey may have suggested that seniors want career
counseling. Perhaps the president indicates that students need
more leadership training or that he is concerned about the high
attrition rates for minority students. Likewise, most programs
end with evaluative data that may take one of the following
forms: No one showed up for your last program session, ten students stayed until midnight asking questions, or the dean of
students doubled your program budget for next year. Each situation provides data about program effectiveness. Knowing the
how, when, what, and why of these kinds of data is useful in
your program planning efforts and should lead to better programs.

As the examples above illustrate, the definition of *data* we will use in this chapter is broad and inclusive. Data are often ignored by people who plan programs because they assume only numerical data are useful. While numerical data are sometimes easier to summarize and interpret, other kinds of data are equally important in the decision-making process. A timely phone call, an astute observation, an insightful perception of a single student, or well-grounded rumors can all be used to design and implement educational programs.

## Role of Data in Program Development

Data are important in the development of educational programs in three important ways:

1. *planning:* using data to determine whether there is a need for the program
2. *monitoring:* using data to determine whether the program was implemented as planned
3. *evaluating:* using data to determine whether the program accomplished what it set out to do

These three functions are interrelated. While different kinds of data are important for the monitoring and evaluating uses, such data play an important role in the planning process as well. It is important to know what kinds of data are important for each use and how the data may be applied in practical work settings.

*Data in Program Planning.* Good program planning requires information that determines whether there is a real need for the program as well as who needs the program, when it should be given, what type of program is required, and how the program should be delivered.

The first issue is the most critical: Is there a need for the program? All too often, staff members ignore the needs of students and develop programs to suit their best interests. Other staff members do the same program time and time again because they are good at doing one kind of program, regardless of what students need. Not surprisingly, when programs are developed without regard for the students' needs, no one attends. Unfortunately, money, time, and no small amount of energy have been wasted by not attending to this fundamental question of whether a program is needed.

Good program design carefully considers who needs the program. Some programs fail because they were designed for the wrong individuals; other programs fail because they were not designed for any given group of students. Too often, student services staff who design programs assume that all students need to participate; however, effective programs meet the needs of a specific group of students. How can these students be identified? Drum and Figler (1973) recommend three sources of data: (1) students, (2) parents, faculty, or staff, and (3) past student records. Data collected from students may take the form of a formal needs assessment survey or the data may be casual conversations with students concerned about special issues. Professional student services staff are not the only individuals on campus with insight into student needs. We often forget to ask others what they think. Parents, staff, and faculty all work with students in a different capacity than student services professionals and possess unique perspectives on which students need what kinds of help.

Data from past student records also provide insight into which students might be needing a specific kind of program. Student retention data compiled from existing records may highlight a problem that has developed over a number of years for which no program has been developed. Analyzing these data resources to identify who drops out and who persists is a good way to begin.

Identifying when a program should be given is just as important as defining who should participate. Providing academic advising about various fields of study to college juniors may result in an ill-fated educational program. Advertising the program to incoming freshmen or sophomores would make more sense. The timing issue is not only related to the developmental status of the students; important data are also provided by the academic calendar. Are there certain periods of time when students are more receptive to the development of their study skills? Are personal relationship problems more likely to occur during the spring semester than the fall semester? Determining the most appropriate time to deliver an educational program requires keeping in close contact with students and maintaining a journal or log of past programming success. If the opportunity arises to give the same program at different times of the day or at several points in a semester, are records maintained about how many students participated in each program? Data about timing also can be collected by including a few simple questions on a needs assessment survey about the most appropriate times to offer programs or to analyze the college data base to determine what hours are heavy class loads.

What type of program is required to meet a particular educational objective? Look at the good educational programs on your campus and analyze why they work. Try to examine records that might indicate the program presentation style, length, sequence of activities, and level of experiential participation. Which program formats work well consistently? Do some types of programs work well with freshmen but not with seniors? Collecting data about these program characteristics and maintaining a journal log, index card file, or a computerized data base will assist program developers with deciding what type of program will be most effective.

How should programs be delivered? Program objectives can be met using a variety of techniques and the selection of the most effective one requires data about relative costs, time commitments, number of staff needed to conduct the program, and other competing priorities. Unless detailed cost accounting occurs, total program costs are difficult to determine. Making evaluative judgments about using one program method or format over another is even more difficult. Most student services staff could not accurately estimate the amount of time they spend in planning and delivering any given program. In addition, evaluative data are needed to determine what worked well in the past. Do students like some program methods more than others? Have student preferences for style and content changed over the last five years? Does the content of a program dictate a special method of delivery? Have the same program objectives been met with two different kinds of programs and what was the relative utility of each method? These evaluative data are extremely important in subsequent program planning.

In summary, the program planning process requires data that help determine whether the program is needed, who needs it, when it should be given, what types of programs work well, and how the program should be delivered. These data need to be supplemented with data from the monitoring and evaluation phase, however.

*Data for Monitoring Program Implementation.* A common complaint among program developers is that the program they designed was never delivered. Often, important aspects of the program are omitted because of time constraints or student attrition, especially if the program is multifaceted and occurs over several time periods. For example, Krone and Hanson (1982) report the problems of student attrition in a study of the impact of various residence hall living options on a measure of student development. Students participated in many different programming activities over a period of two semesters and considerable student attrition occurred when the assessment of student development was made near the end of the project. If students fail to receive the full benefits of a program, subsequent program modification or new program development suffers because the evaluation of the effectiveness of that effort is incomplete. When a program does not work or does not yield the intended effect, how can you tell whether the program was ineffective or whether the students simply did not receive the program treatment? One way to improve the program design process is to keep accurate records on how the program was delivered. Data that help answer the following kinds of questions are most useful in helping to monitor the educational program process:

1.  Did the people for whom the program was designed actually attend? Did other people attend whom you did not expect?
2.  Were all the program elements in the original design deliv-

ered? Were they delivered in the amount of time provided? What shortcuts were taken to "squeeze in" all the program elements?

3. If the program covered multiple time periods, which students dropped out? Did you follow through and find out why they failed to return?

4. What were students' reactions to the total program length? Was too much time devoted to certain aspects of the program at the expense of other elements?

5. Did the sequence of activities in the program facilitate meeting the program objectives? Would a different sequence reduce the amount of time, effort, or money required to deliver the program?

6. Was the program under- or overstaffed? Would experienced staff have been more effective? Did the program provide a good training ground for inexperienced staff?

The primary purpose in collecting data to monitor program implementation is to improve the program as it unfolds and to eliminate making the same mistakes the next time around. Using questions such as these, a simple checklist can be developed to make sure that the program you designed is actually delivered.

*Data for Program Evaluation.* Volumes have been written on program evaluation, but most programmatic decisions can be made if data are available to answer these important questions.

Do students want or need the program or are they aware of an existing program that meets that need? The visibility and awareness of a program are crucial indicators to follow when designing programs. If students are not aware of a program, then efforts should be made to advertise the program or educate students about the need for the program.

How many students participated in the program? Student contact via educational programs is an important evaluative indicator for administrators who must decide how much money, staff time, and physical space should be contributed to reaching a program objective. Programs with a high cost and low utilization are always the first to be terminated. High-cost programs can be justified if the number of students served is high as well. On the other hand, most administrators would support programs designed for special, small subgroups if the associated costs are reasonable.

Student satisfaction is another important indicator for program evaluation. Did the students who participated like the program? Were there parts of the program that could be improved, eliminated, or added? Ultimately, for a program to be successful, students must enjoy participating in it. Word-of-mouth program evaluation among student participants is one of the best indicators that the program goals and objectives were met. If students come to your office asking that the same program be given in their residence hall or student organization, chances are very good that all the necessary program design elements have been achieved and delivered.

Can the program be improved? Few educational programs are perfect and accomplish all the goals for which they were designed. Most programs can be improved the second time around if data are obtained that summarize possible improvements. Questions used to monitor the program delivery can be asked at the end of the program to show whether the objectives were met in a timely fashion for the intended audience.

Program cost accounting is an absolute must. Both direct costs and the indirect costs should be summarized and reviewed by the sponsoring administrators. Direct funds are always spent for materials, audiovisual equipment, and supplies, but collecting and reporting the indirect costs of staff time, overhead, and unanticipated expenditures is equally important. The true costs of producing a quality program are invariably higher than estimated.

When all these kinds of data are available, the toughest decision, requiring many intangible sources of evaluation data, remains to be made. Should the program be terminated? In addition to the "hard" evaluation data about costs, time, satisfaction, and student utilization, data about the contribution of the single program to the overall department, division, and college mission must be assessed. Data must be collected from individuals not directly connected with providing the program. Faculty, regents, parents, and individuals in the local community may lend support for continuing a program when the data indicate that the program should be terminated. The political costs of not providing the program may be higher than the dollar costs of delivering the program. Discontinuing a study skills center at a time when the college is recruiting students with marginal academic preparation could have disastrous long-range implications. Any shift in long-range plans on the part of the institution should be considered in evaluating the worthiness of any single program effort.

## Sources of Data

One basic guiding principle to consider in collecting data for program planning is that, in general, the wider the variety of data sources, the more likely you are to have the information needed to reach the "correct" or at least most appropriate decision (Hanson and Lenning, 1979). Unless there is simply no other alternative (cost, timing, mandate, and so on), no final program planning decisions should be based on a single data source. Having information from a variety of data sources is critical, not only to ensure comprehensiveness but also to provide a means of validating the accuracy of the data collected from individual sources.

Data relevant to program planning can be obtained from a variety of sources, both formal and informal. These data may already exist, or efforts may need to be made to actively collect and solicit additional information. Collecting these types of data may require the use of traditional research methods, survey research skills, or policy analysis. You also should recognize that information gained on a daily basis through contact with students, staff, and faculty provides a rich source of information that is particularly relevant to the program development process. The most critical function of the program developer is to match the available data with the questions and then to determine whether additional data are needed.

*Formal Sources.* Formal data sources may consist of

existing data, whether collected for the specific questions at hand or for other reasons, or data to be collected at some future time. Examples of these formal data sources include:

- *Research literature.* While research conducted at a particular institution is of prime importance, journal articles, books, research reports, and research memos from other institutions should also be considered. These important sources of data are often overlooked by the beginning program developer.
- *Previous research.* Often research conducted by others on your campus will provide insight into the need for a particular program. Any analyses or results, even those not necessarily reported in a formal way, can be reanalyzed in light of new questions that have been raised. These data files might include previously collected survey data, structured interviews, academic performance data, service utilization data, and data from program or project evaluations.
- *Existing data bases.* Most colleges and universities have now developed a computer data base for keeping student academic records. A few institutions have started using student development transcripts to monitor student activity on campus (Brown and Citrin, 1977). Academic performance information—both current and from previously attended institutions—enrollment information, age, ethnicity, names of high schools or previously attended colleges, marital status, number of dependents, major, as well as classes taken and associated grades all provide a foundation for identifying students who may participate in a program.
- *Utilization data.* Many student services agencies and departments on campus keep individual reports and records of how many students utilize their services and when. These data provide important clues to the types of students who already are familiar with at least some of the services or programs offered. Lack of utilization may signal an important area for new evaluation or program development efforts.
- *Previous evaluation data.* Data collected in conjunction with past program evaluation activities, including attendance in-

formation, satisfaction ratings, and long-term program follow-up activities provide additional sources of formal program planning data.

- *Educational policy analysis data.* Nearly all educational institutions examine their educational policies either for internal evaluation or as part of an accreditation site visit. These
reports highlight critical institutional issues and recommend
possible policy or program changes. A careful analysis of
these reports will suggest new types of programs that may be
needed.
- *Concurrent research studies.* Research projects currently
under way may be collecting some of the information
needed for planning your program. Often items or data collection procedures can be "piggybacked" on these ongoing
efforts. Such possibilities should not be overlooked for they
can result in considerable cost savings. Also, similar research
conducted at other institutions can be used in the same manner. Often cross-institutional comparisons provide administrative decision makers an important perspective from which
to judge the data.
- *New research studies.* Using other formal data resources is a
cost-efficient way to obtain information for program planning but more than likely, the specific information you need
will necessitate a special data collection effort or research
study. The data may be collected through such active methods as mail surveys, structured interviews, and/or telephone
surveys.

*Informal Sources.* While informal data sources can provide a rich source of information on their own, perhaps such
data can be most useful in helping interpret or validate data
collected from formal sources. Some examples of informal data
sources include the following:

- *Students.* Pertinent information from students can be obtained on an informal basis from either student leaders, students serving as paraprofessionals, or students using the
services already provided. It may be a simple matter of lis-

tening to what students are saying. Are different students talking about or coming in with the same problems? Or are the same students coming in with a variety of problems?

- *Faculty and staff.* Faculty and staff can also be a useful source of information. Do faculty see an increase in the number of students experiencing academic difficulty in certain areas or an increase in absenteeism? Do staff members who work with students on a regular basis see an increase in the number of students with particular problems or an increase in the severity of the problems? Do either the faculty or staff have concerns about the impact of proposed policy or program changes?
- *Newspapers.* Both campus and local newspapers can provide a barometer of campus and local opinions or concerns. Is there a particular topic that continually appears in the "Letters to the Editor" or the editorial sections pertaining to students or the campus? What is the breadth of support or concern about these issues? Are there local, area, statewide, or national proposed policy changes that may affect students, faculty, or staff?
- *Colleagues.* Colleagues, both at your institution and at other institutions, may be able to provide considerable insight into the program planning and evaluation process. Similar programs in other departments or other institutions may have been tried. A considerable amount of time, effort, and expense can be saved by simply picking up the phone and calling a colleague. Listening and asking questions at professional conferences is another way to use professional peers.

### Assessing the Availability and Quality of Data

In determining what types of data to use in program planning, identifying the potential data source is only the beginning. Some thought must also be given to the availability and quality of the data.

*Availability.* With informal data sources, assessing their availability is only a matter of determining whether the individuals you want to talk with can be reached in a timely fashion so their input can be used. With formal data sources, however, a wider range of factors affects their availability. For example, have the data already been collected or will a special data collection effort be required? If data have already been collected, have they been analyzed in a way that is useful? Are written reports available and where can they be found? If further analyses are needed, are the data in a format that lends itself to easy analysis? Do the data exist on paper documents such as surveys or application forms, or have they been converted to a computer-readable format and if so, do they reside on some computer storage device (that is, diskette, tape, or disk)? If the data reside in such a device, who has the responsibility and custody of the data files? Do you have the necessary credibility to ask that the data be shared?

Other factors may also limit access to data important to the program planning process. For example, are there political, policy, ownership, or legal restrictions that limit the availability of the data to you? Questions of confidentiality under the Family Educational Rights and Privacy Act (the Buckley Amendment) need to be discussed before certain kinds of data can be released and used for program planning.

*Quality.* Assessing the quality of the data sources speaks directly to their usability and reliability. Informal data sources may only require an assessment of previous reliability and accuracy, but often intuition or supporting evidence collected from other sources, either formal or informal, may be required to place confidence in the quality of the informal data used for program planning purposes.

An additional set of questions should be asked about formal data. If data already exist, how current are they? How accurate are the data? (For a more comprehensive discussion of the accuracy of complete data bases, see Martin, 1974.) Have the conditions changed that produced the original data? Was the population or sample used appropriate for the questions now being raised? If a survey instrument was used, how valid and reliable was it? Do the responders to the data collection effort represent an unbiased sample? If the data were from an existing data base, how were they collected and what quality control

checks were made at the time they were entered into the computer? Were the data always collected in the same manner, at the
same time of year, using identical procedures? Are the data
available for all students in the data base or are there considerable amounts of missing data? If the data were collected using a
survey or observational technique, can the behavior, outcome,
attitude, or performance be measured and quantified? How
valid and reliable was the instrument used (Anastasi, 1976;
Oskamp, 1977)? Attitudinal data and measures of student development are particularly difficult to assess (Hanson, 1982).
No single index can be used to measure data quality for a particular use. Hence, common sense and shared evaluation of the
data provide some protection for identifying when it is or is not
appropriate to use. Very few substitutes for experience exist,
however.

## Methods for Collecting Data

Most people think of formal research design and the complicated data collection procedures often associated with these
designs when trying to collect data for program planning. As a
result, very little data are collected prior to or during the initial
program planning process. While good program planning may require, at the appropriate stage, formal data collection procedures, relevant data may already exist. Recognizing, organizing,
and analyzing available data is necessary for the program planning process. The program planner must take a look at the questions that need to be answered, determine what data already
exist, and what additional information should be collected.

The type and quantity of data collected may be restricted
by the resources available for collecting, analyzing, and summar-
izing the data. For example, will the information have to be
hand-tallied or can the computer be used to analyze it? How
quickly is the information needed? Will there be enough time to
prepare a survey effort or must the analysis be restricted to
existing data? If computer support is available, are the resources
available to convert the data to a computer-readable format
through direct computer terminal entry, optical scanned data

sheets, keypunching, or some other method? What software is available to do the analysis and who is available to run the appropriate computer hardware?

*Collecting Informal Data.* When data are used in decision making, timing is a critical issue. If the information is not available when needed, it may not be worth having. Informal data are troublesome because the data sources must be located and contacted; time may not allow gathering data from a wide assortment of informal sources. Too often, the resources that make up these informal data networks are a result of past associations, and individual memory may be insufficient to recall who provided what type of information for a given situation.

The collection of informal data should begin by talking to staff and colleagues about their perceptions of the need for the program and its possible impact. This can be done on an individual basis or through such techniques as "brainstorming" in a staff meeting or a planning retreat. There are several important points to remember at this stage. The first is that all ideas and suggestions offered are as valid as any other and no judgmental decisions should be made at this early point of discussion. This is a data collection phase, with analysis and assessment of the data to come later. Devise some method of monitoring and cataloguing these good ideas. Whether records are kept on simple note cards, a log, or a computerized filing system, do not rely on your memory for all the details.

Student input is necessary, but acquiring such input too early raises some programming problems. During the early stages of planning and data collection, student expectations should not be raised about a "new" program if there is the slightest chance the program will never be developed. Asking questions and collecting student data too early in the process raises expectations that cannot be met and contributes to poor public relations and a loss of credibility among the very individuals the program is designed to help. Not only will your credibility be damaged but the program goals and content may be changed in undesirable ways.

Even in the absence of a specific proposed program, several steps can be taken to quickly identify and access informal data sources. While some of these steps may appear similar to the methods used in the collection from formal data sources, they are not as methodologically rigorous. For example, one of the best sources for informal data is colleagues from other institutions. Active participation in professional organizations is one of the best ways to meet people who struggle with the same programming problems. Also, most professional organizations have "special interest groups" concerned with the same student populations and problems as you. One way to maintain a constant flow of informal data about program ideas is to maintain a list of individuals you meet at conventions, workshops, and professional meetings who have already tried a program along the lines you are considering.

Along with a list of resource people, keep an active file of newspaper clippings (particularly from your student newspaper) targeted at potential or actual areas of interest that fall within your programming responsibilities. For example, student articles may highlight problems in the residence hall, test-taking anxiety, financial aid delivery, and time management.

*Collecting Formal Data.* If data from formal sources are needed, then the first step is to determine what variables or items are relevant to the research questions. Some preliminary indication of these relevant variables may have been gathered from the informal data sources at an earlier stage of planning. These informal clues must be supplemented with information gained from a formal literature review. Starting points for such reviews can be articles and books suggested by staff and colleagues and bibliographies published by professional organizations. Some of the standard bibliographical sources are the Educational Research Information Center, the *Social Sciences Citation Index, Psychology Abstracts,* and the *Index to Statistics.*

Once the relevant variables have been identified, then the program planner must identify the variables for which data already exist and those for which new data must be collected. The list of potential variables is not static but can be modified as the quality and availability of the specific data elements become known and as the program takes shape. An early preview of these data may raise additional questions that require other kinds of data or more current information.

Using existing data solves many data collection problems. However, most computer data base systems contain more data elements than you need to analyze for a particular program planning need. Typically, time can be saved and the number of data processing errors reduced if a new, but smaller, data base is constructed by extracting only those bits of information actually needed for a particular application. Constructing a smaller data base not only reduces the cost of processing but eliminates much of the confusion induced by too much data. Data "overkill" never contributes to good program planning.

The extraction of data elements from an existing computer system should include a thorough documentation describing the original data source and the method used in selecting the data element. If the data are stored in a computer-readable format and the analysis is to be performed on the same computer, then new data files can be created by writing or using existing software. This is not necessarily a task beyond the capabilities of the average program planner. For a discussion of some of the latest user-friendly computer technology, see Martin, 1982. If the information is located on paper documents, such as surveys or application forms, the data may have to be tabulated by hand, entered into a new data file, or coded on summary sheets before data processing may begin.

*Unobtrusive and Obtrusive Measures.* A variety of methods can be used to collect additional data. These methods generally fall into two measurement strategies: unobtrusive and obtrusive. The obtrusive strategies include many of the traditional measurement techniques such as needs assessment or attitude surveys while the unobtrusive strategies include observational methods or the analysis of utilization records.

Many unobtrusive measures may be found on existing data bases, such as grade point averages, course loads, class schedules, receipt of financial aid, residence in college housing, and so on. Additional unobtrusive measures can be developed. For example, utilization data can be gathered by logging the number of students, the hour of the day that they come, and what service component they utilize. In addition, information on what motivated the student to seek the service could be collected. The log need not be complicated; it may consist of a simple check-off or tally sheet filled out by a staff member.

Obtrusive measures require the student to provide information. Traditionally, student services staff have used survey or interview techniques to collect these kinds of data. Survey data can be collected with a variety of methods that usually fall in one of three categories: written questionnaires, telephone interviews, and structured, face-to-face interviews. Using more than one of these techniques eliminates the bias and error that ordinarily occur when only one data collection strategy is used.

Questionnaires are useful for collecting large amounts of data using a common format such as attitude items, opinions, ratings of satisfaction, or evaluative information concerning programs or services. Questionnaires have also been used to collect expressions of perceived need. These questionnaires require a careful review to distinguish between items that measure a "want" and those that measure "need." Questionnaires are most useful when the data collection effort requires either a captive audience (that is, a classroom) or a representative sample. Careful planning and thorough follow-up using mail survey techniques will result in response rates of 60 percent to 70 percent. If the sample is large enough, these questionnaire responses provide information from a wide variety of students. A disadvantage of using questionnaires is that it may take weeks or months of effort to construct a reliable and valid instrument. Every instrument should be pilot-tested on a small sample of students for clarity of directions and specific item content, and other staff members should examine the instrument to verify that the data, once collected, will be usable.

If information is needed quickly and a limited number of questions can be asked, then the telephone survey approach should be considered. The telephone interview allows for in-depth follow-up of specific responses that is not available in the questionnaire approach. The telephone survey can also be used to collect information from the nonresponders of a larger mail survey to determine whether or not there is any nonresponse bias.

Information obtained from structured interviews can provide worthwhile data but the most useful aspect of such information is the richness of detail that elaborates on data gathered through other survey techniques.

## Using Data in Program Development

Data collection is a futile exercise if the information collected cannot be used for program planning purposes. The types of data collected, the methods used to collect it, and the purposes for which the data were intended all influence how the data can be used. Many programs fail because useful planning information is ignored. The responsible programmer must analyze how to best communicate data, when the timing for the data is most appropriate, and who the consumer audience will be. One reason data are not used is that too much data are collected and too little analysis, synthesis, and integration of the results occur. Few program planners want all the details but prefer to know what programs work well, how much it costs to conduct, how long it will take to develop, and who is going to do it. These are "big picture" questions and most data are not summarized in a manner that provides the necessary answers. The following guidelines should help program planners make effective use of whatever data they have.

- *Analyze the consumer audience.* Data cannot be used if you do not understand who plans to use it. You may want the information for your own use but, more often than not, others may need to examine it as well. Whether you provide the data to others or not, the following questions should be asked: Why is the data wanted? What decisions need to be made? What kind of statistics will the user understand? When will the data be needed? When will it have the most impact on the programming decisions? Do the decision makers prefer formal or informal types of data? Do they prefer written reports or verbal briefings? All of these questions shape the way in which the data you collect can be used.
- *Provide intermediate feedback.* Program planning is a dynamic process and data should be used throughout. Waiting

until all of the data are collected may result in the data never being used because all the major decisions are already made. Data analysis and reporting are also dynamic processes and useful information is frequently available during the early data processing stages. Release the results in a preliminary form to interested users as soon as they become available, especially if the data are related to the monitoring function of a current program. Changes can be made and the program improved even with preliminary forms of the data.

- *Present different data for each audience.* Most educational programming efforts are team efforts and the responsibility for decision making is often shared. The person watching the budget and expenses may need data related to previous program costs while the person designing the content may want information about group process techniques or structured program activities. Rarely do all the team members want or need all of the data all of the time. Data are most meaningful when they answer a very specific question, and miscellaneous or irrelevant data actually hinder the decision-making process.

- *Use multiple reporting techniques.* One of the advantages of a careful analysis of your consumer audience is the ability to report data differently depending on the interests and expertise of the program planner. Some individuals like subjective, impressionistic data that illustrate how students "feel" about a particular issue or problem while others want tables of numbers and charts. Knowing which type of data will be most effective for a given individual may mean the difference between the data being used or ignored.

- *Present data in simple, brief, and understandable reports.* Often, data collection and reporting is not successful because too much data are collected from too many people and all of it is presented as important. Program planners rarely want to know as many "interesting facts" about a particular topic as the person responsible for collecting the data. Data should be presented with as much brevity, simplicity, and clarity as possible. Most data summaries should be no more than three or four pages long with one or two tables of data or a simple chart or two. At the beginning, the three or four key points should be made and the remainder of the report used to elaborate the results. Twenty-five-page technical reports should definitely be avoided.

- *Report data in a timely fashion.* Most program planners fail to use data because it just is not available when needed. One of the reasons this occurs is that few planners anticipate data needs. Data collection always takes longer than expected so very careful planning must be done to get the data ahead of time. One way to accomplish this is to conduct anticipatory research. Keep in touch with campus trends and pay attention to minor variations in student issues, problems, and characteristics. These minor variations may not mean a thing or they may provide early clues to later problems. Having a program ready to go just before a crisis hits campus is bound to win the admiration of your colleagues and your president.

## Summary

Good program development demands the collection and use of data. In discussing the role that data can play in the effective design and delivery of educational programs, we identified three major categories of use: planning, monitoring, and evaluating. These uses dictate the kinds of data that should be collected, whom the data should be collected from, and when it should be collected. Deciding the kinds of data to collect requires a good working knowledge of potential data resources on campus, both formal and informal. A great deal of the information useful to the programming process is available in one form or another in existing records. Finding the source of the data may require a survey of newspapers, computer data bases, previous research and evaluation projects, or the collection of totally new data. Collecting the data is only a beginning step, however. An assessment must be made about its availability and quality. And then the consumer audience must be carefully analyzed and appropriate data analysis and reporting techniques selected. The integration of data with purpose, audience, analysis, and dissemination is a dynamic process that leads from one program to the next. Only in this way can data be used to plan programs.

## References

Anastasi, A. *Psychological Testing.* (4th ed.) New York: Macmillan, 1976.

Brown, R. D., and Citrin, R. "A Student Development Transcript: Assumptions, Uses, and Formats." *Journal of College Student Personnel,* 1977, *18,* 163-168.

Drum, D. J., and Figler, H. E. *Outreach in Counseling.* New York: Intext Educational Publishers, 1973.

Hanson, G. R. (Ed.). *New Directions for Student Services: Measuring Student Development,* no. 20. San Francisco: Jossey-Bass, 1982.

Hanson, G. R., and Lenning, O. T. "Evaluating Student Development Programs." In G. Kuh (Ed.), *Evaluation in Student Affairs.* Cincinnati, Ohio: American College Personnel Association (ACPA) Media, 1979.

Krone, K. J., and Hanson, G. R. "Assessment in Student Development Programming: A Case Study." In G. R. Hanson (Ed.), *New Directions for Student Services: Measuring Student Development,* no. 20. San Francisco: Jossey-Bass, 1982.

Martin, J. *Privacy, Accuracy, and Security in Computer Systems.* Englewood Cliffs, N.J.: Prentice-Hall, 1974.

Martin, J. *Applications Development Without Programmers.* Englewood Cliffs, N.J.: Prentice-Hall, 1982.

Oskamp, S. *Attitudes and Opinions.* Englewood Cliffs, N.J.: Prentice-Hall, 1977.

# 7

Margaret J. Barr
Lou A. Keating

✌ ✌ ✌ ✌ ✌ ✌ ✌ ✌ ✌ ✌ ✌ ✌ ✌

# Translating Needs into Specific Program Goals

During her adventures in Wonderland, Alice had a most helpful conversation with the Cheshire cat. She asked, "Would you please tell me which way I should go from here?" With great wisdom, the Cheshire cat replied, "It all depends on where you want to get to." The Cheshire cat's reply is cogent advice for the student services professional. For if we are unsure about what we want to do, where we want to go, and what our programs are designed to accomplish, then we will be most ineffective travelers in the wonderland of higher education.

In the Introduction, emphasis was placed on the importance of developing appropriate, congruent, and attainable goals as a key element in successful program development. This chapter is designed to assist the student services professional in acquiring specific information about goal setting as a key skill in establishing effective student services programs.

Goal setting is not an easy task. Setting program goals is, however, a critical step in the program development process. Goals are important for two reasons. First, program goals provide clear direction for the student services unit and define the accomplishments that should result from any proposed program effort. Second, program goals provide guidance to institutional decision makers by clearly identifying what will *not* be accomplished if the program is *not* supported. In order to set useful program goals, it is important to reach agreement on what a goal is within the domain of student services.

## Program Goals: A Working Definition

Both within and without the field of management, there has been a long-standing debate over the differences between goals and objectives. While attention to such precise definitions may have value in some arenas, it is both futile and nonproductive in the student services program planning process. In fact, Deegan and Fritz (1975) use the terms interchangeably stating that "goals or objectives describe the results we intend to accomplish, what we will have to show for the expenditure of our resources and energy" (p. 26). Odiorne (1965) describes goals as public commitments to accomplish a specific set of tasks and activities. Because goals are public, or at least are shared with the supervisor, they can be viewed as risky. As Odiorne states, "They are attached to the risk that the individual may fail" (p. 102). Lenning (1980) indicates that there are "two types of program goals. The first, outcome goals, focuses on the results the program is intended to achieve. The other type of goals, process goals, refers to how the intended outcomes are to be achieved" (p. 238).

Johnson and Foxley (1980) describe a goal as "a desired future state. Its time frame is long range, and it may be expressed quantitatively or qualitatively. Goals simply state where an individual, unit, or division wants to go" (p. 410). Hanson (1980), although focusing on teaching, provides a different view of goals, stating that "goals provide an opportunity to state our values and philosophy more explicitly, so we must carefully consider what we hope to accomplish" (p. 277). Embedded in these last two definitions is a view of a goal as a dream, a dream that represents a major long-range commitment to our values and to our overarching purposes as a profession. Examples of a goal representing a dream are a university-wide student leadership training program, a greatly improved academic advising system, a new recreation building, and an increase in the number of minority students, faculty, and staff attracted to and retained by the institution. Perhaps these ideal goals will never be achieved, but articulation of our dreams provides a reference point for the development of specific programs and activities. These programs are the intermediate goals that bring our dreams to fruition. Intermediate goals flow from the ideal goal and become specific time-delineated efforts toward the dream. Both the dream and the intermediate goal are important to the program planner: The dream keeps us focused on our values, and intermediate goals help move us incrementally toward that dream.

Broad goals are not reached without meticulous attention to the planning process. Backplanning (Barr and Hurst, 1979) provides one method to help with the process of setting intermediate goals. When a backplanning technique is used, an ideal dream or goal is set for some time in the distant future. Then the program planner works backward from that target date and dream goal to the present time, defining at each step along the way what decisions need to be made, what policies need to be established, and what activities need to be launched in order to meet the larger future goal. For example, in a larger multipurpose university, a dream goal was established of providing improved response time to students in the financial aid office. The method to achieve that goal was to have an on-line financial aid management system installed by 1985. The global goal was based partially on data: paperwork, long response times, staff stress, and a commitment that needy students should receive their aid as soon as possible. The projected financial aid management system cost close to a quarter of a million dollars including installation costs, and the money was simply not available within current institutional resources. Instead of abandoning the ideal program dream of increased efficiency and effectiveness, the program planners employed a backplanning technique. Keeping a target date in mind, program staff planned from that future date to the present time. By doing so, a series of incremental intermediate program goals were established. Each of these intermediate goals was specific and time delineated. Thus, in the first year of the program, (1) computer terminals were installed to eliminate the time-consuming process of looking up basic information on each financial aid recipient, (2) staff training and familiarization with the computer as a resource tool were started, and (3) a series of very concrete specifications for the ultimate system were agreed upon. In year two, (1) a small portion of the system was installed to ease the packaging process, (2) a financing plan was developed, (3) bids for the system were received, and (4) contracts were awarded for necessary outside consultation on system installation. In year three, (1) staff training continued, (2) the system was purchased and installed, and (3) systems testing and modification were accomplished. In year four, the system was on-line and staff duties were reconfigured to support the new approach to the delivery of student financial aid. Without careful attention to intermediate goals, the entire project may have been abandoned and the initial goal would never have been reached.

In addition, the process of setting intermediate goals assists program planners in defining what goals are absolutely unobtainable and in pinpointing goals that are too limited to be useful. Although a step-by-step process to goal setting through development of intermediate goals is time-consuming, it does provide useful and concrete guidance to ultimate goal accomplishment. Unfortunately, articulating the dream and setting intermediate goals in student services programs are complicated by several barriers. These barriers must be addressed to ensure development of meaningful and practical goals.

## Goal-Setting Barriers

There are at least two major barriers in setting goals for student services programs. First, the entire higher education environment is characterized by ambiguous goal statements (Baldridge and Tierney, 1979). The second barrier is the diffuse character of the student services environment. Any number of programs, activities, and services may be part of the student services domain on a particular campus. Under such conditions, it may appear to others, and at time to ourselves, that there are no common goals to unite the enterprise.

*Goals of Higher Education.* The history of American higher education reflects a series of changing goals for colleges and universities. Chapter One by Gary Knock traces the evolution of American higher education and highlights the difficulty of reaching a consensus on the goals for the enterprise. A snapshot of higher education in America today would show great diversity in institutional type, funding source, programs, curriculum, and students served. This diversity fosters lack of agreement on goals for the entire enterprise.

Consensus on goals is even more difficult when the focus is shifted to the individual institution. As long as institutional goals are "kept at an ambiguous and general level, consensus in the institution is easy to achieve. However, as soon as goals are concretely specified and put into operation, disagreement arises" (Baldridge and Tierney, 1979, p. 21). For the very process of setting specific goals means that priorities will be defined and when priorities are defined, someone or something will not be first.

Higher education institutions across the country are struggling with the very difficult task of setting concrete institutional goals. Budget constraints, declining enrollments, and demands for accountability have all been causes of institutional attention to goals. In order to survive, let alone flourish, many institutions must define their mission in new ways and set specific institutional goals. Economic conditions alone are a powerful force in the process of setting institutional goals and forcing a reduction in the number of goals embraced by the institution, as well as reducing the diffuse character of those goals. The institutional concern about goals has a very real and direct effect on student services programs. Specificity at an institutional level requires concomitant concern from all units within the institution with goal setting. For student services units, that task can be particularly difficult.

*Student Services Goals.* Student services divisions, agencies, and programs have had a long history of ambiguous goals. Vague, general goals for student services programs and activities have contributed to the perception that student services units are not a central part of the academic enterprise. Under tight budget conditions, our inability to be specific with regard to program goals and intended outcomes of services has been a negative influence on resource allocation. Often it appears to be fairly easy not to fund a needed position in a student services unit if that unit cannot clearly define the specific ways that position will serve to make a difference for students and the institution.

Part of our lack of skill in goal articulation lies in the roots of our shared profession. Student services programs evolved out of issues and concerns that faculty members had neither the time nor inclination to deal with. During the era of *in loco parentis,* the goals of student services units, although not always agreed upon, were very clear within the academic community. With the demise of the concept of *in loco parentis,* many student services divisions struggled to redefine their goals and articulate their mission within the institution. If we were not to regulate and supervise student behavior, then what was our legitimate role within higher education?

During the last two decades, the profession appears to have answered that question. Agreement has been reached that the roles of service providers, student development educators, administrators, and counselors are all legitimate and needed. As a profession, we have *not* succeeded in translating the goals of student services units to our larger environment. The lack of clear, unambiguous goals for student services programs has been one of our greatest failings as a profession. We need to be able to clearly articulate what we intend to do, what differences will occur as a result of our efforts, and what outcomes the rest of the academic community can expect through the investment of resources in the student services enterprise.

A number of tools are available to assist student services programmers in the goal-setting process. Unfortunately, either through lack of understanding or poor application of these tools, many student services programmers have been reluctant to employ such systems.

## Methods to Assist in Goal Setting

In general, student services professionals have not adopted the goal-setting systems utilized by business and industry. The fear is often expressed that the process of goal setting interferes with effective program delivery. In addition, our product (the educated person) is more complex and less easy to define than is the visible, concrete product of the business enterprise. Thus the application of management tools such as Management by Objectives (MBO) and Management Information Systems (MIS) to goal setting in student services programs appears to be very difficult. In addition, although potentially very useful to the goal-setting process, evaluation and assessment strategies developed within education have often been rejected because of their specificity (Lenning, 1980).

*Management by Objectives.* Wikstrom (1966) indicates there are as many definitions of management by objectives as there are users of the procedure. MBO can be viewed as a philosophy, as an attitude, as an appraisal system, as a planning approach, or as a system for filling out forms and meeting deadlines. Deegan and Fritz (1975) indicate that MBO is merely a tool to assist the organization in moving toward some specified outcomes. Partansontichai (1975) identified the five phases of MBO as: finding the objective, setting the objective, validating the objective, implementing the objective, and reporting the status of the objective. His definition does not differ significantly from a good program-planning process. An MBO program, when effective, requires participation in goal setting by all levels of the organization. It assists in defining what is being done and how tasks are being accomplished, and it sets targets for goal accomplishment by the unit. Deegan and Fritz (1975) provide excellent guidance for the installation of an MBO approach within the context of higher education.

MBO is not a perfect tool for either program management

or goal setting. Levinson (1970) indicates that MBO programs often fail to take into account the personal objectives of professionals and limit the discretion of the individual staff member. Deegan and Fritz (1975) caution against an emphasis on the achievement of objectives to the exclusion of routine and necessary administrative work. Odiorne (1965) warns that in action an MBO system has the potential to stress results without providing the methods to achieve them.

These cautions are very important for the student services programmer. If MBO methods are used in goal setting in student services programs, careful monitoring is needed. An MBO program that deteriorates into paper pushing, endless meetings to set objectives, and overattention to goal setting rather than program implementation is neither useful nor helpful. MBO is one tool for setting goals, but understanding the approach is critical and proper application of the tool is essential.

*Management Information Systems.* Use of data on student characteristics, participation in activities, and budget resources as a basis for setting goals is not a new concept for student services programmers. Housing offices, placement centers, financial aid offices, and other student services units have always used such data as a basis of future planning and goal setting. Advances in computer capabilities and the installation of management information systems have merely provided a greater amount and variety of data to the student services programmer and the institution. The current use of MIS to capture and use data provides both possibilities and problems for student services programs.

Simply put, MIS is a way to organize data about clients, activities, and resources. The key to a successful MIS program lies in the decision of what data is actually needed in the system, that is, transforming data into meaningful information. Too often we become intrigued with the information possibilities, develop a system to capture endless amounts of quantifiable data, and then cannot sort through the data in ways that are useful to the goal-setting process for student services programs. However, a good MIS, structured to provide only the data needed for good decisions, can be a valuable tool in the goal-setting process. For example, Baldridge and Tierney (1979) express their dismay with regard to the amount of institutional misinformation held by administrators and planners within higher education. Obviously program goals based on information rather than misinformation will be more useful and helpful.

The use of quantifiable data as a basis for goal setting has merit. However, several cautions about complete reliance on an MIS system as the basis for goal setting are in order. First, student services program personnel need to decide what data are important. It may be intriguing to know that 50 percent of the junior class come from families with incomes of $40,000 per annum. But unless the data can be used to pinpoint or suggest a possible program intervention, such as one relating to job placement expectations after graduation, such knowledge does not assist in program planning. Second, elaborate MIS programs can absorb enormous amounts of fiscal and human resources within the institution. The question of what actually is needed, in terms of information, needs to be answered early to avoid overcommitment of resources to the mere process of data collection. Finally, Plourde (1976) cautions that MIS programs are problematic when attempts are made to quantify subjective concepts such as the educational value of the total institutional experience. Data can tell us that a student attained a certain grade point average, participated in any number of activities, and had a certain major. By itself, data produced from an MIS program cannot tell us if that student developed or profited by all these experiences.

A good management information system provides some of the data necessary for goal setting. MIS programs and systems are not designed to set those goals; only the program planner can translate the data into meaningful and attainable goals. Chapter Six by Hanson and Yancey provides many useful suggestions for data collection and use of that data in program planning. It is important to remember, however, that data can only begin the process of goal setting. It takes the creativity and energy of program staff to move data-based conclusions to reasonable program goals.

*Evaluation Strategies.* Lenning (1980) categorically states that "to be useful, goals must be transformed into concrete, observable, precise terms" (p. 237). The use of evaluation strategies during the goal-setting process assists with this translation effort. Evaluation questions, when asked during the process of goal setting, focus the goal-setting effort so that program goals clearly state what will be accomplished and who will be the target of the program intervention. Oetting (1980) provides a simple guide to establishing program goals when he states: "First, state the goals of the program, then test them by asking whether that goal would also be true for other programs: teaching, the Girl Scouts, and psychotherapy. To improve adjustment, for example, does not meet the test. It could be a goal for all of them" (p. 146). Oetting's description of the necessary first step in goal setting comes from the perspective of a professional evaluator. It is precisely this kind of specificity that makes evaluation strategies an essential tool in goal setting. Goals are an expression of hoped-for outcomes. Thus, evaluation of the program must be considered as part of the goal-setting process. Focusing on outcomes, on determining what will be different, and on who will be served is the first step in developing good, useful program goals.

One way to assure that this will happen when program goals are established is to use outside evaluators to help in the goal-setting process. At the very least, program planners should be aware of the fundamentals of evaluation and apply those concepts when setting goals. Lenning (1977) and Bloom (1956) have both developed evaluation taxonomies to translate goals into concrete outcome statements. Reviewing research on evaluation strategies and questions may be a critical step in setting program goals. Many times outside evaluators are not available for consultation to program staff. In those cases, one staff member should be assigned to the critical task of focusing program planners in the task of relating overarching purposes or dreams to concrete outcome statements. A goal without a concomitant method to measure whether the goal is achieved is neither useful nor helpful. We need to constantly ask in what ways will we know if a student has grown or developed as a result of the expenditure of human and fiscal resources in a student services program effort. Evaluation techniques used at the time program goals are established will assist in focusing the goal-setting process.

Once global goals for a program effort are agreed upon, then attention needs to be given to specific aims of the program. Oetting (1980) provides particularly pithy advice on how to translate dream goals into intermediate goals. Attention to the question of accomplishment when goals are established will avoid problems later in the program development process.

Whatever technique or method is used to set goals, the important issue is that goal setting becomes an intentional activity on the part of program planners and is an integral part of the program-planning process. The choice of goal-setting tools and methods is not nearly as important as the process of setting goals within the program development cycle.

### Critical Questions in Goal Setting

Definition of goals requires the program planner to move from a generalized idea to a specific, needed outcome. One approach to assure that the process is conducted in a meaningful way is to ask the following critical questions as goals are established.

- *Who sets the goals?* There are many individuals who hold a stake in the higher education and student services enterprises. Inclusion of as many of these shareholder groups in the process of goal setting as is reasonable enhances the possibility of program goals becoming linked to a specified need or priority. To illustrate, if program goals are established to increase the effectiveness of the intake procedure in the counseling center and the support staff is not involved with the process of establishing that goal, problems may result. The support staff may see a program goal of this nature as an implied criticism of their effectiveness. They may be able to tell the program planners that the intake procedures are fine as they are and that the difficulty lies in the telephone system. If all appropriate constituency groups are not involved in the process of setting goals, then an inappropriate, or even worse an unnecessary, program goal may emerge. Most program planning models, including Drum and Figler (1973), Lewis and Lewis (1974), and Moore and Delworth (1976) emphasize the need to centrally involve those who will be affected by the program in the planning process. The insights of representative student client groups, staff members, and supervisors can all contribute to establishing program goals that can and should be met.

- *What conditions will be changed?* The answer to this question requires specification of outcomes. Will more students remain in school after their freshman year as a direct result of the proposed program intervention? Will more returning students seek assistance with resume writing if the program is put in place? Will more students attend concerts, lectures, and plays if more publicity is offered? Whatever the program is to be, proposed outcomes must be specifically delineated. Failure to answer this question as goals are set does not permit sound evaluation of the program endeavor.

- *What will not happen?* The answer to this question may be the most important in the development of goals for a student services program. If the proposed program will not change anything, then why is time, energy, and money being invested in the process of program development? If the changes that result are so miniscule, then why should the program even be funded? If a program means that needed services will not be offered, then we should be able to so state in an uncompromising fashion.

- *Who will be helped?* Focus on the target population is a very important step in the goal-setting process. Just as the goals of higher education tend to be diffuse, so do those of student services programs. In an era of tight resources, one program cannot be all things to all people. Thus, the definition of the target of intervention (Morrill and Hurst, 1980) is a critical step in the goal-setting process. Unless the program is designed to serve a specific population in a specific way, then the program effort may become so diffuse that it is simply not worth doing.

- *What are the program links?* Student services programs are inextricably linked to other units within the institution and to the greater society. The goals of a specific student services program must be related to other programs, activities, and agencies within and without the institution. A careful review of program goals of other units may result in a redefinition of goals of a specific program. Maybe we do not need to do something new, but perhaps we need to just support and enhance what already is available within the community. Under conditions where this question is not asked as part of the goal-setting process, duplication of effort may result and even worse programs with diametrically opposed goals may be established, producing conflict within the institution. Linking program goals to already established efforts minimizes the chances for power, territory, and authority issues arising as the program is developed.

At a minimum, these critical questions must be answered as program goals are being established. If they are not, the goal-setting process may become an exercise in futility and a program may never be effectively implemented. Goals keep the attention of program planners on outcomes and on what is to be accomplished through the program effort. Even if careful attention is given to these critical questions, however, errors can and will occur in the goal-setting process.

## Common Goal-Setting Errors

Odiorne (1965) cites five common errors in goal setting of particular value to the student services program planner: omitting key facts, failure to allow for personal bias, generalizations from bad samples, confusing cause and effect, and failure to plan for normal fluctuations (1965, pp. 122-124). In addition, special care must be given to the error of failure to assess the context when setting student services program goals. Chapter Twelve by Keating discusses many of these goal-setting errors in great detail. Therefore, in this chapter special emphasis is given to only a few goal-setting errors.

- *Omitting key facts.* Often program goals reflect what the program planner would like to be the case rather than the reality of the situation. To illustrate, a staff member in charge of campus cultural programming develops a creative publicity plan with the goal of increasing student participation in on-campus cultural events by at least 50 percent. Great time and effort is put into the program, but student participation decreases rather than increases. Perhaps a more appropriate program goal would have been to examine why students are not currently participating rather than trying to "sell" a program clearly not meeting student needs.

- *Generalizing from bad samples.* This is a frequent error in setting goals for student services programs. For example, a psychologist sees four clients in two weeks, all expressing difficulty with divorces of parents. With such limited data, a program goal of establishing therapy groups for children of divorce is established. Publicity is developed, an initial meeting time is set, and only the original four clients show up. Obviously the sample was not reflective of a general student need.

- *Confusing cause and effect.* Just because two events occur simultaneously, it is a mistake to assume that one is the cause of the other without careful attention to all the surrounding variables. Both may be the result of "some third cause which affects each of them similarly" (Odiorne, 1965, p. 123). Consider the following: The legal drinking age in the state was raised from eighteen to twenty-one. Concurrently, the campus judicial officer embarks on an expensive media program to reduce alcohol violations through the use of media and other intervention strategies. Simultaneously, a local religious center sets up an Al Anon group and eighty students show up. Alcohol violations are reduced and the Al Anon group continues to flourish. Are both of these programs successful because they were put into place or merely because the drinking age change had caused difficulty in getting liquor for underage students?

- *Failure to plan for normal fluctuations.* Program goals are often established without attention to the normal fluctuations that occur within the environment. Goals for programs must be congruent with the student calendar and the normal processes of academic life if student services programs are to be effective. Developing a goal for a series of reading and study skills programs to be offered in the residence halls is only effective if the intervention is scheduled for early in the semester, not at final examination time.

- *Failure to assess the context.* Good programs, to be successful, must be compatible with the institution. To illustrate, a program encouraging older students to return to school will only succeed when the institution is prepared to modify service delivery systems to meet the needs of older students. Encouragement without concomitant program linkages only encourages program failure.

Other errors in goal setting are bound to happen but, just because errors occur, the goal-setting process should not be abandoned. Goals provide both the target and the dream that drive the program development and implementation process.

### Getting Started

Developing program goals takes time, energy, and commitment. The following process guide can be helpful when setting goals for student services programs.

1. *Begin to dream.* Brainstorm, talk, argue, put favorite program ideas on the table, use data to pinpoint unmet student needs, listen, and reflect. Do anything with a program staff that will encourage staff members to look at program possibilities.
2. *Winnow the possibilities.* A creative programming staff will develop more program goals than can ever be implemented. At this stage, call on the experts, others in the institution, staff members who will directly be involved with program possibilities, and students. Find out what needs to be done most.
3. *State your commitment.* Write it down and do not concern yourself with specificity at this stage. Do concern yourself

with stating explicitly the program dream, the goal you will keep in mind through all subsequent planning activity.

4. *Check the dream.* Earlier chapters in this volume talked of the necessity of involving others in program planning. Take the dream to people outside. Check the validity, from their perception, of what you would ideally like to do.

5. *Get specific.* After the dream is stated and verified, it is then important to list intermediate goals and get specific with each one. What will the program actually do? Who will it serve? What will it accomplish? Remember Oetting's (1980) admonishment that program goals should not be able to be applied to three other institutional activities.

6. *Let the goal simmer.* Take some time, get a perspective, and stand back and look at the stated goal. Does it still make sense a week or a month later? If so, proceed directly to program planning. If not, go back to steps 4 and 5.

7. *Plan for evaluation.* Concretely specifying program goals requires that attention be paid to evaluation of the program. If the program goal cannot be evaluated with reasonable cost and precision, it may not be worth doing.

8. *Test the goals agreed upon.* Program goals often mean very different things to different people. Test the stated goal with one or two others not involved in the goal-setting process. Is it congruent with the agency or division mission? Does it contribute to the dream? Is it a goal that can and should be accomplished?

Good goal setting results in good programs. Student services programmers have myriad skills in putting a program together, in using methods and techniques to plan activities. We are not as skilled in taking time at the beginning of the program-planning process to put our goals to a rigorous test. Taking time will result in more effective programs that meet student and institutional needs.

### References

Baldridge, J. V., and Tierney, M. L. *New Approaches to Management: Creating Practical Systems of Management Information and Management by Objectives.* San Francisco: Jossey-Bass, 1979.

Barr, M. J., and Hurst, J. C. "Futuristics: A Tool for Staff Development." In F. R. Brodzinski (Ed.), *New Directions for Student Services, Utilizing Futures Research,* no. 6. San Francisco: Jossey-Bass, 1979.

Bloom, B. S. (Ed.). *Taxonomy of Educational Objectives. Handbook 1: Cognitive Domain.* New York: McKay, 1956.

Deegan, A. X., and Fritz, R. J. *Management by Objectives (MBO) Goes to College.* Boulder: Division of Continuing Education, University of Colorado, 1975.

Drum, D. J., and Figler, H. E. *Outreach in Counseling.* New York: Intext Educational Publishers, 1973.

Hanson, G. R. "Instruction." In U. Delworth, G. R. Hanson, and Associates, *Student Services: A Handbook for the Profession.* San Francisco: Jossey-Bass, 1980.

Johnson, C. S., and Foxley, C. H. "Devising Tools for Middle Managers." In U. Delworth, G. R. Hanson, and Associates, *Student Services: A Handbook for the Profession.* San Francisco: Jossey-Bass, 1980.

Lenning, O. T. *The Outcome Structure: An Overview and Procedures for Applying It in Postsecondary Education Institutions.* Boulder, Colo.: National Center for Higher Education Management Systems, 1977.

Lenning, O. T. "Assessment and Evaluation." In U. Delworth, G. R. Hanson, and Associates, *Student Services: A Handbook for the Profession.* San Francisco: Jossey-Bass, 1980.

Levinson, H. "Management by Whose Objectives?" *Harvard Business Review,* 1970, *48,* 125-128.

Lewis, M. D., and Lewis, J. A. "A Schematic for Change." *Personnel and Guidance Journal,* 1974, *52* (5), 320-323.

Moore, M., and Delworth, U. *Training Manual for Student Service Program Development.* Boulder, Colo.: Western Interstate Commission on Higher Education, 1976.

Morrill, W. H., and Hurst, J. C. (Eds.). *Dimensions of Intervention for Student Development.* New York: Wiley, 1980.

Odiorne, G. S. *Management by Objectives.* New York: Pitman Publishing, 1965.

Oetting, E. R. "A Guide to Program Evaluation." In W. H. Morrill and J. C. Hurst (Eds.), *Dimensions of Intervention for Student Development.* New York: Wiley, 1980.

Partansontichai, V. C. "Management by Objectives." Unpublished thesis, University of Texas at Austin, 1975.

Plourde, P. J. "Institutional Use of Models: Hope or Continued Frustration?" In T. R. Mason (Ed.), *New Directions for Institutional Research: Assessing Computer-Based System Models,* no. 9. San Francisco: Jossey-Bass, 1976.

Wikstrom, W. S. "Management by Objectives or Appraisal by Result." *The Conference Board Record,* 1966, July (3), 27-31.

# Part Three

❧ ❧ ❧ ❧ ❧ ❧ ❧ ❧ ❧ ❧ ❧ ❧ ❧

# Planning and Implementing Quality Programs

Many student services professionals define a program plan as a description of implementation methods. This definition addresses the question of format (workshop versus lecture, individual versus group counseling, and so on). Another definition of program plan centers on administrative detail: What staff will be involved and how will they be scheduled? What is the cost of the program? What materials will be required? Though these definitions are useful starting points, a view of the plan as a listing of procedures does not account for the interactive nature of the programming process. Program plans reflect a series of ongoing and interrelated decisions about the program goal, the institutional setting, and the methods and resources needed to implement the program. It is the orderly arrangement of the outcomes of these decisions that constitutes a program plan. As new decisions are made, the plan changes; thus, program plans

177

are not static, fixed outlines. If they were, Part Three of this book would be little more than an extended procedures manual. In our view, student services program planning requires that the institutional context be assessed and the program goal clearly articulated before development of the final program plan. The context and the goal were discussed in Part One and Part Two of this book. Part Three focuses on the issues critical to program implementation: development of a program model and judicious use of resources.

In recent years, several models have been proposed to guide professionals charged with development of student services programs. Marvalene Styles begins Chapter Eight with a review of those models and their relevance to the program development process. She then addresses the question that plagues every conscientious programmer—how can I translate "models" and "theory" to practice—and suggests an integrative approach to program planning.

The form and nature of our programs are, in large part, determined by the quality and commitment of student services staff. In Chapter Nine, John Baier discusses issues surrounding hiring, training, challenging, and retaining competent staff. After classifying the staff competencies needed to establish successful student services programs, Baier begins with a straightforward discussion of institutional obstacles to establishment of staff development programs. Though staff development programs are often conceived as formal workshops or seminars, this chapter challenges us to view all aspects of our staffing responsibilities (hiring, evaluation, and supervision) as avenues for intentional staff development.

Retaining and challenging quality staff who must work on routine tasks associated with maintaining ongoing programs is a continuing problem. As a profession, we are intrigued by new programs and our literature and convention programs reflect this fascination. However, a large majority of our programming work is directed to program maintenance. In Chapter Ten, Sharon Justice and John Ragle discuss specific techniques for adapting program plans to reflect changes in student, staff, or institutional expectations. They believe that unless we persistently evaluate and market ongoing programs, even the best program will fail.

Effective maintenance assures that most quality programs will continue to receive institutional support. However, changes in staff or in the political or fiscal climate may mean that some student services programs must be drastically altered or eliminated entirely. Arthur Sandeen tackles the difficult questions of program redesign or termination in Chapter Eleven on effective utilization of resources. He first identifies early warning signs that a program is in trouble, and then he recommends basic techniques for repairing faltering programs. Program modification and repair require creative management of staff, dollars, and space. Sandeen's chapter, written from his perspective as a chief student affairs officer, provides practical examples of how these resources can best be utilized to modify troubled programs. When modification doesn't work and a program is terminated, student services administrators must deal with a variety of negative consequences. In the last section of this chapter, Sandeen provides guidelines for responding to staff and political pressures in a humane and ethical fashion.

In some instances, it is a positive step to terminate a student service program. It may have outlived its usefulness or solved a problem. Often, however, worthwhile student services programs fail because of errors in planning or implementation. In Chapter Twelve, Lou Keating identifies common errors that occur at each stage of the planning process and discusses the interrelationship of errors in goal setting, assessing institutional context, and finally in developing a program plan. The chapter focuses on methods of avoiding error in program planning and diagnosing error in existing programs.

The plan is the heart of the student services programming process. It brings all elements of a student services program together to form a practical blueprint for action. If our student services programs are to succeed, it is critical to understand the elements of plan, to know how to recognize and prevent errors, and to learn practical methods for modifying or terminating our programs.

# 8

Marvalene H. Styles

❧ ❧ ❧ ❧ ❧ ❧ ❧ ❧ ❧ ❧ ❧ ❧ ❧

# Effective Models of Systematic Program Planning

Most student affairs professionals spend a significant portion of their working day planning, implementing, and evaluating student services programs. Thus it is surprising that these important tasks receive comparatively little attention in our professional literature and conversations. One reason for this tendency may be that the well-run program is deceptive: It looks so easy. The experienced student services administrator knows that establishing quality student services programs is a complex and difficult task. Successful programming requires that the practitioner (a) understands the historical place of student affairs in higher education (see Chapter One by Knock; Fenske, 1980), (b) possesses a wide variety of skills and competencies, (c) has a comprehensive view of the goals and mission of higher education, and (d) believes that the university should facilitate what Brown (1980) suggests as goals of education: intellectual, emotional, moral, and physical development. The successful programmer also understands the context of higher education—that while "the espoused theory of academicians is apolitical, the applied theory is political" (Styles and Fiedler, 1981, p. 83). Experienced practitioners always account for the university's political influences when planning new programs. These influences include complex, multiple power clusters, such as governing boards, the formal administrative structure, faculty and faculty governance groups, student government groups, staff groups, and community power groups.

The first assumption made in this chapter on program development is that managers of student services areas comprehend the multiplicity and complexity of higher education institutions and apply this knowledge to their particular campus. A second assumption is that managers and planners of student services share a common professional foundation that serves as an anchor to program planning. Third, it is assumed that student services professionals accept as a part of their mission the promotion of student development in the education of college students. Fourth, there is an assumption that student services professionals will master the skills to comprehend the politics of higher education. Finally, and perhaps most important, must be the student affairs professional's willingness and competence to perform in a role that is often viewed as marginal and peripheral to the academic mainstream.

## Program Development Models

Student services professionals are guided by a variety of program planning models.

The models presented in this section are not independent, either in the history of their development or in their present application in the profession. Basic commonalities surface in all models. Each model is presented for the same purpose: to encourage purposeful planning of programs that will provide the best educational opportunity to a college population. These programs must augment the regular academic classroom process, thereby expanding and balancing the mission of education.

Current models for program development reflect earlier

foci on foundations in student personnel. Contemporary models embrace the science of human development in addition to foundations. Collectively, the models reviewed direct the program planner's attention to needs assessment, goal setting, planning teams, staff development, evaluation and accountability, modes of implementation, resource management, and environmental assessment.

Much more attention is needed, however, in areas that relate to application of contemporary theories; contextual considerations such as historical, political, and fiscal contexts; theory to practice; marketing strategies; forecasting and trend analysis; demographic considerations; resource management; and time framing. None of the models addresses the role of student affairs professionals in the emerging science of futurism.

Some of the most frequently cited models focus on specific program areas within the profession of student services. Examples of models presented here that target specific areas or themes include: Kaiser (1972), Drum and Figler's (1973) focus on outreach programming for counseling, Lewis and Lewis's (1974) emphasis on environmental change strategies, and the ecosystem model discussed by Aulepp and Delworth (1976), which suggests mapping strategies to promote a fit between the student and the campus. Other more generic models emphasize the application of remedial, preventive, and developmental principles in the planning of students' life experiences in higher education. Representative samples, chosen for their generic foci, are Morrill, Oetting, and Hurst's (1974) cube, Moore and Delworth's (1976) training model, and Miller and Prince's (1976) model.

Regardless of the selected model, there are standard variables that guide all program planners in the preliminary stages. Chickering (1981) suggests that each institution consider the following variables to ensure that student services programs address students' development:

1. a statement of clear objectives and a focus on internal consistency
2. consideration of the size of the institution

3. understanding of the curriculum, or teaching and evaluation
4. awareness of residential hall arrangements
5. consideration of clusters of friends, groups, and student cultures

It is likely that program developers will find components in numerous program models that will facilitate their efforts at a given time. Each institution can best identify models or components of models to effectively serve the purposes on its campus.

*Lewis and Lewis's Schematic for Change.* Prerequisite to building programs in student development is an examination of values and talents that are operationalized within a campus setting. Lewis and Lewis (1974) suggest that student development professionals are change agents within the university. Change agents must thoroughly understand the university environment, including the values and talents within that environment. Change agents must also be active self-examiners who are willing to employ six stages in program planning.

The planner, in stage 1, identifies the institution's values and the values of significant constituencies within the institution. Planners may discern the magnitude of the undertaking.

Stage 2 is the identification of congruent and incongruent behaviors that impact on identified values. In this stage, one examines the true test of institutional commitment—resource allocations that include budget, personnel allocation, space, location, and written and unwritten procedures and policies.

In stage 3, the planner analyzes the system microscopically. A detailed analysis of causal factors that contribute to the existing situation permits the change agent to identify barriers as well as enabling forces within the university. Barriers may include both the hostile and neutral forces that contribute to institutional inertia. In identifying enablers, care must be taken to ferret out the talkers and the doers and to strategize in a manner to include both in the planning.

It is not uncommon that student affairs professionals neglect the inclusion of the extrasystemic support system. Stage 4 invites the professional to be purposeful about inclusion of potentially potent groups that are external to the university, such as alumni and other community organizations. Having completed stages 1 through 4, the planner prepares a step-by-step strategy (stage 5) that guarantees that all players execute designated roles and operate with knowledge of a shared master plan. Finally, in stage 6, the planner oversees the continual assessment of effectiveness and ensures that appropriate introduction of new interventions will occur.

These six stages highlight the necessity for stated values and behaviors to be congruent so that a healthy climate exists among all campus constituencies. The change agent, therefore, needs organizational and fiscal support to act on the institution's goals and values.

One responsibility of the change agent may become that of selling the values of student development programming. Where this becomes necessary, a process similar to a force-field analysis is an enabling tool for the identification of support groups or a "nucleus of kindred souls" (Lewis and Lewis, 1974, p. 321). The role of change agents is a rather serious and often tedious role for student development professionals. Nevertheless, it has become increasingly apparent during this era of budgetary retrenchment that change agent strategies are vital skills for the professional in promoting student services on campus.

Lewis and Lewis's change strategies invite student services professionals to organize purposeful environments. The environment is viewed as the client, and planned change becomes the goal. Appropriate change strategies involve an identification of systems values, an awareness of talents, and an awareness of context. Utilizing these procedures, clarification can be achieved for all members of the university on the scope of permissible change, the knowledge of goals and behaviors, the reaction of constituencies to new stimuli, the possibility of alternative strategies, the institution's mores, and the identification of authority and power.

The Lewis and Lewis model is valuable largely for its emphasis on becoming a change agent in the organizational bureaucracy of higher education.

*Ecosystem Model of the Western Interstate Commission for Higher Education (WICHE).* The ecosystem model is a design application of an ecological view of institutions of higher education. This view focuses on the environment as a major determinant of student behavior. The model studies the relationship between people on campus and those features of the environment that affect various students and student groups. The assumption is that once those features or "environmental referents" are identified, then they can be influenced. The influencing process is termed "environmental design" or "redesign." Put in more mundane terms, we should fit the place to the person rather than helping the person "adjust" to the place.

Similar to the Lewis and Lewis model, the model by Aulepp and Delworth (1976) underscores the necessity to select institutional values (step 1) and to translate those values into goals (step 2). The next step is to design environments to match the goals (step 3), followed by the creation of an environmental fit for students (step 4). A measurement of students' perceptions (step 5) is valued over the usual quantitative assessment of needs. Students' behavior must then be monitored (step 6) in order to determine the nature of the fit between the environment and the student. This monitoring is, of necessity, both quantitative and qualitative in nature, so that data can be fed back into the design (step 7). Steps 1 through 7 are interactive and interdependent.

Ecomapping can occur at three levels: Level 1 or macrodesign involves designing environments for an entire campus community. In level 2 or microdesign, the planner identifies a target population and studies environmental effects on that population. Level 3 or life space design seeks to understand the individual student's relationship to the campus environment. The goal of all ecosystems design is to build a living and learning environment that maximizes opportunities for students to develop.

Environmental assessment takes into consideration those established variables that influence students' college experiences (either positively or negatively). An example of the environmental structure as it relates to students' adjustment would include a review of the cluster groups such as sororities, clubs, and fraternities in relation to their accessibility for ethnic minorities. Where elitist groups are condoned, either overtly or covertly, the nonmainstreamed student, who typically is an ethnic minority, a woman, a disabled person, or an older student, receives messages that relegate his or her status to a secondary position. The designer has several options on identifying this aspect of the environment, such as lobbying for a policy review or developing programs for clubs on the subject of sexism or racism. The goal of any of these program interventions would be to alter the environment to create a better student-environment fit.

*Drum and Figler's Outreach Model.* Although Drum and Figler's (1973) outreach model is directed to counselors in student services, the model has broader applications in student services programming. Outreach programs have increasingly received endorsement as a viable tool of student services delivery. Perhaps the initial selection of counseling was appropriate because the clinical one-to-one mode of service delivery in this area planted doubts about the fiscal viability of counseling in higher education. Thus, outreach programming, a multimodal developmental model, is presented to counselors and counselor educators as a tool for increasing the scope of services and the user population. It was also a significantly new and meaningful modality to delivery programs to students and other campus constituencies.

Outreach does not mean a mere expansion of the same services to the same populations. Outreach can make sufficient impact upon a student population only if it involves all potential helpers, advocates environmental change, offers many options for self-development, and initiates contacts with students.

Seven dimensions of the outreach model are proposed to direct actions of the program planner: (1) problem awareness, (2) intervention targets, (3) setting, (4) directness of service, (5) number of helpers, (6) counseling method, and (7) duration of counseling.

Problem awareness may occur in relation to manifest behaviors of students. For example, student affairs professionals may identify a need for a problem intervention through documented observations of epidemic eating disorders or suicidal ideations. Other programs may be directed to students who are flooding the placement offices anxiously seeking jobs.

In assessing intervention targets, the planner determines the appropriateness of working with individuals, formal groups, informal groups, or the institution. Within the institution, the setting that seems most conducive to the program may include an office, a residence hall, an activities building, a classroom, or the natural environment. Directness of service, as applied by Drum and Figler, will indicate whether the planner applies a personal helping interview to the target population or uses other modalities, such as groups, self-help, or community resources.

It is undoubtedly valuable to identify the various helpers available for outreach services. Student affairs professionals, through this identification, are encouraged to examine and train other groups for service delivery, such as paraprofessionals, teachers, lay people, or "naturalistic counselors" (Drum and Figler, 1973, p. 21). The method of delivery, which ranges from individual services to computerized and educational roles, and the duration of the delivery are vital questions to pose prior to the action.

The Drum and Figler model highlights the need to address environmental concerns and suggests that our helping community extends beyond trained student affairs professionals. Further, it demystifies the role of professional helpers by prescribing self-help programs. This model also provides for an evaluation of student consumers and of all persons providing services for them, and it describes ways in which research may be used to provide planning data. Such data may identify positive and negative valences of each program and each strategy employed. The outreach modality employs dimensions of service delivery that are concurrently remedial, developmental, and preventive. An important contribution of outreaching is the possibility of mainstreaming student services in the academic community, thereby educating the community and expanding the programs.

*Miller and Prince's Future of Student Affairs.* Miller and Prince (1976) identify three domains of student development: cognitive, affective, and psychomotor. In this design, interventions, programs, or functions grow out of theories of development. For each intervention, program, or function, goals are set, assessment occurs, and change strategies are designed.

In setting goals, the target population is identified as either individuals, groups, or the organization. Developmental modalities may include instruction, consultation, or milieu management. Student development professionals design instructional activities that are appropriate and productive for students' growth in other (nonclassroom) environments, such as residential centers, counseling centers, career development centers, placement centers, cultural/activities centers, student government centers, and student organizations.

Evaluation is a key component in the model. Assessment, according to Miller and Prince, is a broad function to help students understand their growth and direct student affairs professionals to build programs that promote students' development. A unique feature of the Miller and Prince model is the intentional focus on empowering students to understand their behaviors, to integrate feedback, and to assess their progress. The consultant's role is especially valuable because the student affairs professional is often viewed as an outsider in the educational hierarchy. Student affairs consultants are enabling agents to campus groups in helping them to set goals, develop leadership and power, and make decisions (p. 106).

Miller and Prince call attention to the application of organizational development in student affairs. Accordingly, organizational development theory and practice form a body of tested information in which student affairs professionals must acquire skills. The skills will direct consultation actions that focus on strategies to sell the goals of student development to the campus community. Application of organizational development strategies is particularly difficult for student affairs professionals because it serves to test the true understanding of student development theory and its application on a particular campus.

The Miller and Prince model frames a perception of the future of student affairs by identifying three domains of student development: suggesting intervention competencies, recognizing target populations, and designing stages for students to assess their progress. There is assurance that evaluation plays an integral role throughout the program.

*Morrill, Oetting, and Hurst's Cube.* In designing the cube, Morrill, Oetting, and Hurst (1974) addressed the timely question of the effectiveness and efficiency of a one-to-one modality of service delivery in counseling. Like the Drum and Figler model, counselors were the target population. Nevertheless, one readily discerns the applicability of the model to other student services programs.

The cube describes three dimensions of counselor (and other planners') functioning: (1) the target of intervention, (2) the purpose of intervention, and (3) the method of intervention. (For a more detailed analysis of the cube, see Chapter Five.)

The cube's first dimension includes a focus on the individual as target, recognizing that often the alteration of one's "knowledge, attitudes, perceptions, responses, etc." (p. 356) is best accomplished through a one-to-one contact. The model augments this one-to-one pattern by suggesting that the primary group, associational group, and the institution or community may become targets for program planners. The primary group is one that has the most influence on the individual, such as the family unit or close friends. The associational group is either chosen by the individual or it becomes a chance affiliation. Classes, clubs, fraternities, and sororities are examples of associational affiliation. In one's institutional or community affiliation, members are aware that they are a part of the community, but they will not necessarily meet or have any personal contact.

The second dimension of the cube defines the purpose of the intervention, which may be remediation, prevention, or development. Remediation suggests that corrective measures must replace some dysfunctional aspect of students' programs; prevention relates to the strengthening of present and future skills to counter potential problems; development turns attention toward "enhancing the functioning and developmental potential of healthy individuals and groups" (p. 357).

The method of intervention may include direct service, consultation and training, and media. Direct service delivery has been the predominant method of intervention, and there are times when it is the appropriate mode of delivery. Exclusive reliance on direct service delivery poses disadvantages, namely: "(a) the cost, both in money and in scarce professional time; (b) the limitation of being unable to deal with large numbers of clients; and (c) the resultant inability to reach some groups of clients or provide some kinds of programs" (p. 358).

Because of the stated limitations above, a second alternative of consultation and training is proposed. Morrill, Oetting, and Hurst (1974) view this alternative as a critical mode for expanding the work force. The student affairs professional trains other people such as the paraprofessional, who will work with client populations, thus reaching the target population through others. The final method of intervention is a broader utilization of media. Computer-assisted programs, radio, newspapers, and television are examples of diversified applications of media. It is important to capitalize on this diversity to maximize opportunities to influence both individuals and groups.

*Moore and Delworth's Training Model for Student Services Programs.* Moore and Delworth (1976) provide a systematically outlined procedure that potentially ensures sound planning. The five-stage model directs the planner from the stage of program initiation (stage 1), through the development of a training program (stage 2), the implementation and evaluation of the pilot test (stage 3), the review of each program component based on experiences gained in pilot testing (stage 4), and a combined procedure of program maintenance and observations of directional spin-offs (stage 5). The program-planning stages are carried out by a planning team composed of individuals representing various constituencies and possessing needed skills and knowledge.

Germinal ideas are probably born in the minds of professionals several times each day. When an individual has an idea for a course of action, it becomes the responsibility of the planning team to assist with the exploration of the idea. If appropriate resources are available to the planning team, planning then advances to the stage of assessing the extent of the need among consumers. Adequate assessment techniques will minimally include a search of the literature, a review of campus records, demographic data and documents, informal unobstructive data such as attendance patterns at various events, a search for related campus programs, and a sample survey of potential consumers, including empirical data and perceptions.

The training program prescribed by Moore and Delworth

(1976) is explicitly designed to set behavioral goals. It asks what behaviors students or consumers will display when the goals are achieved and what specific behavior changes would occur if a narrowly defined goal were set. The training program that complies with the behavioral objectives of the planner is an investment in an effective and efficient operation. It is, therefore, advisable to give careful consideration to the quality of the chosen trainers. An astute trainer will introduce modes of operation that are both welcomed by the trainees and responsive to the organization's needs. The training program, like all other components in the model, will have a carefully designed evaluation procedure and a preparation for pilot testing.

Implementation of the training program's pilot test follows the completion of the training program. In this stage, program publicity is designed to inform and recruit consumers. Prior to selecting participants, preparation of a rigorous evaluation and perhaps a research design, enables the planner to establish how participants will become involved in the program. For example, one may decide that experimental and control groups are desirable for a particular program. Finally, program maintenance options are explored with an awareness that planners will carefully monitor data collection and readdress appropriate issues as they arise. The planning team observes new ideas as they emerge and ensures that a systematic process is followed before acting on new ideas.

## Developmental Theories

Developmental theories are especially useful to student affairs professionals because they describe particular patterns of growth for a diversified student population. Generally, these patterns are described in life-cycle stages that focus on age-linked developmental tasks, role-related life structures such as work and relationships, and life transitions that signal changes and discontinuities (Weathersby and Tarule, 1980).

Levinson (1978) sees life structures as patterned choices made by an individual in relation to significant life roles (for example, education, occupation, and family). Adults build and alter life structures; in so doing they exercise the right to choose. A life transition engages the individual in "a thoughtful confrontation with the reality of one's own choices and experiences; necessitates a change in viewpoint, a change . . . [seen] as transformative" (Weathersby and Tarule, 1980, p. 18).

A comprehensive summary of developmental theory is provided by Widick, Knefelkamp, and Parker (1980) who organize theorists into four categories: (1) psychosocial realms, (2) cognitive developmental theories, (3) maturity models, and (4) typology models. There is, however, one inherent danger in dividing developmental theorists into distinct types. Such categorization reinforces the belief that isolated parts of the individual can be developed without consideration of the whole. Holistic developmental program planners embrace all theories that facilitate the movement of students toward and through tasks that kindle human growth.

Erikson's (1959) earlier works recognize the lifelong stages of human development. A major value of his studies in planning students' programs rests with Erikson's notion of the predictability of the life cycles. For the traditional college student who is embarking on an identity formation or separation from home, student development theorists may predict and prescribe programs that promote movement through these stages. Likewise, as college populations shift, programs may be planned to address those tasks that correlate with their life stage.

Kenneth Keniston (1968) ferreted out one of Erikson's particular stages of development, the adolescent stage, and substituted the term *youth* to more appropriately demonstrate the absence of definitive boundaries during this period of one's life. His illumination on this stage is especially important to the student services professional because typically this is the college-age population. He would suggest that since this group is "neither psychological adolescents nor sociological adults" (Widick, Knefelkamp, and Parker, 1980, p. 82), special attention must be devoted to the struggle to balance societal (college) boundaries with the self.

In introducing the term *ego-identity status,* James Marcia's (1966) work became yet another amplification of Erikson's life stages. Critical to his theory are two factors: (1) "the experiencing of crises, a time of uncertainty and active search, and (2) the making of commitment, particularly in the occupational and value (ideology) spheres" (Widick, Knefelkamp, and Parker, 1980, p. 84). Included in Marcia's identity statuses are:

1. *the achieved-identity student:* has matured through the mastery of a crisis and confirmed commitments in both values constructs and vocational goals; essentially anchored in realism
2. *the moratorium student:* struggling with crisis situations and engaged in an identity search
3. *the diffused-identity student:* ambivalent, without purpose, and without roots
4. *the foreclosed individual:* has achieved identity from others, perhaps parents, without experimentation; externally oriented.

Arthur Chickering's (1969) vectors of development received widespread attention in *Education and Identity.* His seven vectors—developing competence, managing emotions, developing autonomy, establishing identity, freeing interpersonal relationships, clarifying purpose, and developing integrity—suggest a hierarchical pattern in college students' development. The central vector toward which all other vectors magnetically gravitate is the establishment of identity.

Developmental theorists also underscore the need to understand intellectual development, or the way in which people perceive, think, and reason. In any discussion of cognitive development, Piaget (1964) is a common reference point. He postulated two sequential stages of development. The readiness stage is one in which preparation for forward movement is examined. During the second phase of attainment, the individual puts into action the capacity to reason and think.

Although Widick, Knefelkamp, and Parker (1980) acknowledge contributions of numerous other cognitive development theorists, they chose the works of Perry (1970) and Kohlberg (1969) as exemplary. Perry's scheme encompasses both intellectual and ethical development as demonstrated in four categories: dualism, multiplicity, relativism, and commitment in relativism. In the dualistic phase, one views the world in absolutes, that is, right/wrong, good/bad, either/or terms. A more pluralistic notion is acquired in the phase of multiplicity where judgment is reserved. An even more advanced level is that of relativism where the world is viewed in relative terms and the cognitive thinking patterns are more advanced and complex. Finally, Perry's stage of commitment in relativism describes a responsible person who views the world pluralistically and who is able to become committed. Unless an individual chooses one of Perry's delay tactics—such as temporizing, retreating, or escaping —passage through those four phases would be normally expected.

Kohlberg (1969) has added another dimension to Piaget's work by studying moral reasoning. In many ways, his work parallels that of Perry. For example, in the preconventional level, the individual's acceptance of cultural rules or rules of authority, that is, parents, denotes the absence of independent moral reasoning. In this stage, one responds to the pleasure-pain principles. At the conventional level, the individual is extremely loyal and committed to conformity to a referent group, that is, family, fraternity. On the other hand, the postconventional person is capable of abstract and independent thoughts, is considerate of consequences for action, and is committed to defining moral values independent of a referent group.

Douglas Heath's (1977) theory of maturity provides a more comprehensive representation of how a theory may encompass all aspects of human development. After reviewing Heath's principles and applications of the theory, Widick, Knelfelkamp, and Parker (1980) concluded that it falls short of accomplishing the tasks of educating the total person. The model provides a matrix that summarizes the behavioral qualities of a mature person in four categories: intellect, values, self-concept, and interpersonal relationships. Each of the four categories has a behavioral outcome quality that corresponds to five dimensions: (1) capacity to symbolize experience, (2) capacity to become allocentric (other-centered), (3) capacity to become progressively integrated, (4) capacity to stabilize and resist disruption, and (5) capacity to gain autonomy. While it is useful to examine these outcomes, a program planner is struck with the reality that intuition and influences are the tools to employ in the application of Heath's theory. Theory-to-practice methodologies are once more overlooked.

A theory such as that of Patricia Cross (1971) that directs attention to sociological differences has become increasingly valuable as education becomes more pluralistic in its student population. Multiethnic, multilingual, multicultural, multiage, multiphysical and mental abilities and disabilities, multieconomic, and many other heterogeneous labels can be ascribed to today's students. Cross uses the generic term *new student* to describe the members of the changing population whom she believes have difficulty with mainstreaming because their values are atypical of the achievement orientation patterns in higher education. The definition of new student must undergo constant reexamination, for even in Cross's scheme, there is no recognition of the new student who is usually female, often of the mid-life, reentry age, and from a socioeconomic and achievement background that may exceed the college mainstream. Likewise, there are new ethnic minority influxes that defy traditional achievement expectations of minorities. Universities' refusal to customize programs to these new populations has resulted in a new wave of alternative education, both in business and industry as well as in a wellspring of nontraditional educational institutions. It has also resulted in unstable enrollment patterns for traditional universities.

An example of a theory that reflects psychological differences is found in the works of Roy Heath (1964). Heath's emphasis on individual differences and sequential stages of development is not unlike other models. His unique contributions, however, lie in the recognition of the struggle between the inner self and the outer (rational) self. The fully mature person is described by Heath as the "reasonable adventurer" who possesses: (1) intellectuality, (2) close friendships, (3) independence in value judgment, (4) tolerance of ambiguity, (5) breadth of interest, and (6) sense of humor.

In their recommendation to practitioners on applications of theory, Widick, Knefelkamp, and Parker (1980) present two theory types. Informal theories allow us to "make implicit connections among the events and persons in our environments and to act upon them everyday" (p. 111). Formal theories "act as counterforces to our highly personal world" (p. 111). Formal theories presented in this chapter, as well as others, serve as guidelines to program planners.

Student affairs practitioners must be mindful of limitations posed by the research practices in human development theory. Neugarten (1963) and Gilligan (1977) highlight major differences in developmental patterns of females. Perhaps age-linked norms and development are better understood when couched in the context of male Anglo identity. Some recognition of sex differences is emerging. Cultural, socioeconomic, and ethnic norms are less understood.

## Future of Program Development

It is my belief that the chief function of student services is to plan programs that facilitate psychological maturity. Before achieving this goal, student services professionals must become comfortably anchored in theory and research that link programs with the developmental needs of the campus population. Student development principles are integral to the process of education. When institutions fail to support equally all aspects of education as outlined by Brown (1980), outcome measures of students' education have been affected. Sprinthall, Bertin, and Whitley (1982) reviewed research findings to determine the influences of undergraduate education. Examination of replicated studies indicate that "traditional measures of academic achievement in college including grade point average are not associated with accomplishment in adulthood" (p. 42). What was discovered, however, is consistent with the belief that maturity is the outcome of education. "Psychological maturity has been found to have a significant relationship to postcollege accomplishment. Promoting psychological maturity as a component of the college experience is a very feasible alternative for colleges and universities as a contribution to the accomplishment in adulthood for their graduates" (p. 42).

Student affairs practitioners must continually question the persistence of leaders in educational institutions who maintain the narrowly focused perspective that the classroom experience is practically the sum total of education. Job satisfaction and some postcollege life satisfactions variables have been found by D. H. Heath (1976, 1977) to be closely correlated to psychological maturity. Sprinthall, Bertin, and Whitley (1982) note that developmental education as a model and psychological maturity as an educational outcome are reasonable goals for student services professionals of the future.

Futurists Toffler (1980), Ferguson (1980), Naisbitt (1982), and Capra (1982) suggest that we are currently in the midst of a major transformation in society. Yet our actions as student services professionals have reflected a basic apathy toward futurism. We are experiencing the rise of a new culture and a decline of the old that will produce new concepts, new ideas, new values, and new social and institutional organizations (Capra, 1982). According to Marilyn Ferguson, the transformation will be led by people whose "lives had become revolutions... they found themselves rethinking everything, examining old assumptions, looking anew at their work and relationships, health, political power and 'experts,' goals and values" (1980, p. 24).

A new role emerges for student affairs professionals in the examination of futurism. We have the option of becoming futurists and true leading-edge leaders, or we can become observers of the transformation. I suggest the former is our responsibility. It is time for us to claim our expertise and enter into the mainstream of a rapidly transforming society. Our program planning models must reflect this awareness.

*Expanding the Goals of Education.* Goals of education must be clearly delineated and endorsed before program planning can be pursued (see Chapter Seven). We need clearer descriptions about our evolutions that would also point to definitive prescriptions for our future.

Brown (1980) offers five prescriptive goals of education:

intellectual, emotional, moral, physical, and social development. Brown's prescriptives could be significantly enhanced if they were expanded to include spiritual development and cultural development as goals of education. As applied in this context, spiritual development is not construed as religious practices. Spirituality addresses the essence of human existence, or the energy and vigor that connect humankind with the universe. College students flounder excessively in their spiritual development partly because student development educators limit their interpretative spheres to religious practices or covertly deny the importance of spirituality.

As an explicit goal, cultural development would highlight the diversity of humanity and transcend the current dominant focus of education on Anglo-Saxon, masculine, Western patterns. Multicultural, multiethnic, and multilingual values can be mainstreamed in our culture by deliberately building program strategies that render this society more conversant in other languages and cultural appreciations. This focus transcends the monolithic fortress of Western left-brain (rational) dominance and introduces diversity.

I believe that the ultimate goal for education is human maturity, which serves as the apex for student development programming. Human maturity is a lifelong process that signifies a hierarchical direction. Regression may occur but forward movement is always directed toward maturity. Maturity, as an absolute state, can never be fully achieved; one is always in the process of advancing toward a higher level of maturity. During one's life span, some individuals achieve maturity at a higher state than others. Humans are, therefore, always challenged with the constant process of becoming and growing. Education, too, is a lifelong learning process. We are never stagnant in our developing capacities. We become increasingly focused and self-directed as we advance up the maturity scale.

One major transitional point, noted for its discontinuity, is the mid-life transition that gives the illusion of becoming increasingly focused while introducing a set of challenging variables. The consistency of this mid-life pattern underscores an often disruptive cycle of human development during this age-linked period. Student development educators will prepare for their mid-life transitions and organize students' programs in a manner that prepares them for this growth stage. The mid-life transition stage serves as one example of the importance for student affairs practitioners to fully understand theory and become cognizant of the application of theory to practice.

*Application of Theory to Practice.* How does the program planner take the leap from a knowledge of theory to its application? Theory is valuable to the extent that it provides guidance both *descriptively* and *prescriptively*. One of the problems in anchoring student services in theory is that human behavior theories have been largely descriptive, that is, they describe various patterns or stages of development without prescribing interventions that facilitate development. The practitioner is left with an inferential responsibility in making prescriptive program plans. The practitioner must ask some of the following questions in order to apply developmental theory.

1.  According to developmental stages established by Erikson, Keniston, Marcia, and Chickering, what programs must I introduce to enhance students' cognitive development?
2.  Since cognitive theories add another dimension to human development, what kinds of prescriptive ideas should I introduce from Piaget, Perry, Kohlberg, and others?
    a.  How can I introduce Piaget's paradigm of perceiving, thinking, and reasoning?
    b.  If, according to Perry's theory, I recognize that a group of students is operating dualistically, what can be organized to advance them to multiplicity, relativism, and commitment? How can growth be facilitated for an individual student who is at the dualistic stage in life?
3.  At a time when sociological variables such as age, gender, ethnic identity, and sexual orientation pose special challenges to student services professionals, how can we incorporate Cross's theory and Levinson's life structure choices in program planning?

In translating theory to practice, the student development educator is aware that values are transmitted through techniques and methods. Overriding values that are rooted in our philosophical principles and foundations are found in the concept of person-centered teaching (Rogers, 1983). Carl Rogers reiterates the importance of building an interpersonal climate that fosters trust, empathy, and deep respect for the student and the facilitator. Using a person-centered approach, student development educators are concerned that (1) students enjoy shared power, (2) staff are excited with the facilitative interactions with students, (3) a creative climate will flourish, and (4) empathic understanding of the learning experience is practiced. The person-centered student development educator enjoys the exciting challenge of introducing process-oriented, empathic values in university communities that traditionally adopted linear learning styles.

Rogers (1983, p. 121) invites us to become "facilitators of learning." The facilitator understands that learning does not necessarily occur as a result of teaching skills, knowledge, lectures, and resources, but "the facilitation of significant learning rests upon certain attitudinal qualities that exist in the personal relationship between the facilitator and the learner" (p. 121). Students are in need of personal relationships that sometimes may be available mainly through the efforts of student development planners. Our techniques will be effective to the extent that we model person-centered values.

*Model for Future Program Development.* Figure 1 illustrates the significant interactive functions in planning student development programs. Each connecting arrow demonstrates a two-way interaction that connotes the necessity of both descriptive and prescriptive input. Developmental theories and goals of education are at the base of an open-ended pyramid, signifying that these elements are pervasive throughout a life span. Both human development and education are lifelong processes. Program development models serve as interventions that impact on education and human development.

The ultimate goal in life is psychological maturity, which

**Figure 2. Psychological Maturity.**

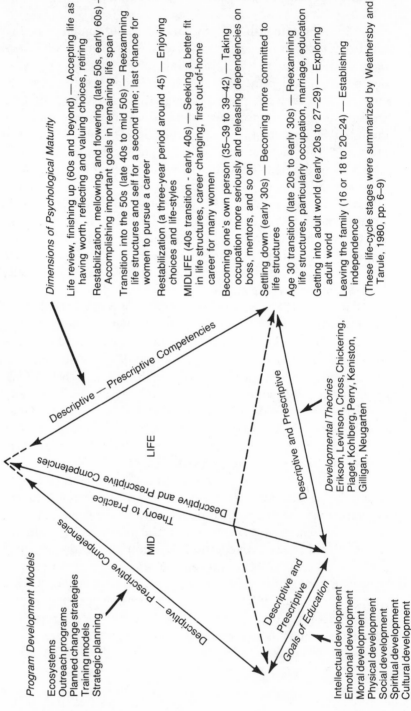

*Dimensions of Psychological Maturity*

Life review, finishing up (60s and beyond) — Accepting life as having worth, reflecting and valuing choices, retiring

Restabilization, mellowing, and flowering (late 50s, early 60s) — Accomplishing important goals in remaining life span

Transition into the 50s (late 40s to mid 50s) — Reexamining life structures and self for a second time; last chance for women to pursue a career

Restabilization (a three-year period around 45) — Enjoying choices and life-styles

MIDLIFE (40s transition - early 40s) — Seeking a better fit in life structures, career changing, first out-of-home career for many women

Becoming one's own person (35–39 to 39–42) — Taking occupation more seriously and releasing dependencies on boss, mentors, and so on

Settling down (early 30s) — Becoming more committed to life structures

Age 30 transition (late 20s to early 30s) — Reexamining life structures, particularly occupation, marriage, education

Getting into adult world (early 20s to 27–29) — Exploring adult world

Leaving the family (16 or 18 to 20–24) — Establishing independence

(These life-cycle stages were summarized by Weathersby and Tarule, 1980, pp. 6–9)

Descriptive — Prescriptive Competencies

*Developmental Theories*
Erikson, Levinson, Cross, Chickering, Piaget, Kohlberg, Perry, Keniston, Gilligan, Neugarten

Descriptive and Prescriptive

LIFE

Descriptive and Prescriptive Competencies

Theory to Practice

MID

Descriptive — Prescriptive Competencies

Descriptive and Prescriptive

*Goals of Education*

Intellectual development
Emotional development
Moral development
Physical development
Social development
Spiritual development
Cultural development

*Program Development Models*

Ecosystems
Outreach programs
Planned change strategies
Training models
Strategic planning

is hierarchically achieved as one masters various developmental tasks. Midway, the pyramid is a discontinuity that represents the mid-life transition. Theory-to-practice is in the central axis because all other dimensions of the pyramid feed into the central point. Program planning in student affairs will underscore the value of theory and will acknowledge the significance of all other dimensions of the pyramid.

*Areas of Special Concern.* Student services professionals of the future will be required to pay particular attention to several specific areas.

- *Research.* Student development educators of the future will view research as a central function of their service delivery. An obvious limitation of program development models is the absence of multi-institutional and longitudinal research (Astin, 1970). Equally valid is the need to ensure population sampling that represents multiethnic groups, women, the aging population, disabled persons, and persons of alternative life-styles. Rigorous research on the impact of student affairs on the educational outcomes or maturity of students can advance student services toward the centralized mainstream of education.
- *Assessing special populations' needs.* Perhaps the most neglected area in program development for student services is the aggregate of special considerations that results from the sociological typology described by Cross (1971). Theorists feed data to practitioners and vice versa. Both are guilty of focusing research designs and, consequently, program development on the middle class, Anglo, heterosexual, able-bodied, young adult, male population. Little is known about women's development; less is known about ethnic minorities' developmental patterns and the developmental patterns of disabled persons. The needs of an older student population, the needs of lower socioeconomic groups, and the needs of the increasing number of out-of-the-closet gays are barely recognized as worthy of research. Nevertheless, all these groups have appeared on college campuses in increasing numbers. Considerations of their needs cannot be left to chance. Spe-

cial needs assessment in the future will reach out to address this emerging majority group with a view toward prescribing sensitive programs.

- *Balancing bureaucracies.* Student development programmers must master the art of functioning in political and apolitical environments that enforce a status of "marginality" (Silverman, 1980). Being marginal has the potential advantage of empowering the student development manager to become what Silverman labels a "leading-edge leader." A student affairs leading-edge leader is successful in direct proportion to the extraordinary demands for strength that his or her position dictates.

  The major challenge for leaders in student programming is to balance the impetus that comes from the university's "machine bureaucracy," the "professional bureaucracy," and the "political bureaucracy." Professional bureaucracy is found in the directional guidance from professional organizations and student development theory. The machine bureaucracy is represented in the university's politics. It is unlikely that the university's machine bureaucracy will be knowledgeable about the professional issues in student development programming. The political bureaucracy encompasses external power forces that impact directly and indirectly on programming. The chief manager or program planner has the responsibility of translating and implanting this information throughout the university. Since educators exists in an historical, political, and financial climate, an appropriate contextual response from student affairs can create a base of strength.

- *Managing power and influence.* The astute program planner recognizes the difference between managing power and influence. Many student affairs positions do not offer comparable formal power to their academic counterparts. For example, the title of dean of students, no matter where it appears on the organizational chart, is not accorded equal status to that of vice-president for academic and faculty affairs. The person in the position, however, does sometimes carry a great deal of personal power or influence. There are distinct differences between personal power and position power. Management of both powers is critical to mastering bureaucracies. Other resource management responsibilities become apparent such as (1) managing budget, (2) managing skills, (3) managing data and information, (4) managing public images, (5) marketing programs, and (6) managing goals, people, space, and work load.

- *Internal evaluation and accountability.* Most student services agencies have adopted systems of accountability. This is merely a way of tracking programs and resources and feeding these back into a planning system (Styles and Hull, 1979). Unless extremely careful evaluation modalities are designed, it will be impossible to establish a cause-and-effect relationship of students' behavioral changes. Evaluations must be qualitative as well as quantitative in student services, for it is only through these measures that one can discern the meanings of changes and experiences for clientele. Evaluation must be translated into language understood by those in the machine bureaucracy, such as retention and career futures. Where psychological maturity becomes the goal of student development and the goal of education, outcomes must be measurable. Process or ongoing evaluation is equally as important as outcome evaluation. The organization's needs can be more easily defined and justified when both efficiency and effectiveness measures are obtained (Styles and Hull, 1979).
- *External reviews and accreditation agencies as program development tools.* Beyond regular accrediting agencies that exist in higher education and beyond accountability measures, not all divisions in student affairs are privileged with evaluation by external review agencies. When there is an absence of such agencies, a student development planner is responsible for identifying review teams external to the campus. The team must be objectively selected to ensure that no particular administrative point of view is enforced. This review is designed to parallel the well-established accreditation teams in the academic community.

*Strategic Planning as a Method.* When an organization adopts a policy of strategic planning, the entire institution must be prepared to move in that direction. Should the institution experience inertia, the student affairs units can choose to adopt strategic planning methods. As this happens, it guarantees that the compartmentalization that has typified educational planning can no longer survive. In strategic planning, the part relates to the whole. Therefore, a continued exclusive focus on the mission of intellectual development in education yields to a more integrated perspective. Strategic planning allows an organization to overcome institutional inertia (Styles and Fiedler, 1981). It enables institutions to move beyond that inertia to a maintenance and program development posture.

Kotter and Murphy (1981) define strategic planning as the process of developing and maintaining a strategic fit between the organization and its challenging marketing opportunities. It demands clearly defined goals and mission statements from the top level of administration before becoming an integrated part of the formal institutional hierarchy. Detailed planning becomes the role of program planners. Kotter and Murphy (1981) present the following six stages in strategic planning.

1. A careful analysis of the environment (today's and tomorrow's): All models previously presented for discussion in this chapter include some aspect of environmental assessment and needs assessment. Strategic planning introduces the role of forecasting for tomorrow's environment as well.
2. A review of major resources as the key to an expected accomplishment: Such a review should include tangible and intangible resources and outline strengths and weaknesses of each.
3. Goal formulation or goal setting: Goal setting occurs within the context of assessed needs and assessed resources. This process allows planners to design realistic programs that have greater opportunities to experience success. Successes of established goals are vital both to the student services deliverer and receiver.
4. A cost-effective strategy to carry out goals: The manager

needs to determine which of the available alternative strategies is most cost effective

5.  The culture, structure, and people to carry out the new design: Not only will training be necessary in some cases, but it may become necessary to change organizational norms, cultures, structures, and people. What is delightful about strategic planning is that it views cultures, people, and resources as dynamic entities capable of moving toward and away from assumed structures.

6.  An overhaul of the organization's systems of information, planning, and control: The system of information may well be the major source of power on campus. Withheld information may become a powerful tool. It is critical to the planner to identify all sources of information and to determine how information is disseminated and applied.

Strategic planning is a dynamic, continual process of balancing stages 1 through 6. To implement such a process assumes that there exist (1) the capacity to assess the internal and external environments, the "machine bureaucracy," the "political bureaucracy," and the "professional bureaucracy," (2) an adequate system of accountability, (3) goal setting and goal formulation to fit the organization, the staff, the students, the administrators, and the external communities, (4) performance reviews that are tied to goals, and (5) procedures for evaluating effectiveness. Strategic planning precludes isolated programming by units within student affairs and organizes services for the entire division.

A strategic planning team will represent various planning groups, both inter- as well as intraorganizational in scope. Thus, community advisory boards may become as central to the planning as faculty and staff. Students are certainly consulted and collaboratively involved in planning their development.

## Summary

Program development is the most critical function performed by student services professionals. Efforts must be made to build responsive programs that are anchored in descriptive theories that promise prescriptive direction to program planners. When program development is successful, it has the potential of influencing the campus community as well as the external communities. Program development must represent systematic, purposeful planning that reflects the priorities of the organization and the institution. Other communities external to the institution must also be considered in program planning. Often an informal assessment of perceptions of these external communities is adequate. More ongoing formal assessments are needed within our campus communities.

Program planners in student affairs must view as obligatory their role to expand education beyond cognition to a more integrative, all-encompassing model of human development. Earlier models encouraged student affairs professionals to employ environmental assessment, change strategies, training programs, outreach programming, population targeting, and planned interventions. Evaluation procedures are viewed as essential in all models. It is recommended that future models pay greater attention to comprehensive goals of education, applications of theory to practice that incorporate both descriptive and prescriptive dimensions, scholarly research procedures, purposeful population sampling and assessment, expertise in balancing bureaucracies, division-wide strategic planning, knowledge of how to manage powers and influences within the university, and internal and external accountability procedures. This perspective suggests a framework for units within student affairs to examine their internal goals and determine how they augment the larger division of student affairs and the ultimate mission of the institution through strategic planning. It further underscores that theoretical applications are essential to program development and that constant upgrading of theories will occur through scholarly research.

## References

Astin, A. W. "The Methodology of Research on College Impact." *Sociology of Education,* 1970, *45,* 437-448.

Aulepp, L., and Delworth, U. *Training Manual for an Ecosystem Model.* Boulder, Colo.: Western Interstate Commission for Higher Education, 1976.

Brown, R. D. "The Student Development Educator Role." In U. Delworth, G. R. Hanson, and Associates, *Student Services: A Handbook for the Profession.* San Francisco: Jossey-Bass, 1980.

Capra, F. *The Turning Point: Science, Society, and the Rising Culture.* New York: Simon and Schuster, 1982.

Chickering, A. W. *Education and Identity.* San Francisco: Jossey-Bass, 1969.

Chickering, A. W. "Potential Contributions of College Unions to Student Development." In W. M. Klepper (Ed.), *The Impact of College Unions and Their Programs on Today's Students.* Stanford, Calif.: Association of College Unions—International, 1981.

Cross, K. P. *Beyond the Open Door: New Students to Higher Education.* San Francisco: Jossey-Bass, 1971.

Drum, D. J., and Figler, H. E. *Outreach in Counseling.* New York: Intext Educational Publishers, 1973.

Erikson, E. *Identity and the Life Cycle: Psychological Issues.* New York: International Universities Press, 1959.

Fenske, R. H. "Historical Foundations." In U. Delworth, G. R. Hanson, and Associates, *Student Services: A Handbook for the Profession.* San Francisco: Jossey-Bass, 1980.

Ferguson, M. *The Aquarian Conspiracy: Personal and Social Transformation in the 1980s.* Los Angeles: Tarcher, 1980.

Gilligan, C. "In a Different Voice: Women's Conceptions of the Self and of Mortality." *Harvard Educational Review,* 1977, *47* (4), 481-517.

Heath, D. H. "Adolescent and Adult Predictors of Vocational Adaptation." *Journal of Vocational Behavior,* 1976, *9,* 1-19.

Heath, D. H. *Maturity and Competence.* New York: Gardner Press, 1977.

Heath, R. *The Reasonable Adventurer.* Pittsburgh, Pa.: University of Pittsburgh Press, 1964.

Kaiser, L. R. "Campus Ecology: Implications for Environmental

Design." Unpublished paper, Western Interstate Commission for Higher Education Task Force on Epidemiology, Campus Ecology, and Program Evaluation, Boulder, Colo., 1972.

Keniston, K. "Social Change and Youth in America." In K. Yamamoto (Ed.), *The College Student and His Culture.* Boston: Houghton Mifflin, 1968.

Kohlberg, L. "Stage and Sequence: The Cognitive Developmental Approach to Socialization." In D. Gaslin (Ed.), *Handbook of Socialization Theory and Research.* Chicago: Rand McNally, 1969.

Kotter, P., and Murphy, P. E. "Strategic Planning for Higher Education." *Journal of Higher Education,* 1981, *52* (5), 470–488.

Levinson, D. J. *The Seasons of a Man's Life.* New York: Knopf, 1978.

Lewis, M. D., and Lewis, J. A. "A Schematic for Change." *Personnel and Guidance Journal,* 1974, *52* (5), 320–323.

Marcia, J. "Development and Validation of Ego-Identity Status." *Journal of Personality and Social Psychology,* 1966, *3* (5), 551–558.

Miller, T. K., and Prince, J. S. *The Future of Student Affairs: A Guide to Student Development for Tomorrow's Higher Education.* San Francisco: Jossey-Bass, 1976.

Moore, M., and Delworth, U. *Training Manual for Student Service Program Development.* Boulder, Colo.: Western Interstate Commission for Higher Education, 1976.

Morrill, W. H., Oetting, E. R., and Hurst, J. C. "Dimensions of Counselor Functioning." *Personnel and Guidance Journal,* 1974, *52* (6), 354–359.

Naisbitt, J. *Megatrends: Ten New Directions Transforming Our Lives.* New York: Warner Books, 1982.

Neugarten, B. L. "A Developmental View of Adult Personality." In J. E. Birren (Ed.), *Relations of Development and Aging.* Springfield, Ill.: Thomas, 1963.

Perry, W. *Forms of Intellectual and Ethical Development in the College Years: A Scheme.* New York: Holt, Rinehart and Winston, 1970.

Piaget, J. "Cognitive Development in Children." In R. Ripple and V. Rockcartte (Eds.), *Piaget Rediscovered: A Report on Cognitive Studies in Curriculum Development.* Ithaca, N.Y.: School of Education, Cornell University, 1964.

Rogers, C. *Freedom to Learn for the 80s.* Columbus, Ohio: Merrill, 1983.

Silverman, R. J. "The Student Personnel Administrator as Leading-Edge Leader." *National Association of Student Personnel Administrators (NASPA) Journal,* 1980, *18* (2), 10-15.

Sprinthall, N. A., Bertin, B. D., and Whitley, J. M. "Accomplishment After College: A Rationale for Developmental Education." *National Association of Student Personnel Administrators (NASPA) Journal,* 1982, *20* (1), 37-46.

Styles, M., and Fiedler, L. "Management Styles." *Proceedings: 30th Annual Conference of University and College Counseling Center Directors.* Fontana, Wisc., October 11-15, 1981.

Styles, M., and Hull, S. "Career Planning and Placement." In G. Kuh (Ed.), *Evaluation in Student Affairs.* Cincinnati, Ohio: American College Personnel Association Media, 1979.

Toffler, A. *The Third Wave.* New York: Morrow, 1980.

Weathersby, R. P., and Tarule, J. M. *Adult Development: Implications for Higher Education.* Washington, D.C.: American Association for Higher Education, 1980.

Widick, C., Knefelkamp, L. L., and Parker, C. A. "Student Development." In U. Delworth, G. R. Hanson, and Associates, *Student Services: A Handbook for the Profession.* San Francisco: Jossey-Bass, 1980.

# 9

John L. Baier

❧ ❧ ❧ ❧ ❧ ❧ ❧ ❧ ❧ ❧ ❧ ❧ ❧

# Recruiting
# and Training
# Competent Staff

We know they're out there. We've often described them in our position announcements. "Wanted: Individuals who understand student development theory, group dynamics, and computer technology. Must also counsel, teach, supervise, design student development programs, and manage a budget. Candidate must pay interview transportation costs. M.A. required. Salary: $15,000 a year."

Clearly, no one individual can fulfill all the expectations implied in most student services position descriptions. We couldn't afford to hire anyone who did! Yet we continue our search for that outstanding staff member who will make all the difference in our programs. The search is frustrating, for today's student services professional must possess a wide variety of skills and abilities. Even the apparently simple task of advising residence hall government requires skills in counseling, conflict management, program planning, and budgeting, to name a few. How much more complicated are the competencies required of staff charged with "consultation" or "systems change." In some settings, it may still be possible to work as a specialist in a specific student affairs area. In recent years however, even the specialists—the psychologists, admissions recruiters, health center nurses—are being asked to "reach out" to the campus community and to cooperate with allied professionals to develop new programs. These changing and expanding role expectations carry with them skill requirements that may be outside the specialists' area of expertise.

A central task of the student services administrator has always been to assure that quality staff are hired, trained, and challenged. Changes in staff role expectations coupled with more limited staff mobility patterns underscore the need to assign as highest priority the selection, support, and development of quality staff.

## Defining Quality Staff

What do student services professionals mean by quality staff? To a large extent, the definition of quality staff is prescribed and limited by the demands of the specific job and supervisor. Therefore, when defining quality, two questions must be resolved: (1) What are the minimum competencies and competency levels required of *any* student services professional? (2) What competencies and competency levels are required of quality staff in this *particular* job? Answering either question requires an understanding of the term *competence*.

Delworth and Yarris (1978) define competence as a combination of cognitions, affect, and skills. They then group the competencies required of new student services professionals into four categories: (1) agency goals, policies, and procedures; (2) ethical concerns; (3) basic communication skills; and (4) job-specific knowledge and skills. These competencies could be viewed as the basic or "core" skills, knowledge, and affective capabilities prerequisite for any student services position. In a report to the American College Personnel Association (ACPA) Executive Committee, Hanson (1977) endorses six other competencies: goal setting, consultation, milieu management, instruction, evaluation, and assessment. These six are more advanced or higher-level competencies that more experienced professionals could reasonably be expected to possess.

Ideally, student services professionals' training would be directed to acquisition of a clearly defined group of "core" or minimum competencies (similar to those defined by Delworth and Yarris), followed by second-level competencies, and so on. Unfortunately, the profession has not yet agreed on such precise standards, and graduate programs continue to teach from their own unique curriculum. Therefore, responsibility for identifying competencies required of quality staff and then selecting and training that staff continues to rest with the individual supervisor. While these tasks may appear to be fairly straightforward, student services professionals must make personnel decisions in the context of institutional policies and procedures. Thus, the successful supervisor does not begin the staff selection or training process without first considering the effect of common institutional employment practices on the overall staffing strategy.

## Employment Practices

Contemporary student services administrators must hire, fire, promote, and train staff in accordance with collective bargaining agreements, personnel policies, and many other legal or procedural requirements. These institutional rules and regulations often restrict administrators' ability to reward competent staff members or to terminate unproductive or incompetent employees. Some personnel procedures require that promotions, transfers, or raises be based on length of service rather than on merit, and some affirmative action requirements have led to staff being selected on the basis of sex, ethnicity, or disability in order to fill quotas or goals. While the intent of these regulations is laudable, these organizational constraints can hinder the ability to select and support quality staff.

Budget constraints also limit administrators' ability to obtain and maintain quality staff. Lack of merit increases and travel funds can lead to low morale, and lack of staff recruitment funds hampers hiring efforts. Budget restrictions in one or more critical areas can also result in political infighting, staff burnout, "protective" posturing, and other nonprofessional behaviors.

Another obstacle to the hiring and challenging of competent staff is the lack of professional preparation or "certification" standards for student affairs. In most other professional areas (law, medicine, teaching, engineering, accounting), there are designated degree programs and certifying examinations or agencies that monitor entry into the profession and the performance of people in the field. With the exception of some staff in counseling and health centers, this is not the case in the student personnel profession. During the last forty years, thousands of people have entered student personnel work from a variety of academic disciplines. The numbers of "student personnel"–trained and educated professionals have increased significantly in the last decade. However, master's and doctoral programs in the student personnel area vary widely in curriculum and in quality. In fact, the curricula and the ultimate value of these student personnel preparation programs and their graduates have been severely criticized for many years by people inside and outside the field. In the past, many graduate programs taught student personnel workers to become counselors, advisers, managers, and quality control engineers. More recently, a number of programs have shifted their focus to teaching a series of micromanagerial tasks, such as budgeting, management by objectives, legal responsibilities, and affirmative action guidelines (Prior, 1973; Rhatigan, 1975). Despite these changes, Dewey (1972) reported that "effective practitioners of artistry and skill (in student affairs work) may be successful in spite of and not because of their professional preparation" (p. 63).

There is no single way to overcome these obstacles to selecting and supporting quality staff. Student personnel professional associations are monitoring preparation standards, and employee groups are reviewing hiring and grievance practices. Certainly student services professionals have an obligation to challenge policies or procedures that interfere with efforts to support and develop competent staff. There is a limit, though, to any individual's ability to overcome all the obstacles to staff development embedded in common employment practices. And some employment issues, such as some budget constraints, are beyond our control. However, given our limitations, there are steps that student services practitioners can take to assure quality staff.

## Selection, Supervision, and Evaluation

After considering the institutional context framed by common employment practices, the next step in assuring quality staff is to devise procedures that will lead to hiring of the most qualified individuals. In most cases, these procedures include analyzing the position, specifying skills and knowledge required for success in the position, and conducting an affirmative and open search. In general, student services professionals do an excellent job of conducting open selections for we know that shortcuts at this stage will decrease the likelihood that a suitable candidate will be located. Unfortunately, however, strict adherence to defensible selection criteria and affirmative search procedures does not guarantee a quality hire. As stated earlier, no one individual can reasonably be expected to possess the range of competencies needed in many student services positions. In addition, even the most careful screening and interviewing process does not always lead to a good hire. We've all seen the person who interviews well but cannot do the job once hired, and even the best hire must be followed by careful supervision and evaluation. When the wrong candidate is selected, the supervisory responsibility is even greater.

Effective supervision can greatly stimulate the professional and personal growth required to develop and maintain quality staff. Through proper supervision and evaluation, an employee's strengths and weaknesses can be identfed and appropriate staff development activities can be designed. Thomas and Good-Benson (1978) outline three conditions required for effective supervision to occur: the supervisee and supervisor understand each other's duties and responsibilities, have mutual respect for each other, and are able to work together. When these conditions exist, it is more likely that staff supervision and evaluation will be a developmental process.

Generally accepted steps for proper evaluation and supervision include discussion of the employee's specific duties and identification of the specific skills and knowledge the employee should possess to fulfill those duties as efficiently and effectively as possible. In general, it is not difficult to identify needed competencies and employee strengths and weaknesses. The challenge is to then specify a program of developmental activities and goals for correcting the deficient areas and enhancing strengths. Though some employees are able to follow through with such programs independently, most supervisors find that a referral to a specific development activity assures that a minimum level of staff growth and development will occur. In addition, no one supervisor can or should possess the expertise to train his or her staff in all required skill areas. Thus, staff development programming is critical to our central task of establishing effective student services programs.

## Staff Development Programming

Staff development programming can serve a wide variety of purposes. Many who enter the field from other courses of study may require basic information regarding the mission of student affairs. Also many of the student personnel–trained professionals who entered the field during the past twenty-five years were trained for a different focus than currently exists in student affairs today. Organized staff development programs can enable us to bridge the gap between the theory taught in graduate training programs and the practical knowledge gained on the job. Such training can also provide older staff members with the skills or knowledge needed to deal with new problems.

Student affairs divisions have been slow to develop "in-service" staff development programs. Many student affairs administrators tend to see the immediate task that needs doing as much more important than an ambiguous goal of skill improvement. The positive relationship that exists between participating in staff development activities has yet to be linked to professional performance and merit increases. Though many of the skills required of student affairs practitioners lend themselves readily to in-service training, few systematic staff development program efforts have been established in student affairs organization. In a national study of staff development activities in student affairs, Miller (1975) reported that only one of every five institutions of higher education had made a formal policy statement concerning off-campus in-service activity for student personnel workers. On-campus in-service education, when provided, received only one tenth of the total staff development budget and had a low organizational priority.

This apparent lack of support for structured staff development efforts might be attributed, in part, to the difficulty of identifying the components of a successful staff development program. In an article on professional development activities, Rhatigan and Crawford (1978) described the problem this way: "In spite of the importance of professional development, its components are imprecisely understood. No doubt different kinds of work require different modes of assistance, and perhaps some fields find this easier to manage than others. Many large industrial organizations are effective in offering a planned sequence of management training experiences to selected employees. Other relatively formal models have been tried by various professionals. But how does one become a better dean of students? The answers may depend on one's age, sex, training background, current position, personal and professional affiliations, available resources, and whatever individual experiences one can find. Of course, the vagaries of style, attitude, values, energy, and circumstances intrude to complicate our understanding" (p. 45).

At this point in time, the answers *are* individual in nature and the staff development needs reflect the diversity of the profession. Therefore, student services divisions or offices must make available a wide variety of staff development opportunities.

Such comprehensive staff development programs consist of two categories of activities—campus-based and off-campus programs. Campus-based activities include seminars, workshops, short courses, and similar offerings. Off-campus programs include regional and national conferences, site visitations, and professional institutes. The extent to which a given institution utilizes each type of program will depend on its geographic location, its fiscal resources, and its developmental needs. Most comprehensive staff development programs, however, will need to rely more on campus-based activities and programs to meet their in-service needs than on off-campus programs. Although participation of staff members in professional association conferences, meetings, committees, and commissions is valuable and stimulating, most institutional budgets and work assignments don't allow very many staff members to actively participate in off-campus programs and professional associations. It is much more cost-effective for a student affairs division to bring in a speaker to address the entire professional staff than it is to send the entire staff to a professional conference at which the same individual may be the keynote speaker. Thus, by developing a balanced and comprehensive campus-based staff development program, more staff needs can be addressed at less cost to the institution.

Typically, campus-based comprehensive student affairs staff development programs have the following objectives:

- to provide programs and opportunities from which staff may learn about and keep up-to-date on current issues and trends in higher education and student personnel work
- to provide opportunities for staff to identify and learn those new skills necessary to better perform their duties in accordance with changing needs and new technology
- to provide opportunities for staff to explore new ways to solve old, new, and perplexing problems in student affairs
- to provide incentives and training experiences for staff to try and apply old skills to new programs and administrative challenges
- to provide professional experiences and opportunities that motivate staff members to grow personally and professionally

As should be evident, an effective staff development program does not occur by chance. Instead, time must be invested to design, administer, and evaluate the program, and money made available to implement the effort. A well-balanced, comprehensive program at a medium- to large-size school could cost from several hundred to several thousand dollars per year to administer. Costs at smaller colleges would be proportionately less.

Effective staff development programs are generally administered by a staff development committee or a staff development coordinator. Committees at a medium- to large-size college or university will usually consist of five to ten staff members who spend one to two hours per week planning or delivering staff development activities. Successful programs require that each member of the professional staff spend one to two hours per month participating in some type of staff development activity. At small colleges, only one to two people may be needed to plan and administer the program, but staff member participation time should be the same as at larger colleges.

Staff development programs need to be centrally coordinated, encouraged, and supported, but not all activities need to be directed at all staff members in all departments. Effective staff development programs must address a wide variety of topics and concerns and must be appropriate to different levels and types of student affairs staff. Some programs should transmit information pertinent to division programs and policies. Others might address university or college concerns about student personnel work and higher education issues. Other programs might be designed to teach specific skills, such as the use of microcomputers and word processors, food preparation techniques, clerical tasks, financial aid packaging, program advisement, and conflict resolution. Skill development seminars in food management areas might be directed only at employees in housing and union operations responsible for food services. Similarly, a program that instructs staff members in computerized packaging and processing of financial aid might be offered as a part of a regular financial aid department staff meeting for financial aid staff members. On the other hand, informational programs of general divisional or university-wide interest might include and be directed at as many staff members as possible.

The benefits of effective staff development activities far outweigh the costs. A well-defined, administered, and attended staff development program can help improve staff morale, stimulate creative problem solving, increase staff productivity and efficiency, facilitate goal setting, improve staff skills, increase staff awareness of the importance of keeping current and up-to-date, and raise skill levels. In short, staff development programs facilitate the development of a competent staff.

Many colleges and universities have recently developed and implemented comprehensive staff development programs. As reported by Merkle and Artman (1983), Canon (1980), and Wanzek (1977), the more successful staff development programs are generally those that are division-wide in scope, are vigorously supported by the chief student affairs officer as an integral part of the division's priorities, and are administered by a professional development committee or high-placed officer in the student affairs administrative structure.

There are five steps involved in the planning and implementation of successful staff development programs: determining needs, defining objectives, designing the program, implementing the program, and evaluating the program. Staff needs can be determined by reviewing staff evaluations, conducting staff surveys, surveying directors and supervisors, or simply by asking staff members at random what types of activities or programs they feel would be helpful to them or their employees for better performance of their assigned duties. Once needs have been determined, program objectives should be defined that address those needs. Having determined needs and defined program objectives, a program should then be designed that can accomplish the stated objectives. Merkle and Artman (1983) have defined a staff development program "as a planned experience designed to change behavior and result in professional and/or personal growth and improved organizational effectiveness" (p. 55). Based on that plan, or design, the program can then be implemented and evaluated against its stated objectives to determine its effectiveness. By following this simple procedure, it is possible to establish numerous successful staff development programs.

## Vehicles for Staff Development

The variety, nature, and scope of staff development programs that could be utilized to accomplish the development and maintenance of a competent staff are limited only by our creative abilities, management skills, and fiscal and human resources. Programs that have been successful in a variety of campus settings are described in this section.

*Staff Newsletter.* One basic but important staff development activity is the publication of a periodic staff newsletter. The newsletter can include news of future activities; profiles of selected staff members, departments, or programs; recognition of individual staff member accomplishments; and a periodic message from the vice-president or dean. Many newsletters also publish lists of recommended readings and conferences, as well as information on selected college functions or departments. If published five or six times each academic year in an inexpensive manner, the newsletter can be an important staff development tool. Many benefits are derived from such short, timely, and inexpensively produced newsletters. The newsletter provides an inexpensive and effective way for a staff development committee to communicate on a regular basis with the entire staff as well as to promote future staff development activities. Staff and department morale increases because staff members know that their accomplishments will be reported to their colleagues. Receiving a copy of the newsletter also serves as a reminder to all staff members that they are a part of a larger organization.

*New Staff Orientation Activities.* These are activities designed to introduce new staff members to the institution, to the division of student affairs, and to other staff in individual departments. Staff orientation often means assisting new staff with finding suitable living accommodations in the community, arranging tours of office facilities, meeting with other staff members, and visiting the personnel office. Supervisors may show audiovisual presentations about the department, division, college and community, university policies and procedures, and cultural activities or may provide written material on college structures and activities. Many student affairs divisions sponsor an event at the beginning of each school year for all new and old staff members to get acquainted. The dean or vice-president usually attends this function and outlines goals for the coming year.

Well-run orientation activities set the proper climate for more in-depth staff development programming. Systematic staff orientation programs can relieve anxieties about a new position in a new place and reduce the time it takes a person to feel comfortable relating to new people in a new environment. Orientation activities also remind current staff members that the organization is constantly changing. In student affairs we have long espoused the virtues and importance of orientation programs for new students. The same arguments and benefits apply to orientation programs for new staff members.

*Coffee Hours.* Coffee hours provide a time for informative conversation and the discussion of current issues that are, or should be, of interest to the staff. Coffee hours are quite informal and usually include time for both a speaker and social interaction. The programs should be short, scheduled at about six-week intervals on different days and times, and held in different campus locations, with a wide variety of guest speakers. There are a number of ways to program a coffee hour series. Each year a different theme or focus could be used. For example, the theme could be a "Focus on Student Affairs," featuring presentations by the individual departments; or a "Focus on Higher Education," featuring addresses by key college administrators or special guest speakers from other campuses. Another approach would be to have a variety of topics covered each semester, with the emphasis being on introducing the staff to as many different people, areas of campus, and issues as is possible. Through the coffee hour, senior staff members can be introduced to new ideas and trends in higher education and student personnel work, challenging them to look at ways to apply old skills or programs to new ideas and problem areas. At the same time, the programs are fun and nonthreatening, require little preparation on the part of participants, and provide an opportunity to interact informally with staff colleagues from other departments.

*Workshops and Seminars.* Half-day or day-long workshops or seminars are often utilized to provide in-depth training for selected staff groups. The expanded length of the programs allows for more detailed presentation and discussion of pertinent information than does the coffee hour approach. Advance readings or other forms of preparation may be required of participants. The program can be either voluntary or required, depending on the nature of the topic and the importance of the information or skills being taught. Workshop formats should vary according to topic, audiovisual materials used, and facilities. Examples of possible workshop topics are "Women in the Working World," "Nonverbal Communication," "Legal Concerns Facing Student Affairs Professionals," "Program Budgeting," "Management by Objectives," and "Computer Systems."

Because of their longer length, workshops and seminars are more difficult to schedule. The periods between semesters and between spring semester and summer session offer excellent times for scheduling workshops of this type. Staff members' work loads are generally lower at this time of year, and adequate blocks of staff time can usually be found to allow a large number of people to participate in the entire workshop. Since no travel is required for staff members on the campus to participate, the cost of sponsoring a workshop on your campus is much less than sending a group of staff members to a national or regional meeting dealing with the same topic.

*Mini-University Programs.* Based on the "free university" model common on college campuses during the late 1960s and early 1970s, the student affairs mini-university was developed by Meyerson (1974) and his colleagues at the University of Nebraska. The program has subsequently been adapted for use at several other universities.

A typical mini-university staff development program consists of ten to twenty short skill development courses offered over a short period of time (usually two to three weeks). Mini-university courses differ from workshops in that the topics can be covered in hourly meetings spread over a period of time that allows more staff members to attend the offered courses than is possible with the single-day workshop approach. The mini-university format also allows for the subject to be covered in more depth. Especially popular courses are usually offered each semester or repeated the following year. Volunteer course instructors can be drawn from within the division of student affairs, the university faculty and administrative staff, or from the community. Course topics generally involve professional knowledge and skills but may also focus on personal development.

A properly designed mini-university program should achieve the following objectives: (1) provide staff the opportunity to study timely issues and concepts in higher education and student personnel work; (2) provide staff the opportunity to interact with resource people who have acknowledged expertise; (3) provide staff the opportunity to interact with one another; and (4) provide staff the opportunity to learn pertinent student affairs management and administrative skills. Examples of courses that have been included in mini-university programs are "The University and the Courts," "Human Interaction and Communication Skills," "The Freshman Year," "Affirmative Action and Equal Opportunity Programs," "Stress Management," and "Supervisory Techniques."

Evaluation of the established mini-university programs (Meyerson, 1974; Beeler, 1977; Baier, 1980) have indicated a broad base of staff satisfaction and support and a high level of staff participation. Through the mini-university format, it is possible to address a large number of development areas under a single program umbrella, and course offerings can be updated on an annual basis as changing needs and staff competencies dictate. The program is easy to organize, administer, and evaluate, requiring a minimal amount of staff time to implement. By using student affairs staff members to serve as course instructors, the mini-university program offers the staff an opportunity to gain instructional experience. In addition, the mini-university approach provides a suitable format for staff members to share their special skills, competencies, and interests with their colleagues. Such instructional experiences serve as an excellent training ground to sharpen audiovisual aid and oral presentation skills.

*Student Affairs Program Grants.* Traditionally, student

affairs staff members have had limited opportunities or encouragement to apply for "research and development" grants that could fund pilot project programs, research efforts, and staff training and development programs. Departmental budgets typically do not allow for this type of budget flexibility, and the usual sources of grant money have generally not funded student affairs programs and research studies.

A number of student affairs divisions, however, are fortunate enough to have access to small sums of locally generated funds, such as revenues from vending machines profits, bookstore profits, student services fees, laundry service profits, foundation money, and alumni association contributions. If it is possible to assemble $500 to $2,000 per year of this type of funding, a student affairs program grant can be established. Meyerson (1976) reports a high level of staff participation and satisfaction with the program grants that were funded at the University of Nebraska.

The student affairs program grant can be used to fund those activities that might lead to improvement of delivery systems for student services, new educational programs, expansion of individual or collective staff development efforts, or an increase of staff resource efforts. The administration of a program grant is relatively simple. An individual staff member or group of staff members develops a proposal and submits it to the vice-president's or dean's office for consideration. Grant requests should be limited to requests for the seed money (usually $100 to $500) needed to achieve the program objectives. Proposals could fall into one or more of the following categories: (1) more effective delivery of student services, (2) educational program development, (3) improvement of research and evaluation efforts, (4) new and innovative departmental staff development programs, (5) improved coordination of programming and communication with other university officers and personnel, (6) improved communication with students or student groups, (7) improved communication or joint programming with academic departments and faculty members.

Proposals should be evaluated by the chief student affairs officer and other selected readers according to established criteria such as: (1) relationship of the proposal to one or more of the designated categories, (2) creativity reflected in the proposal, (3) potential benefit to the target population, (4) method for measuring and evaluating program activities, (5) coordination of program sponsorship, and (6) long-range benefits of the proposal to the division and university.

Careful use of program grants can motivate staff to think and act creatively. Because the design of a grant program closely parallels the methodology and criteria used by many private and government grant-giving agencies, student affairs staff members are provided with a real opportunity to learn how to successfully write grant requests, to think through the principles of accountability, and to plan for program research and evaluation.

*Self-Instruction Training Modules.* Self-instruction training modules in specialized areas of administration and management modeled after self-instruction programs used to learn foreign languages make excellent training aids for staff development. Programmed self-instruction books, cassettes, and computer programs can be internally produced or commercially purchased in accounting, program budgeting, affirmative action procedures, leadership training, computer programming, time management, conflict resolution, group dynamics, and other skill areas. Internally produced modules can also teach information about various university and division programs and policies. Maintaining a reference library of these resources in the dean's or vice-president's office and making them available to student affairs staff on an individual basis is a way of developing new skill competencies among untrained or older staff members and also can be used to complement staff orientation programs. Self-instruction modules allow for staff training and information transmission to be accomplished on a "flexible time" basis and at an instructional speed determined by the individual staff member's needs and schedule. They also ensure that all staff members are being exposed to the same information on a given topic and provide for a convenient method for disseminating information on new policies, structures, or programs to large members of staff members in an efficient and timely manner.

*Research and Literature Reports.* A staff development

program that is easy to implement is to include a review of current research or a literature report at departmental or divisional staff meetings. Ideally, all staff members would be expected to give a short, oral report on an assigned journal, research report, or book at a designated meeting during the year. Since most staff groups meet on a weekly or biweekly basis, ten to twenty minutes of each meeting could be devoted to an oral report. Over the course of a semester, six to ten journals, reports, or books can be reviewed using this method. This activity provides an opportunity for staff to improve their oral reporting abilities. Additionally, it also compels staff to read at least one professional publication or book each semester. Rhatigan and Crawford (1978) report that approximately 25 percent of student affairs administrators read professional journals and only about 12 to 15 percent read professional books. Therefore, in order to increase the incidence of staff members keeping current with the literature, this rather simple staff development technique should be considered.

*Temporary Staff Assignments.* Frequently, middle management or upper-level staff members take a semester or yearlong leave of absence for health, personal, or professional reasons. These leaves create temporary vacancies that can either be left vacant (depending on how critical the vacated position is to the organization) or can be filled on a temporary basis. These temporary vacancies provide a unique way to offer a challenging "in-service training" opportunity to another member of the staff. For example, if the assistant to the vice-president for student affairs needs to take a six-month leave, one of the department heads could be assigned to fill the assistant to the vice-president's position for the six-month period. In turn, the associate director of the department affected can assume the director's position on an interim basis, and the assistant director can assume the associate director's responsibilities, and so on down the line, until a position is reached that can be left unfilled for a six-month period of time without causing great harm to the functioning of the department. By making these temporary assignments, a number of staff members are given the chance to try their hand at someone else's job. The interim appointees are offered an opportunity to learn about new aspects of the division or department's functions and to gain a sense of appreciation for others' responsibilities, job expectations, and stresses. These temporary assignments also give the chief student affairs officer a chance to view the administrative talents of some junior staff members and give staff members the opportunity to find out whether they possess the talents and professional ambition to fill those positions on a permanent basis. By creatively filling temporary vacancies in the manner described, staff morale, learning, and competency can all be readily increased without spending any money or significantly disrupting the normal functions of the organization. In fact, the normal functions of the organization are frequently improved as a result of these temporary assignments. The fresh vision and energy level that interim appointees bring to the department and division often lead to improved operations, programs, and services.

*Interdepartmental Staff Exchanges.* Interdepartmental staff exchanges are a variation of the temporary staff assignment concept. However, instead of waiting for a temporary vacancy to occur, two staff members from different departments are paired; and for a six-month or year-long period, they literally exchange positions with one another. During the exchange period, they do each other's job. In the process they learn about the other department, different management and leadership styles, and the similarities and differences between selected student services programs and activities. They also gain an appreciation for the specific skills required for staff members in another department and the day-to-day nature of their work. Staff exchange programs serve many of the same purposes that practicums and internships are designed to do in graduate preparation programs, but they have the additional benefit of reducing "burnout" and staff complacency. Staff exchanges can give a few staff members each year a chance to change jobs and try something new without having to quit their job or permanently relocate to another department, area, or university.

*Mentoring.* Closely related to both temporary staff assignments and interdepartmental staff exchanges is mentoring.

Mentoring is a process through which a more experienced staff member provides one-to-one, professional guidance, advice, information instruction, and encouragement to younger, less experienced staff members. Most student affairs administrators can readily identify one or more individuals who have "mentored" them at a critical time in their professional careers. Unfortunately, most of these mentor relationships occur by chance. This need not be the case, however, for mentoring to be effective. Mentor relationships can be formally developed and established within a student affairs division on most campuses. The concept of setting up a formal mentoring structure within a student affairs division is similar to what fraternal organizations have been doing under their big brother/big sister programs. It is also similar to what we have been doing for decades with the assignment of resident assistants to each floor in our residence halls and the assignment of group leaders or advisors to orientation groups.

For mentoring to be effective, the mentor must be secure in his or her job, not threatened by younger staff members, able to communicate clearly the rationale used for making decisions, able to delegate tasks effectively, and able to teach younger people how to do their jobs effectively. Unfortunately, the student affairs profession does not currently have an abundance of people with those characteristics. Therefore, although mentoring can be a most beneficial and effective staff development technique, it is one of the most difficult to implement as an ongoing staff development program. Whenever it can be set up, however, it should be.

*Piggyback Activities.* Many colleges and universities have active continuing education divisions and collegiate and departmental units that sponsor a variety of seminars, workshops, noncredit short courses, and other programs. Many of these sponsoring agencies are anxious to find cosponsoring departments to share the program's expenses and ensure enough participants to make the course/program successful. Student affairs departments should take advantage of these staff development opportunities by "piggybacking" on someone else's activity. Piggybacking is one of the easiest ways to provide a wide array of staff development programs with minimal effort and expense. The personnel office, purchasing department, accounting department, continuing education division, college of business, college of education, and law school are just a few of the units that frequently sponsor activities that might be of value and interest to student affairs staff members.

## Summary

Any experienced student affairs administrator will testify to the fact that having the "right people" in the "right places" generally makes the difference between success and failure of a particular student services program. We must have competent staff to ensure successful student services programs. Developing and maintaining a staff who possess all the knowledge, skills, and talents needed in student affairs today does not occur by chance. It takes coordinated and intensive efforts in staff selection, staff supervision, and staff development programming.

Although there are many legal and regulatory obstacles to achieving staff competency, they are not impossible barriers to overcome. Our need for professional growth and development, like education, never ends. We all need to attain higher levels of competency in new and emerging areas of professional knowledge and skill development. Proper supervision and staff development programming offers each of us the opportunity to grow and seek greater professional competence and fulfillment. Only with a competent staff can most student services programs succeed.

## References

Baier, J. L. "Evaluation of Mini-University Staff Development Program at Texas Tech University." Unpublished research report, Texas Tech University, 1980.

Beeler, K. D. "Mini-U: A Promising Model for Student Affairs Staff Development." *National Association of Student Personnel Administrators (NASPA) Journal,* 1977, *14,* 38-43.

Canon, H. J. "Developing Staff Potential." In U. Delworth,

G. R. Hanson, and Associates, *Student Services: A Handbook for the Profession.* San Francisco: Jossey-Bass, 1980.

Delworth, U., and Yarris, E. "Concepts and Processes for the New Training Role." In U. Delworth (Ed.), *New Directions for Student Services: Training Competent Staff,* no. 2. San Francisco: Jossey-Bass, 1978.

Dewey, M. E. "The Student Personnel Worker of 1980." *Journal of the National Association of Women Deans and Counselors,* 1972, *35* (2), 59-64.

Hanson, G. R. "Stop the Bandwagon . . . ACPA Wants to Get On." Committee report submitted to the American College Personnel Association Executive Council and Commission Chairperson, University of Texas at Austin, 1977.

Merkle, H. B., and Artman, R. B. "Staff Development: A Systematic Process for Student Affairs Leaders." *National Association of Student Personnel Administrators (NASPA) Journal,* 1983, *21,* 55-63.

Meyerson, E. "Mini-University Provides Staff Training for a Big University." *College and University Business,* 1974, *56,* 31-33.

Meyerson, E. "A Technique to Motivate Staff to Improve the Quality of Student Life." *Southwestern Review,* 1976, Winter, 16-18.

Miller, T. K. "Staff Development Activities in Student Affairs Programs." *Journal of College Student Personnel,* 1975, *16* (4), 258-264.

Prior, J. J. "The Reorganization of Student Personnel Services: Facing Reality." *Journal of College Student Personnel,* 1973, *14,* 202-205.

Rhatigan, J. J. "Student Services versus Student Development: Is There a Difference?" *Journal of the National Association for Women Deans, Administrators and Counselors,* 1975, *38,* 51-59.

Rhatigan, J. J., and Crawford, A. E., II. "Professional Development Preferences of Student Affairs Administrators." *National Association of Student Personnel Administrators (NASPA) Journal,* 1978, *15* (3), 45-52.

Thomas, L. E., and Good-Benson, P. "Supervision: A Key Element in Training." In U. Delworth (Ed.), *New Directions for Student Services: Training Competent Staff,* no. 2. San Francisco: Jossey-Bass, 1978.

Wanzek, R. P. (Ed.). *Staff Development.* Developmental Series Monograph 1. DeKalb: Division of Student Affairs, Northern Illinois University, 1977.

Sharon H. Justice
John D. Ragle

10

❧ ❧ ❧ ❧ ❧ ❧ ❧ ❧ ❧ ❧ ❧ ❧ ❧

# Building
# and Maintaining
# Program Quality

Program maintenance, at a successful level, requires initiative, enthusiasm, and responsibility in order to assure that quality services are being provided. Unfortunately, the connotations of maintenance are not very positive. Maintenance usually refers to the grimy work of changing the oil in a car, checking for leaky pipes in the basement, or the menial chores of washing and cleaning around a house and yard. The chores of maintenance are usually regarded as tedious, tiresome, and uninteresting.

### Misconceptions about Maintenance

The glory in student services programming usually goes to the innovators. That which is new, improved, or new *and* improved—different in any way—catches the attention of organizational superiors and colleagues and this recognition may well be accompanied by increases in salary, status, or responsibilities.

This desire for innovation affects not only the aspiring professional but also those who have risen to the positions of dean or vice-president. Harway (1977) reported that college and university administrators regarded creativity as a behavior they greatly value in their professional subordinates. When asked to indicate which of eighteen behaviors are rewarded by educational institutions, 55 percent of the chief student affairs officers and 64 percent of the presidents and chief academic officers chose creativity. For both, creativity ranked above such behaviors as "willingness to accept authority" and "effectiveness in dealing with students."

With such fascination with creativity and innovation, established student services programs that do not regularly evidence some major change are often perceived as stagnant. This perception is supported by several myths.

*Needs Always Change.* The assumption is often made, for example, that student needs are constantly changing and as a result, the programs that serve these students are expected to "keep up." Some basic needs, however, remain the same. The need for clean, safe, comfortable housing, the need for readily available health care, the need for financial assistance, the need for rules by which to live within a campus community, or the need to introduce students to the campus environment and register them for classes remain unchanged. Programs addressing these types of student needs tend to produce little excitement among professionals and little professional recognition. Preparing to open a new residence hall on a campus garners a great deal of attention and support, but preparing to open that same hall for the tenth time ten years later is hardly noticed.

In the Introduction, providing essential institutional services was identified as one of the three overarching purposes of the student services enterprise. Yet programs engaged in that process and doing it well often do not receive the recognition associated with such essential work.

*Staff Stability.* Similarly, low turnover among staff over a five- to ten-year period may create the impression that a program could not possibly have the vitality that new staff members would offer. How could anyone stay with a student services program for five years and not be burned out? We believe it is possible, but only if careful attention is given to the difficulties surrounding effective program maintenance. When staff members in well-established programs are being evaluated, they often hear their superiors say, "Your program has been a strong one in the past, but what have you done *lately*?" The perception is that maintenance is not enough.

Needless to say, student services programs do occasionally lose their vitality and grow stagnant. Sometimes innovative programs are created for the wrong reasons. Just as university campuses often reflect the latest fashion trends, student services professionals sometimes get caught up in the desire to showcase the latest trends in the profession. Unlike faddish clothing, however, these programs are seldom put away even in the face of limited resources. Between the extremes of faddish innovations and outright programmatic stagnation lies a middle ground of effective program maintenance.

This chapter will define and illustrate the characteristics of effective program maintenance and identify some of the warning signs of programmatic stagnation. In order to illustrate the concepts to be presented, examples from student services programs at a variety of fictitious colleges and universities will be cited.

## Features of Effective Program Maintenance

Effective program maintenance requires attention to detail, constant monitoring, constant assessment, and the willingness to spend the time and energy on subtle program improvements. Student services programmers responsible for maintaining quality programs must be particularly attuned to the small changes occurring within the external and internal context of their program and must work to maintain their skills and competencies to respond to such changes.

*Monitoring Feedback.* In a well-maintained program, evaluative data are collected each year in order to monitor student response—no matter how long the program has been established or how well it has been received in the past. A number of good resources are available to assist in this task, including the work of George Kuh (1979). If a program has always been successful, complacency can set in and valuable feedback can be lost.

For example, the new student orientation program at Bledsoe University serves approximately 3,000 new students in a three-day residential summer program each year. For the past ten years students have been asked to complete an extensive evaluation on the last day of each session. As each year has passed, a few items on the questionnaire have been modified to reflect changes in the program, but the format of the questionnaire that asks about the overall effectiveness of the program has remained the same.  Each year the overwhelmingly positive feedback has been gratifying for the staff and the data have been utilized in planning programs for the next year. If these are the only uses made of the data, however, some of their potential has been lost. Subtle changes in the feedback over time may represent a more significant change in students' response to the program and may reveal aspects of the program that need attention. While the positive feedback at Bledsoe University was in the 94th to 96th percentile for several years, that figure has slipped for the past three years to the 90th or 92nd percentile. While such a small change in the feedback may or may not pinpoint any particular problem for the program, it should generate some further investigation. The staff member who examines the data each year without some reference to possible trends may form the impression that there has been little, if any, change in the evaluation, but the nuances in the data would have been overlooked.

Moreover, overwhelmingly positive feedback—for example, feedback above the 90th percentile—may turn attention away from a closer examination of the remaining unsatisfied minority. A closer scrutiny of the data might reveal that many of the unsatisfied students were older than average and may have felt awkward being thrown together with a group of eighteen-year-olds; or perhaps many of those 300 students were enrolled in the same academic program and their dissatisfaction is not with the program as a whole but with specific problems in the curriculum; or perhaps most of the dissatisfied students are transfers from senior colleges who already feel they understand the ways of college life but nevertheless chose to attend the program in order to learn more specific information about Bledsoe University. Neglect of this corrective feedback from even a small number of students will eliminate the opportunity to enhance the orientation program at Bledsoe University in some significant ways.

An additional form of feedback from students is attendance. Although attendance is certainly not the sole indicator of the quality of student services programs, it may demonstrate that the program offered is not meeting the needs or wants of students. Many times, however, student services programmers interpret a lack of attendance in other ways: The weather was bad. Publicity was poor. The location was hard to find. It was a bad day of the week. It was too early in the day. It was too late in the evening. It should have included food. There were too many other activities on campus that evening. Indeed, many of these factors may affect attendance, but if attendance is consistently low at programs or if the number of clients served by an agency continues to be small, then the feedback is clear.

Another way of gathering feedback from a student perspective is by means of student advisory committees. Although members of a student advisory committee may not currently be utilizing the service as clients, they offer a point of view that could otherwise be lost. Lott College is primarily a commuter institution, although a small portion of the student body lives in residence halls. The health center, located in the residence hall complex, conscientiously surveys those students who use its services to gain information about the quality of patient care and the availability of services. Unfortunately, most of the health center's clients are residential students because commuter students find it difficult to park anyplace nearby. An advisory group composed of a true cross section of the student body at Lott College might be able to point out the limited scope of the health center's services.

A third way of gathering feedback is to seek out faculty members, administrators, and student services colleagues who can offer an external perspective on the program. The perspective of a staff member from inside a student services program is limited by the very commitment and amount of effort it takes to operate the program. From the perspective of a program staff member, the constraints of scarce resources, the limited availability of staff, and the very inertia of a well-established program can be so tangible that it is difficult to see beyond to ways in which the program could be improved. Outsiders who have a basic understanding of the program objectives and operations can provide valuable insights about ways to increase program effectiveness with students. For example, in order to prepare student services staff members to better serve disabled students in a variety of agencies, faculty members from special education or rehabilitation counseling departments may be asked to share their expertise.

Student services colleagues may also be called upon for informal consultation. Staff members who handle walk-in clients in a variety of settings—including counseling center, study skills center, dean of students office, and career center—may find they all have difficulty accommodating students who are in a crisis because each agency is organized to serve students on a first-come, first-serve basis. Many times a clerical staff member is left to handle the situation. Consultation between agency staffs experiencing difficulty as well as discussions with the campus health service that has a successful walk-in service may benefit all programs.

*Ongoing Reconceptualization.* The initial conceptualization of a program usually includes an examination of the appropriate theoretical foundations, the specification of goals and objectives, and the articulation of how this particular program would be of benefit to students. Once the program is under way, this work of conceptualization is often set on the shelf and rapidly begins to collect dust. The demands upon staff to deliver the program usually overshadow the need for continual reexamination of the theory, conceptual models, and new research findings that might enhance the program efforts.

Staff members who work with parents' orientation programs, for example, may seldom stop to reexamine the conceptual bases of what they are doing, simply because the parents' needs for information and support seem so immediate. While those immediate needs may be met, an exploration of theories of adult development (Erikson, 1963; Levinson, 1978), new findings about single-parent households or the models used in parents' programs on other campuses might give staff members a new perspective on what they are doing and help them articulate more clearly the value of their efforts. Reexamination does not mean that the current successful program base should be abandoned. Instead the process serves to refine and expand the understanding of the original base in order to support program goals.

*Maintaining Accountability.* In a new student services program, the need for accountability is well recognized because staff members realize that the program will have to be justified. The resources devoted to the program are expected to yield specific, demonstrable results. Procedures for budgeting, allocation of staff time, and evaluation are usually established to account for the link between resources and results.

In a long-established program, those accountability systems may come to be neglected altogether or elaborated to such an extent that they become burdensome. Staff members, for example, may end up spending most of their time documenting what they do not have time to produce.

In a well-maintained program, the accountability system is neither lax nor excessively rigorous. One is often forced to choose from among the various options for documenting the use of resources. Consider, for example, a leadership development program. With regard to resources, one might choose to document the total value of materials and supplies, determine the dollar value of every hour of staff time devoted to the project, and then calculate the cost per student served. Yet the amount of staff time spent in documenting every moment devoted to the project and the resulting frustration may outweigh the benefit of such refined accountability procedures. Documentation instead might focus on results by concentrating on the subsequent achievements of participants in leadership training programs, administering pretests and posttests at all training events, or sending out trained process observers to assess the skill levels program participants display in the meetings of their various organizations. The zeal reflected in using every conceivable means of evaluation, however, may inadvertently derail the program's progress in actually achieving its goal.

*Reconnaissance.* In the learning skills center at Hargrave Community College, the staff has long offered extensive programs in speed-reading, note taking, and test anxiety reduction. The quality of the programs has been excellent and the staff has made a conscientious effort to keep the program up-to-date by incorporating the latest research findings and newest techniques. The programs were developed at a time when the student body at Hargrave was largely college-bound. The local economy has changed in such a way that the typical Hargrave student is now more vocationally oriented. The number of students the center serves has gradually declined, but staff members are at a loss to understand why. What the learning center staff has been missing is an effective effort in campus reconnaissance.

In the military, reconnaissance means an attempt to observe or survey the enemy's strength or position in order to gain a strategic advantage (Justice and Ragle, 1979). In a student services program, reconnaissance means the continuing effort to remain informed regarding the context of the program. Unless staff members take time to look up from their day-to-day routine, they often miss changes in the context that significantly affect the program. These changes may occur, for example, in the political climate of the institution, the composition of the student body, the needs that students present, or the availability of resources. In the learning skills center at Hargrave, the staff failed to detect the change in the composition of the student body and, as a result, continued to offer programs that no longer met student needs.

Reconnaissance on a campus means keeping one's ear to the ground in a variety of ways. Staff members can take the initiative by staying abreast of campus news, spending some time with students away from the office, maintaining social contacts with student services colleagues as well as other faculty and staff members, reading brochures and reports produced by other agencies, attending a variety of events on campus, and serving on institutional committees. In the case at hand, greater effort in information gathering by the learning center staff might have resulted in a deemphasis on reading for speed and a growth in reading for the detail needed to understand technical manuals.

*Maintaining Visibility.* Just as it is important to be aware of a changing campus context, a student services program must also keep the campus community aware of its current activities and events. No matter how many students a program serves or how well the program is working, an older program can easily be overshadowed by a newer or more innovative one.

To maintain visibility among student services colleagues and other administrators, staff members can circulate written reports about the work of the program, serve on institutional committees, maintain social contacts, invite university officials to attend events sponsored by their program, and initiate meetings with colleagues and other officials to discuss program problems and successes. These activities are similar to those discussed in relation to reconaissance, and each activity offers the opportunity for both gathering and sharing information.

To maintain visibility among students, staff members must continue to "market" their events and services. Student services professionals sometimes assume that students will automatically know that their programs exist. A corollary assumption is that knowledge of programs will breed use of services and participation in activities. For example, outreach programs have become prominent in counseling centers all over the country (Drum and Figler, 1973; Morrill, Oetting, and Hurst, 1974). Staff members in such agencies may forget that students who have never been exposed to a counseling center with a full range of services would have no way of knowing about them or assessing the potential value of such services in helping them cope with normal problems. Thus, it is not enough to distribute the outreach schedule every semester; more marketing is needed.

*Sustaining Coalitions.* Like the work of reconnaissance and maintaining visibility, the work of sustaining coalitions requires ongoing communication—in particular, with those agencies and programs to which one's own program is most closely related. Most programs are to some extent interdependent with other programs or agencies, and these liaison relationships have to be maintained. One type of interdependence involves those agencies with which a program works most closely in order to accomplish program goals and provide student services. A second type involves those agencies or university officials who provide political support for a program. In both of these ways, no program is an island (Barr and Keating, 1979).

For example, Berger College is a small residential college with an extensive recreational sports program. The intramural sports aspect of the program is organized primarily through the residence halls. Resident assistants play a key role in motivating students to participate, organizing teams, explaining rules, and keeping the programs competitive but friendly in tone. The funding for the program comes from student fees administered by the student government.

In order to maintain this program, staff members must attend to both types of coalitions. By collaborating with the housing staff in the training of resident assistants (RAs), the recreational sports staff can ensure that the RAs will be prepared to handle their responsibilities. However, the recreational sports staff may have to be flexible with regard to scheduling training for the RAs, since RAs have many other responsibilities. Likewise, by working with the officers of student government, programmers can try to ensure that they have ample opportunity to justify and defend the expense of the intramural program. The coalition with student government may require furnishing more information than staff ordinarily would prefer to share with student groups.

The give-and-take of sustaining these kinds of coalitions is not unlike maintaining a marriage. For the partnership to work, there must be a sense of shared purpose, an allowance for different points of view, a willingness to compromise, and strong two-way communication. Such coalitions cannot be taken for granted because the cast of characters is likely to change frequently. As staff members come and go, the new ones must be thoroughly oriented to the coalition relationship that binds the two agencies or groups.

*Nourishing Staff.* In innovative programs, staff morale is naturally high; but in a well-established program, staff members may feel a lack of opportunity to make a unique contribution or to grow professionally.

Chapter Nine reviews a number of specific staff development programs, including temporary assignments and interdepartmental staff exchanges. There are also methods to help staff continue to grow and develop within current job roles. One way to help staff members feel challenged is by sharing or trading tasks in such a way as to "stretch" their capabilities. Too often tasks are rigidly identified with an individual job description and the staff level. For example, the director of residence life at Kramer College has traditionally coordinated the selection and training of resident assistants. Specific tasks in the process were delegated to hall coordinators but the scope of these tasks was always limited. The hall coordinators and the director of residence life have worked together for approximately three years and for each of them the process has become routine. In an effort to stretch the capabilities of the hall coordinators, the director might delegate the coordination of selection to one and the coordination of training to the other and choose to share some of the more routine tasks himself. This arrangement might provide the hall coordinators the challenge they are seeking without taking unfair advantage of them.

When less experienced staff members undertake these kinds of tasks, however, it may be necessary for the director to invest additional time and resources in staff development; yet the benefits in morale make this worthwhile. Moreover, staff members in this situation must feel the freedom to fail. If they fear punishment for trying or even suggesting something that does not work, the change in their responsibilities will not yield benefits in either morale or productivity. The residence hall director in this situation may also incur some risk. In an innovative program, university officials can be very forgiving when something new is tried and does not work. But in a well-established program, the competency of the director is often suspect when what appears to be a routine undertaking goes awry. The director of residence life must be willing to accept this risk.

A second way to help staff members feel challenged is to avoid defining every detail of the tasks they are to perform. Every staff member has a right to expect some clarity in what is expected, but a supervisor should leave some margin for individual creativity and initiative. In the case of the director of residence life, for example, assigning one of the hall coordinators the task of RA selection may not achieve its intended purpose if the coordinator is told exactly how to do it. The director has to be willing for the coordinator to approach the task differently and has to be able to assign the project in terms of what would constitute a successful outcome. To illustrate, rather than expecting the coordinator to use the current applicant evaluation form, the director might specify that the selection process needs to include a written evaluation that is behaviorally oriented and is based upon criteria agreed upon by the staff. For every other aspect of the selection process, success would need to be defined in a similar way.

One common problem for supervisors in a well-established program is the tendency to take staff members for granted. It is easy for a supervisor to lavish praise upon a staff member who is just learning the various aspects of the job but to forget the staff member who has been doing that job well for a number of years. Praise and appreciation remain important no matter how many times the job has been done. Likewise, it is easy to remember to offer corrective feedback to a new staff member but to neglect to offer that feedback to the more experienced staff member. If feedback is offered in a respectful way, it can be accepted by even the most experienced employee.

## Program Adjustments

At the beginning of this chapter, the work of program maintenance was compared to the grimy work of automotive and other kinds of maintenance; but to many individuals, working on a car can be intrinsically motivating and enjoyable. Tinkering with the adjustment of the carburetor or the timing, installing more efficient shock absorbers, customizing the interior, or grinding the valves do not imply that anything on the car is broken, but merely that with a few adjustments the car may run more smoothly or be more comfortable. Such is the case with well-maintained programs. Constant tinkering provides an opportunity to enhance what is already working satisfactorily.

*Attention to Detail.* Tinkering may mean giving attention to the mundane details of a student services program. For example, the placement service in the college of business at Gardenview University serves hundreds of employers and approximately 2,000 graduating seniors each year. The placement service keeps resumés on file and provides assistance to students preparing for interviews. The competition for interview slots is keen, and the logistics of getting the right resumé to the right recruiter and sufficient information about each company to the prospective employee have become quite complicated. On the whole, the operation of the placement service is going smoothly, but a little tinkering could provide some improvements, particularly in the area of interview sign-up.

In the past, interview times have been assigned on a first-come, first-serve basis, but this has resulted in long lines and, on occasion, students camping out overnight to be first in line. An alternative procedure might be to give each qualified student 500 points per week with which to bid for interview slots. Students would then be forced to prioritize among prospective employers but would increase their chances of interviewing with the companies in which they are most interested. The long lines and the resulting loss of sleep and study time would be eliminated. It is also possible that adjusting other relatively routine aspects of the program such as the filing system for resumés, arrangement of physical space, or the hours of operation might yield similar benefits.

*Employing New Techniques.* Sometimes tinkering involves using new techniques. In helping students prepare for interviews, for example, the placement service might choose to utilize such techniques as role playing, videotaping interviews for feedback, or training students as interviewers so that they can better understand the corporate interviewer's perspective. Although these techniques are not necessarily new, they might be of some benefit to the students and ultimately the placement program.

*Using Technology.* A third form of tinkering may involve the application of computer technology to student services programs. In many cases, this requires additional resources, but the benefits to students may be enormous. At the Gardenview University placement service, for example, computer technology might be used to enhance the way in which candidate information is supplied to employers and vice versa. A computer system could be set up to give an employer lists of qualified applicants, depending upon the qualifications the company is seeking. Lists could be generated to include all finance majors with a 3.0 or better grade point average (GPA), all finance majors who were involved in at least one campus activity, all marketing and management majors who are seeking employment in a particular city, and so forth. For the students, lists could be generated to include all the companies in a particular state willing to interview accounting majors for management positions, all manufacturing companies willing to consider finance majors with a given GPA, and so forth. The possibilities are endless.

Spending the time and energy on tinkering with or adjusting the program is a necessity for a well-maintained program. The program that embraces new ideas, techniques, and technology in a positive manner will not stagnate.

## Warning Signs of Program Stagnation

Genuine programmatic stagnation is difficult to detect. There are a few objective indicators that a program has grown stagnant, but they are fairly gross measures. A loss of attendance, negative feedback from students, high staff turnover, or absenteeism among staff may be signs of programmatic stagnation but may also indicate other problems. High staff turnover, for example, may be a sign of poor supervision rather than an indicator that the program itself is in trouble. Careful attention should be given to the gross indicators of program stagnation and appropriate corrective measures should be designed and introduced if possible.

Equal attention should be given to the more subtle signs of program stagnation evidenced most often by staff attitudes and perceptions of their role and function. For example, have you ever heard yourself or student service colleagues say: "This program has been the same for so long. Let's do something to make it different." On the surface such a comment would seem to indicate an openness to change, but it may actually be a sign of stagnation. Staff members may be so hungry for professional stimulation that change for change's sake seems appealing. In this situation, proposed changes are not based upon refinements in the basic mission or goal of the program. The prospect of small-scale improvement is not appealing because the desire is for a more drastic change.

Comments such as "if things are going well in my program, people will notice; I shouldn't have to tell them" may be a sign of stagnation, for they indicate a complacency about keeping one's program visible. One cannot assume that people will notice what a program is achieving, and taking the initiative to tell people about the program is not necessarily the same as "tooting your own horn" about your individual accomplishments.

A third warning sign is flashed when you hear "if people on my campus are doing something I should know about, it is their responsibility to tell me." Attempting to remain oblivious to changes that may be occurring in the campus context usually indicates a loss of interest in adapting one's program to address new circumstances. The work of reconnaissance is not so laborious that it should elicit this reaction.

Aversion to continued evaluation is another subtle sign of program stagnation. Staff members in a stagnant program can usually think of many reasons to discontinue evaluation. One of the most popular is the thought that some programs do not need to be evaluated because the program will continue regardless of what the feedback says. For example, a campus judicial service may elude evaluation because the function seems so basic, but feedback from accused students about the fairness of the process and counseling skills of staff members might be helpful in maintaining the program's viability.

Unwillingness to assess new ideas may be detected in such statements as "I hear about new ideas at conventions, but I know none of them would work on my campus." Sometimes we associate new ideas with whole new programs and forget that new ideas may include small ideas as well. While it may be true that the programs one hears about at conventions could not be transplanted just as they are to your campus, exposure to these programs should stimulate some ideas about ways in which one's own program might be modified.

Lack of attention to training of new staff also indicates program stagnation. One positive aspect of intentional and thorough training of new staff is that it forces the supervisor to articulate clearly what the program does and why. If you expect the new staff member to make a unique contribution to the program and not merely to be a cog in the program machine, it is important that he or she understands both the theoretical underpinnings and the practical aspects of the program.

If you hear "I really think I have my job under control now—maybe I'll look for other ways to get involved on campus," be alert. An eagerness among staff members to reach out and expand their campus contacts may be beneficial in maintaining visibility and reconnaissance for the program. Yet, taken to extremes, this eagerness to get beyond one's own program may mask simple boredom. The program may not provide sufficient stimulation to hold the staff member's attention.

Finally, the most obvious stagnation sign is expressed in the following view: "The program is going well as it is. Why take chances with change?" As has already been noted, a well-maintained program involves some acceptance of risk. This statement, however, may come not only from colleagues within your program but also from those in interrelated programs. To avoid stagnation, it is necessary to overcome this resistance without disrupting the coalitions that have been carefully built to support the program.

Although hearing yourself or a colleague say one or more

of these things may be a warning sign of programmatic stagnation, it is not necessarily so. It may, however, prompt you to focus appropriate attention on aspects of the program that need improvement.

## Summary

This chapter has attempted both to identify the characteristics of a well-maintained program and some of the warning signs of stagnation. A well-maintained program is not based on myths such as the needs always change, staff stability is a sign of laziness, and innovation must be embraced for vitality to continue. Well-maintained programs instead monitor feedback, expand the conceptual base, maintain accountability, assess the context, maintain coalitions and visibility, and nourish staff. Well-maintained programs require attention to detail, willingness to risk, and willingness to use technology if appropriate. In its own way, the challenge of effectively maintaining a student services program is as great as the task of innovation. With initiative, persistence, and enthusiasm, the rewards of program maintenance can be even greater.

## References

Barr, M. J., and Keating, L. A. "No Program Is an Island." In M. J. Barr and L. A. Keating (Eds.), *New Directions for Student Services: Establishing Effective Programs,* no. 7. San Francisco: Jossey-Bass, 1979.

Drum, D. J., and Figler, H. E. "Achieving Total Outreach Potential: A Seven-Dimension Model." *Impact,* 1973, *3* (2), 5-17.

Erikson, E. *Childhood and Society.* (2nd ed.) New York: Norton, 1963.

Harway, M. "Management Style and Philosophy of the Student Personnel Administrator." *Journal of College Student Personnel,* 1977, 18 (4), 255-262.

Justice, S. J., and Ragle, J. D. "Once You've Got It, How Do You Keep It?" In M. J. Barr and L. A. Keating (Eds.), *New Directions for Student Services: Establishing Effective Programs,* no. 7. San Francisco: Jossey-Bass, 1979.

Kuh, G. (Ed.). *Evaluation in Student Affairs.* Cincinnati, Ohio: American College Personnel Association Media Publication, 1979.

Levinson, D. *Season of a Man's Life.* New York: Knopf, 1978.

Morrill, W. H., Oetting, E. R., and Hurst, J. C. "Dimensions of Counselor Functioning." *Personnel and Guidance Journal,* 1974, *52* (6), 354-359.

# 11

Arthur Sandeen

❧ ❧ ❧ ❧ ❧ ❧ ❧ ❧ ❧ ❧ ❧ ❧ ❧

# Assessing
# Program Utility
# over Time

One of the ironies of the 1980s in student services is that the best-trained staff in the profession's history have arrived at a time when institutional resources are very scarce. With the exception of computer science, medicine, accounting, and some engineering fields, this problem has been echoed in most academic disciplines as well. George Bonham (1983) has referred to the current period as the "fallow years." Whatever name is attached to this decade, the contrasts between it and the booming 1960s and early 1970s in higher education have been made so frequently that they do not need repeating here.

Large numbers of young professionals currently serving in student services positions bring a new sophistication to their work. Knowledgeable about human development and organizational theory, they have expectations that frequently exceed the resources available to them. This has often resulted in discouragement and frustration, and in some cases, in decisions to

252

leave higher education. In the current climate, there is less and less naiveté among bright, young scholars in higher education, and those in student services are no exception.

Those who have the primary responsibility of delivering effective student services programs for their institutions face increased pressure to ensure that the limited resources are used effectively. The drive for accountability has been widely discussed in recent years. Often neglected in these discussions have been the conflicting publics to which student services programs are frequently directed. Meeting the needs of one group may be vigorously opposed by those who do not share the political, religious, or economic views of the group being served. Moreover, the criticism comes from such diverse groups as students, community organizations, board members, faculty, parents, or legislators. Some student services administrators react by avoiding programs that may invite objections, and in the process fail to fulfill their educational obligations to the institution and to the profession. In the 1980s, however, such vigorous public scrutiny is applied to almost all institutional programs and even the most bland do not escape criticism.

The student services leader in this decade is also faced with sharply increased expectations on the part of students, their families, and the community. While the parental or custodial role in its traditional context is largely gone, the number and quality of various institutional services expected by various publics have risen significantly in recent years. Consumerism in all its forms is a reality on campus and is especially reflected in student services areas such as admissions, housing, food services, financial aid, and placement. Prospective students and their parents now shop for institutions in the same way they may shop for an automobile or an insurance policy. They are seeking the best return for their investment, and with their educational purchase, they expect the promised services to be delivered.

The current financial climate in higher education forces the effective chief student services administrators to engage in daily competition for institutional resources. Walker (1979) suggests that university resources are distributed not in strict conformity to an overriding management philosophy but as a result of bargaining in which conflicting interests compete with one another and trades are made. Student services programs that attempted to isolate themselves from academic affairs or business affairs were seldom effective in years past. Now, such isolation is impossible. Increased competition for institutional resources has forced student services administrators to sell their programs to others not familiar with and sometimes skeptical of their language, educational goals, and style. Able student services leaders must become more aware of other institutional programs, exert influence on these programs, and demonstrate the benefits gained from student services activities.

Another factor compelling effective use of available resources is the increased emphasis upon individuality. The drive in years past has been upon a "melting pot" mentality. Now each ethnic, political, religious, academic, or social group strives to promote and retain its special character. This fact of contemporary American life has significant implications for student services programs and policies. The goals are more complex and the potential for conflict is greater. Thus the need for sensitive and thoughtful planning increases.

This chapter will address four major questions regarding effective resource utilization. The questions, discussed from the perspective of a chief student services administrator, are as follows:

1.  What are the indications that a program is not meeting its goals?
2.  What techniques can be used to force program modification if efforts are not meeting goals?
3.  What skills in resource management are necessary for successful student services programs?
4.  What pressures may arise when a program is terminated, and how should these pressures be addressed?

## Diagnosing the Problem

A sensitive chief student services administrator receives many indications about the effectiveness of programs simply by listening and observing. For example, a special orientation program designed for entering students with poor academic preparation is likely to attract considerable attention from faculty, academic administrators, student services staff, and others. Some faculty and staff may be determined to see such a program fail, as they feel it is a waste of institutional resources. They may go out of their way to inform the chief student services officer of their views, various shortcomings they have observed, and the "bleeding heart" attitude of the program director. The program director, aware of such criticism, tries even harder to prove the value of the program. There may also be a vocal group of supporters so strongly committed to the program that they label as elitists any who question its worth. Moreover, they publicly state that the institution needs a strong and courageous student services officer who will stand up for what is right for the college. The chief student services officer who knows the literature, has consulted with colleagues on other campuses about their experiences with similar efforts, and has stayed relatively close to students in the program will not be misled by such biased incantations. Relying exclusively upon the weekly reports of the director will likely result in a one-sided assessment of the program's success. Informal personal observations and conversations with participants provide understandings and insights not otherwise available. Using a predetermined evaluation instrument is, of course, an obvious way to gain another indication of whether the program is meeting its goals. Objective data can also be collected in a short period of time to assess the impact of the program on students' academic success.

It is often difficult for those who have designed and implemented programs to effectively evaluate those programs. Despite efforts to achieve a certain professional detachment, there is an understandable ego involvement that sometimes takes precedence over objective assessment. This is especially true with new or younger staff members who may be determined to demonstrate their worth to the institution, to their colleagues, or to students. More experienced student services staff may also be defensive and protective of programs they have initiated. They may display ownership behavior regarding a certain campus or student territory that they have staked out. Additionally, they may feel that their years of experience should make their efforts immune to criticism or questions from others. Despite these difficulties, it is usually not advisable to exclude those responsible for developing and implementing programs from program assessment efforts.

Effective program planning requires the chief student services officer to have a clear understanding with those responsible for the program regarding this method of program assessment, who will conduct it, and when it will be done. With highly visible programs, it is often beneficial to invite a credible and objective group of faculty, students, or outside consultants to serve as an advisory board. This group must be constituted in such a way that its members remain independent in their judgments. If the chief student services officer simply invites well-known friends of the program to serve the board, the group will be viewed by skeptics as nothing more than an in-house cheerleading organization. Given the opportunity, however, an independent advisory group can frequently identify shortcomings and problems that others miss and may be the student services leader's most effective assessment tool.

Even when clearly formulated plans and goals exist, programs may still fail to meet their purposes. For example, an institution seeking additional freshmen to solve an underenrollment problem may initiate a new program of no-need academic scholarships. Lack of response from prospective students is an obvious indication that this particular program approach was not effective. Similarly, a counseling center, in an effort to serve the special needs of Hispanic students, begins a program of open hours at the center, during which time these students can visit a counselor without making an appointment. Again, simple lack of response on the part of students provides a clear indication that the program goal is not being met.

In most cases, indications of program problems are not so obvious. Moreover, the participation of large numbers of students in a program does not necessarily signify either that the program is successful or that it is meeting its goals. Substantial numbers of students may respond positively to an invitation to attend a weekend leadership development retreat, but they may not be the particular kinds of students to which the program was directed. Or, the execution of the program may be faulty, due to the poor planning of staff, inadequate organization, or underdeveloped skills of the workshop leaders. The student services administrator in such cases may receive conflicting indications of the program's success and most likely will need to rely upon his own notion of program standards in that particular field. To rely exclusively upon responses of student participants or staff observations is usually insufficient.

While student feedback can be an important indication of program effectiveness, it can also be very misleading. Its obvious weakness is that it is severely limited by what those students may happen to know or what they have experienced. For example, students living in traditional residence halls were surveyed to ascertain their reaction to living in some new residence halls that would include classrooms, faculty offices, laboratories, and libraries. The overwhelming response from these students was negative, as they claimed such facilities would be an invasion of their own living space. The institution decided to build the new facilities anyway, and after only one year of occupancy, over 90 percent of the students reported that they enjoyed the halls. In fact, the new facilities became the most popular halls on the campus.

Another institution that was constructing a large performing arts theater on its campus surveyed undergraduate interest in classical concerts, ballet, and opera. The survey results confirmed the biases of most of the staff; that is, the students indicated little enthusiasm for such a program. However, in the first year of operation, student demand for tickets became very heavy, and student access to these classical events became a controversial campus issue. Again, this was a case of relying too heavily upon "student opinion" as an indication of likely student participation.

What does this mean for the chief student services administrator? No case is being made for autocracy or disdain for student or staff opinion. Nor is one being made for a coy sort of political maneuvering, so as to satisfy all groups involved, which is impossible anyway. The effective chief student services administrator will look for indications of growth in students who participate in programs, do the necessary professional homework, and know what excellence in programs (both content and process) is all about. She will be sensitive enough to the campus environment to understand that a small, quiet program may grow rapidly in future years; she will be strong enough to discontinue programs that are of poor quality, that cannot be afforded, or that are an unproductive use of staff time. She will be a diplomatic defender of programs that receive negative attention from the media, the campus president, or other critics, when the program deserves defending; and she will be sensitive to the delicate needs of other student services staff whose professional lives and egos are closely identified with "their" programs. Most important, it is the responsibility of the chief student services administrator to insist that the primary indicators of educational programs be student growth and development.

## Program Modification Techniques

Most staff associated with the development of a program are not very enthusiastic about external efforts to modify it. Nevertheless, this is necessary from time to time, especially if an institution is serious about its efforts to conduct effective educational programs with its limited resources. The disappointment and frustration felt by staff who have their program modified is a more attractive alternative than seeing the education of students shortchanged by mediocre programs. This, of course, is the responsibility of the chief student services administrator. When program modifications are indicated, the process used by the student services leader to achieve change may be as important as the content of the change itself.

*Get Involved.* For example, a staff member in the placement bureau has conducted a career day for prospective teachers each semester for the past two years. The response and participation from students and area school boards has been quite low. This costly, ineffective program can be terminated by the chief student services administrator, despite the insistence of the programmer that its future is bound to be positive. Simply informing the staff member in charge of the program that it should be discontinued will accomplish that objective but may very likely affect the future efforts of that staff member as well. A more effective technique would be to conduct a joint evaluation of the program with the staff member. Contacts can be made with students and school boards to determine why they did not participate and to review the planning and publicity for the program. This direct, positive participation by the supervising administrator is more likely to result in better future efforts.

But what if there is resistance to change? What if a program has been in existence for many years and staff feel that the program is functioning effectively? What if there are inadequate resources to continue to support the program? How can the chief student services administrator force modification in a program when this becomes necessary?

*Shift Program Responsibility.* One obvious way to force program modification is to shift administrative responsibility. For example, the student services administrator is aware of the advances made in recent years in outdoor recreation programs for students. Yet the campus intramural sports director is resistant to this development, and so the campus program has not kept pace with other institutions. A practical solution is found by the student services administrator by assigning responsibility for the outdoor program to the student union director, who is very enthusiastic about the opportunity. It can be argued, of course, that this is not the ideal way to achieve the goal, but it often gets the job done. Not infrequently, however, the solution is temporary, because the program is now split and the two parts inevitably become competitive with one another. Eventually, another solution must be found.

Another avenue for shifting responsibility is illustrated by the high cost of the inpatient services of the student health service. An evaluation indicates that an average of only two of the eighteen available beds are occupied. Moreover, students are complaining loudly about the high level of the health fee and are questioning what they receive for the fee. The medical staff is very protective of the inpatient beds, insisting that they are an essential service on a residential campus. The local hospital is willing to enter into a contract whereby it will guarantee to provide at least four beds per night to the college's students for a fee that is only 40 percent of the current inpatient service. This alternative is an effective technique that shifts responsibility for the program, retains the service, and reduces the cost of the program as well.

*Move the People.* Of course, not all problems result in such happy solutions for all concerned. The most distasteful technique to force program modification is to terminate a staff member and replace that person with another. If the staff member is not performing or simply does not have the training or skills necessary to achieve the program results, it is the responsibility of the chief student services administrator to take such action. Being in the "people business," student services administrators probably delay such action too long, either hoping for change, or somehow ignoring the obvious solution to the problem. A mediocre program can be turned around by a new and creative person, and such action may be the most responsible and effective decision the student services leader can take.

In some institutions, some individual staff have been permitted to "do their own thing" and conduct programs on isolated themes for small groups of students. This may cause a very serious problem for the administrator who knows that the institution cannot afford the luxury of individual staff members establishing their own program agendas. For example, a senior staff member in the student development center spends a large percentage of her time on a program she developed for handicapped veteran students. It is well received, and the staff member meets frequently with the fifteen students who participate in the support program. However, the most pressing need for the center is to provide academic and career advising services to all 2,500 freshmen at the college, and this staff member spends less than 10 percent of her time on this. The chief student services administrator may have to force a program change in this situation by assigning the staff member to the academic advising program, where the greatest need lies. Moving staff to new assignments must be done in a way that respects their professional pride. This can be accomplished by consulting with them before and after the move and by joint exploration of the new program alternatives. Demonstrating a commitment to their continuing professional growth is also likely to assist staff who have been moved to new responsibilities.

Quite often, a program may benefit if the staff responsible for it are granted the opportunity to examine other such programs on similar campuses or at national conferences and seminars. If there is resistance on the part of staff to participate in such experiences, the chief student services administrator can require it, although this would be unusual. Even required professional development can provide staff with new ideas and a new perspective and enthusiasm. Canon (1980) argues that student services staff have an obligation to themselves and to their clientele to actively engage in their own professional growth.

*Change the Plan.* A program may be essential to an institution, but there is inadequate support from regular institutional resources for it. The pressure on student financial aid offices in recent years has been very high, yet there have rarely been sufficient resources to handle the demand for timely delivery and personal financial counseling for students. To force a program modification in such circumstances, the chief student services administrator may institute a financial aid application fee to increase the financial resources for the office. Or support dollars and staff may be shifted from another student services office to financial aid in order to meet the need. Yet another technique would be to seek special state legislation for earmarked support for student aid delivery. In the same manner, alumni may be seeking more assistance from the placement office, but the staff is already overloaded with the job needs of undergraduates. A program modification here can be achieved by charging the alumni a user fee sufficient to provide the service.

A program may be functioning reasonably well, but the chief student services officer has seen several other more effective programs and knows that some improvements must be made. For example, the undergraduate resident assistants in the residence halls may not have really changed their role much over the past ten years, and the prestige of the position on campus may have declined. The chief student services administrator feels that the program can be improved by increasing their salary, strengthening and broadening the selection process, augmenting the training effort, and developing some regular, campus-wide recognition for these students. Each of these program modifications may have to be "forced" upon the housing director, who may be defensive about this long-standing program. To force such changes, the most effective student services leader will work closely with the staff in designing, implementing, and evaluating changes. If the results can demonstrate the benefits of these changes, the administrator's credibility and effectiveness with the staff will be enhanced.

In a similar situation, the campus registration program may be years out-of-date because the director has not developed his own skills in data processing and computer-assisted techniques. The results are high costs of personnel, a bulky record system, and complaints from students and faculty. While the quickest way to achieve program modification would be to terminate the director, the chief student services administrator does not want to do this and is convinced that there will be more benefits for the institution if the director can be convinced to learn these essential skills. A solution is found by the student services leader, who arranges a six-month sabbatical for the director, who will use this time to enroll in a special off-campus instructional program in data processing. While reluctant at first, the director returns to his job, eager and confident about instituting the needed changes. A program modification has been effected, and there is a minimal amount of disruption.

Johnson and Foxley (1980) argue that with declining resources, the manager—the chief student services administrator—must ensure the most effective use of staff time. With limited institutional resources, and with vastly increased information and knowledge available about the developmental needs of students, program planning and modification are essential. No matter what technique is used to stimulate program modification, it is the responsibility of the chief student services administrator to establish a campus-wide educational program that most effectively meets the institution's goals within available resources.

## Resource Management Skills

Administrators in higher education have responsibility for managing the basic resources of people, space, and dollars. The activities of the chief student services administrator are no longer concerned exclusively with the psychological or student conduct problems of undergraduates. In the 1980s, the responsibilities of that administrator have increased and may range from counseling and intercollegiate athletics to student financial aid and the campus bus system. Thus, the skills needed for effective resource management have also increased.

*Staff Resources.* Perhaps the most valuable skill needed for effective resource management is the ability to hire talented and dedicated staff. With staff turnover so infrequent in the 1980s compared with fifteen years ago and with very few new positions being established, great care and sensitivity must be given to the hiring process (Keller, 1983). The opportunities for institutions to improve their student services program by hiring new staff have never been greater than at present. There are substantial numbers of well-trained professionals available throughout the country.

Matching the talents of the applicant to the needs of the position in order to achieve the optimal fit is a difficult task. In recent years, it has become common practice to establish campus- (or community-) wide search and screen committees to aid in the selection process. Often, these committees have served the affirmative action needs of institutions well and have encouraged a more open and democratic approach to the hiring process. However, at times such committees have been composed of persons not well informed about the needs of the open position, or even about the nature of student services work itself. In such cases, persons recommended for the position may not be well suited for it and, if hired, will not serve the needs of the institution effectively. The chief student services administrator has the responsibility to avoid such problems, and the appointment of persons to search committees is a critical part of the successful effort to hire talented staff. Clear, written instructions should be provided to each member of the search committee, and their responsibilities, time schedule, and limitations should be thoroughly explained. Adequate flexibility in the hiring process must be retained by the chief student services administrator, so that he may accept or reject the committee's recommendations at any step of the process, and this should be clearly understood in advance. After all, the administrator in charge will be held accountable for the newly hired staff member's performance or lack of it, not the committee. There is a balance, of course, that must be sought by the chief student services administrator. A committee that is composed only of persons who are friendly to the administrator's point of view will have low credibility and most likely will not represent the diverse needs of the campus. Finally, the use of a committee should never be allowed to become an end in itself; it can be an effective aid to the person responsible for the hiring decision, if careful planning is done.

Another skill that is needed in the successful hiring of staff is the ability to accurately define the responsibilities of the job. More hiring mistakes result from this failure than any other. If an institution fails to be clear in the expectations it has for a new staff member, the result is usually confusion, frustration, and poor performance. It also results in staff leaving their positions early because what they were expected to do on the job turned out to be something quite different from what they were led to believe during the hiring process. Clearly written position descriptions are necessary but sometimes not sufficient to ensure understanding. The hiring administrator should discuss the job expectations in detail with each applicant before any offer is extended.

Hiring the right staff for the job is very important; using the available staff on the campus is also very important in successful resource management. The chief student services administrator, of course, has the responsibility to use all her available human resources in the best ways possible to meet the institution's needs. This requires the skill to establish priorities and to decide that certain functions need more staff support than others. For example, there may be six full-time staff in the very busy student activities office, but as enrollment is declining, the most pressing need is for more staff to visit high schools and recruit new students. Thus, the chief student services administrator may need to reassign three of the student activities staff to this admissions function. In this age of specialization, it may be argued that staff expert in one area are not well suited for work in another aspect of student services, and indeed this may be the case. Some staff may thus have to be terminated, and those with more specific training hired. However, through an effective staff development program, student services staff can become knowledgeable and skilled in aspects of the total program. Both the individual staff and the institution will benefit from such retraining.

While many staff have highly developed skills in one area, it is not at all unusual in the 1980s for staff to have a wide variety of skills and experiences. Not only are these staff very valuable to their institutions but they are also in demand by others. Student services staff working on small, residential campuses have divided their time among placement, orientation, financial aid, admissions, student conduct, and housing for many years. Such staff are often more able to adjust to shifting institutional priorities and problems than their more specialized colleagues on larger campuses.

The skillful student services administrator can extend the available resources by the use of part-time staff, paraprofessionals, community support personnel, and volunteers. On many campuses, a large proportion of the student services function is carried on by such people, and the success of the entire program depends upon them. The following examples illustrate various ways staff resources can be extended. The doctoral-level counseling psychologist in the counseling center can extend her influence and program several times by use of graduate interns, residence hall volunteers, and paraprofessional group trainers for special sessions. The director of the international student program can greatly extend the impact of his program by recruiting volunteer host families, churches, and other community support groups. The coordinator of academic advising can improve the quality of that program by inviting retired faculty to spend a few hours per week as "mentors" for new freshmen. The admissions director can expand the impact of the recruiting program by training some upperclass students to speak at high schools around the state and at alumni gatherings. In each of these examples, the costs to the institutions are minimal, and the opportunities to increase the human resources available are extensive. The chief student services administrator must ensure that part-time volunteer staff are given effective supervision by a qualified professional. Without vigorous and regular supervision and evaluation, programs may quickly become sloppy, misdirected, and inefficient (Winston, Mendenhall, and Miller, 1983).

With the difficult problems facing higher education in the 1980s, the chief student services administrator will have to make some unpleasant choices and decisions in resource management. Most of the time, this involves people, since more than 80 percent of most student services budgets consists of personnel support. When changes have been made, every effort must be made to minimize disruption so that the quality of the division's work does not suffer. While no such change is easy, the skillful chief student services administrator will consult widely with staff and involve as many of them as possible in the decision-making process. If priorities and problems are reviewed in an open atmosphere of trust, then it is far more likely that even unpleasant decisions will be accepted. Just as important, the chief student services administrator will have demonstrated genuine concern for the staff and their futures by using a process that encourages frank discussion of problems and priorities.

*Fiscal Resources.* The management of fiscal resources requires a variety of administrative skills. The student services leader must clearly articulate and persuasively argue the goals of the total student services effort. This task must be carried out with an audience that is often unfamiliar and perhaps unsympathetic with the student services function. In most cases, persons representing student services in such discussions will do well to avoid the use of professional jargon. At best, this jargon is highly suspect by outsiders, and it often results in outright hostility. The skillful student services administrator will be successful in securing fiscal resources for the division to the extent that the proposed programs are likely to improve or enhance the success of the institution and its goals. The student services leader must demonstrate that the allocation of dollars will result in better service, increased retention, or more effective education. In the 1980s, the chief student services leader is competing with other major academic and administrative officers of the institution for scarce dollars, and a forceful, clearly stated, jargon-free proposal has the best chance of survival.

The effective use of clearly presented data may enhance the skillful student services leader's efforts to secure resource dollars. An argument for a particular program can be much more persuasive if real data can be presented that support effective results. A proposal to hire three additional financial aid staff becomes more attractive when data are presented that indicate that two additional staff will enable the admissions office to make actual offers of financial aid packets to students one month earlier. This argument, which can be tied to an improved enrollment picture, will generally be better received than one that focuses on "improving counseling opportunities." The use of data to support program proposals for increased dollars is essential but does not guarantee support. Others in the competition also have good data, and there are finite resources available.

Resources can often be secured by entering into agreements with academic departments, student organizations, or community agencies. This approach usually requires some adjustment and compromise in the content of the program. However, it can enhance the attractiveness of the proposal because the shared responsibility may enable the institution to conduct the program for fewer dollars. The chief student services administrator of the 1980s may find that such arrangements are not only attractive but necessary for the survival of certain programs.

Another skill in fiscal resource management that has become increasingly important in recent years is the solicitation of funds from outside sources for program support. Long a standard operating procedure in many academic disciplines, it is now a common practice in student services as well. A chief student services officer who relies exclusively upon the funds that can be secured from the regular institutional operating budget is unlikely to be providing effective leadership. While there are limits and guidelines that should be applied to efforts to seek outside support dollars, professional staff in student services may be pleasantly surprised with their efforts in this area. A technique that can be used by the chief student services administrator in budget hearings with staff is to insist that program proposals include efforts to secure outside support for their programs. This can encourage a more self-reliant and creative posture on the part of those seeking support and, when successful, can greatly extend institutional programs. It may also encourage student services staff to collaborate more often with faculty colleagues in developing program proposals that have a potential for broad impact.

Some chief student services administrators have found that the offer of incentives to staff can stimulate creative activity and can make it more likely that they may secure funds on their own. For example, if an alcohol abuse prevention program cannot be supported in full, the chief student services officer may offer to fund half if the staff can secure the other dollars from private sources. Such an approach may challenge staff to explore other funding options.

*Space Resources.* The management of space is very important to the success of student services programs. The student services administrator competes with other administrators for office space, programming areas, counseling space, or space for recreational activities. As the institution understandably views classroom or laboratory space as its first priority, student services leaders often start at a disadvantage with academic administrators. For example, the chief student services administrator may have excellent data to support the argument that a new building is needed to house the major student services functions, thus serving students more efficiently. However, there are limited capital support dollars available, and the institution opts to construct a new computer science facility. As a result, many student services leaders have found that their best approach is to join with other campus groups, usually academic or administrative departments, in proposals to secure additional space.

In some institutions, space is allocated on the basis of formulas that relate primarily to faculty-student ratios or to total student credit hours. Unless some change is made in the basic formula, space for the student services function may rarely be generated. It is the responsibility of the chief student services administrator to point out these problems and to urge a revision of the formula to reflect the space needs of the student services function.

Imaginative student services leaders are often on the cutting edge of change and may introduce programs that are not initially received with much enthusiasm. Such reactions may make it very unlikely that any campus space will be provided for the program. This was often the case when childcare programs were begun several years ago. Space was initially secured in such places as churches, residence halls, or community support facilities. After a few years of demonstrated effective service, it was easier to locate more acceptable facilities. Such a strategy may be necessary if innovative programs are to be initiated; later they can be housed in on-campus facilities.

Occasionally, student leaders and student organizations may offer their support for the space needs of student services. While such offers may be tempting, caution should be exercised in accepting them. Student support should not be sought for financial or political reasons within the institution. This tactic may be resented by other administrators and can lead to negative consequences such as accusations of purposeful manipulation.

Resources for people, dollars, and space do not come easily, and substantial efforts and skills are required to secure and retain them. The chief student services administrator must be a statesperson—sensitive to the needs of staff, expert in evaluation, creative in fiscal management, and persuasive in presenting resource management ideas.

## Program Termination

In the 1980s, many programs will be reduced or terminated because of lack of funds. One way to help staff understand this reality is to involve them in creative efforts to secure outside funds, thus increasing their autonomy. The leadership must be taken by the chief student services administrator, and joint efforts to solve the problem can go a long way in building confidence and staff morale.

With limited resources and changing needs, it is inevitable that some programs will be discontinued. A vigorous evaluation effort will indicate that some programs should be terminated, and financial considerations will necessitate some reductions as well. Because these terminated programs served the needs of various groups, it is likely that real pressures may be placed upon the student services staff by those who have benefited from them. Questions, criticisms, and demands may come from students, parents, faculty, other student services staff, community members, board of trustees members, or legislators. Moreover, persons in charge of terminated programs may have professional objections of their own regarding the problems created by program termination. How can these situations be handled so that program disruptions and pressures on staff are minimized?

*Staff Issues.* A difficult concept for new staff to learn is to maintain a healthy professional distance from a program for which they are responsible. Too much ego involvement blurs one's ability to evaluate the program's effectiveness and often gets in the way of realistic efforts to change it. When a program must be terminated, it does not have to be received as a personal failure by the responsible programmer, and a maturing professional person will understand this. It is certainly understandable, even desirable, for staff to argue vigorously for the survival of their programs. But when a decision is made, the professional staff member must move on to other ideas and efforts.

Not all pressures arising from program termination can be handled so easily. If criticism becomes intense, some staff will need support and assistance. Such pressures are not uncommon, and some staff can handle it better than others. Thomas (1979) argues that a critical management responsibility is consideration for the staff involved in a terminated program. They need attention and support. Chief student services administrators should be experts in handling criticism, and at times they will need to intercept this for some of their staff. For example, when a remedial reading program was terminated, the criticisms and demands from former users became so intense that the former coordinator of the program decided that he was going to leave the profession. The chief student services officer not only counseled this staff member but publicly supported him, assuring the critics that she, not the program coordinator, was responsible for the termination.

In many cases, the person in charge of the eliminated program must be reassigned to another area of responsibility. This can cause great pressures, of course, and the chief student services administrator should make every effort to minimize them. The department that inherits a newly reassigned staff member may not be overly enthusiastic about the opportunity. The chief student services administrator must prepare the receiving department by explaining reasons to them in advance and by requesting their support. If added expense dollars, space, or travel money can be included in the reassignment, the receiving department may be less resistant. Perhaps most importantly, all staff should be encouraged not to become so professionally specialized that they only develop their skills in one limited area. A diversity of programming talents in student services has always been a great asset, and in the 1980s it is a professional necessity. Staff assignments, job descriptions, and staff training efforts should all reflect this need. If staff must be terminated, efforts can be made to assist them to find other employment and to secure additional skills. For staff who are assigned to new duties, a period of time and special training may be arranged so that the staff member can learn the needed skills. Ideally, staff will have been encouraged to broaden the base of their professional skills and will be able to adapt to such changes. For example, a campus decided that it would discontinue its active recruiting program of National Merit scholars. The person in charge of this effort was informed that the position would be eliminated as well. However, it was possible to immediately place her in a financial aid position because she had taken the initiative to be involved in that office during the past three years and had taken additional post-master's course work in counseling at the same time.

Sometimes staff faced with program termination can be

encouraged to think positively about ways to reestablish the program. Often this can be done, even after the fact, by meeting with "the opposition" and demonstrating to them the benefits of one's efforts. Meeting with pressure groups is important; meeting with student groups fulfills an educational obligation as well. For example, a student committee may vote to discontinue an exercise program for handicapped students. The staff member in charge, convinced that the student committee members are simply unaware of the need on the campus, decides to find ways to educate the committee about the lives of handicapped students. This approach accomplishes an important educational objective; in addition, the staff member is likely to get the program reinstituted by the student committee.

*Political Issues.* The most difficult program termination decisions to handle are those decisions based on reasons other than changing educational goals or financial exigency. If a staff member is convinced that a program has been canceled because of political reasons or that the publicly stated reasons for termination are not truthful, the most professional response may be to resign, rather than to continue to be associated with any organization that one cannot respect. Reasonable efforts should be made, of course, to achieve an understanding or compromise, but such drastic action as a resignation may be a proper response. At one institution, for example, a staff member developed an effective walk-in counseling program for student drug abusers. The program was serving a substantial number of students and had been in existence for four years. A conservative board member felt that the program encouraged drug abuse on the campus and gave the college a bad name. The board ordered the president to terminate the program, but the only publicly announced reason given was lack of funds. The president and the chief student services officer, fearing a loss of their jobs, refused to admit openly the actual reasons for the action. The programmer in charge, after unsuccessful efforts to discuss the matter with her superiors, decided to resign.

In such situations, a strong and resourceful student services administrator would have anticipated such action and would have kept both the president and the board well informed about the program. Moreover, she would have established a community advisory group for the program when it was established to broaden its support and visibility. Board members and others who may be skeptical of such efforts can be invited to the campus to observe personally what the program is doing and who the people are who run it. Even with such efforts, the program may be terminated. It is the obligation of the chief student services officer to support the program, the staff member in charge of it, and the objectives it is seeking. The student services leader must demand that the reasons given for the termination be the actual ones. If this is not possible, then the reasonable course of action for the chief student services administrator is to seek other employment as well.

While the above example certainly is not unrealistic, most situations do not call for such drastic action. Quite frequently, the best way to assist a programmer in dealing with the pressures of a terminated program is to get this person involved right away in another worthwhile effort. The variety of tasks pursued in the student services enterprise provides a number of alternatives. Occasionally, a program similar to the one terminated can be established with some minor variations or a name change. A program called "sexual assault recovery service" may have raised too much controversy and attention because of its name; labeling it "women's support group" may accomplish the objectives of the program and may avoid the negative publicity.

Because of limited resources and changing needs, programs will be discontinued, and this will often create pressures for responsible staff. It is the responsibility of the chief student services administrator to ensure that the issues are dealt with openly and honestly and that sensitive attention is given to the personal and professional needs of the staff programmer.

## Summary

Few chief student services administrators currently practicing have escaped actual reductions in staff, dollars, equipment, or space. Many have addressed these difficult problems effectively, resulting in actual improvements in institutional services. Others have watched their programs diminish in size and quality. Newton and Caple (1983) argue that a creative management response to the problems of austerity is to use the crisis as an opportunity to generate new alternatives. The vigorous scrutiny applied to all higher education programs, both from within and without the institution, will continue. Thus, it behooves student services leaders to learn the best ways of using the available resources. At stake is the educational future of the students and the credibility and viability of the student services profession itself.

## References

Bonham, G. "The Fallow Years." *Change,* 1983, March, pp. 3-4.

Canon, H. J. "Developing Staff Potential." In U. Delworth, G. R. Hanson, and Associates, *Students Services: A Handbook for the Profession.* San Francisco: Jossey-Bass, 1980.

Johnson, C. S., and Foxley, C. H. "Devising Tools for Middle Managers." In U. Delworth, G. R. Hanson, and Associates, *Student Services: A Handbook for the Profession.* San Francisco: Jossey-Bass, 1980.

Keller, G. *Academic Strategy: The Management Revolution in American Higher Education.* Baltimore, Md.: Johns Hopkins University Press, 1983.

Newton, F., and Caple, R. B. "Managerial Leadership." In R. B. Winston, W. R. Mendenhall, and T. K. Miller (Eds.), *Administration and Leadership in Student Affairs.* Muncie, Ind.: Accelerated Development, 1983.

Thomas, W. "Exit Valor, Enter Veracity." In M. J. Barr and L. A. Keating (Eds.), *New Directions for Student Services: Establishing Effective Programs,* no. 7. San Francisco: Jossey-Bass, 1979.

Walker, D. E. *The Effective Administrator: A Practical Approach to Problem Solving, Decision Making, and Campus Leadership.* San Francisco: Jossey-Bass, 1979.

Winston, R. B., Mendenhall, W. R., and Miller, T. K. "Managing Human Resources: Staffing, Supervision, and Evaluation." In R. B. Winston, W. R. Mendenhall, and T. K. Miller (Eds.), *Administration and Leadership in Student Affairs.* Muncie, Ind.: Accelerated Development, 1983.

Lou A. Keating

ᘛᘚᘛᘚ ᘛᘚ ᘛᘚ ᘛᘚ ᘛᘚ ᘛᘚ ᘛᘚ ᘛᘚ ᘛᘚ ᘛᘚ ᘛᘚ ᘛᘚ

# Common Pitfalls
# in Program Planning

It's happened to all of us. The program failed. The students
didn't attend the seminar on career planning. The faculty didn't
read the advising handbook. Funding for the recreational sports
program was cut. The report on the critical need for childcare
was shelved. The list is endless. What happened? Why did the
program fail? In retrospect, the cause may be apparent. We
didn't advertise the workshop widely or perhaps the timing was
wrong. Vowing never to make *that* mistake again, we painstak-
ingly develop programming expertise in a trial-by-error fashion.
But all too often, we cannot identify any obvious error. The
need for the program was carefully documented and the design
carefully piloted, and it still didn't work. How do we find out
what happened?

Roberts (1978) claims that many university deans are
"obsessed with uncovering what went wrong. We spend hours
investigating factors that led to failure" (p. 48). However, a review of professional journal and convention program topics indicates that the obsession is a private one. The norm on campus,
at professional meetings, and often with our colleagues is to dis-

cuss what works or at least what might work. The conspiracy of silence about program failure is pervasive, and at times it seems that admission of program error violates a sacred professional taboo.

The taboo may be grounded in a defensiveness born of our history as the institutional stepchild. "Student services emerged and evolved by default, by taking over necessary and unpopular tasks abandoned by trustees, administrators, and faculty" (Fenske, 1980, p. 3). Hungry for respect, we justify our services to faculty and to other administrators while overlooking or rationalizing program shortcomings among ourselves. The taboo may be related to the profession's historical gap between the theorists and the practitioners, the evaluators and the doers.

However the taboo came to be, such avoidance behavior is professionally irresponsible and ultimately self-defeating. The battle for institutional resources is intensifying, and flawed student services programs are inviting targets for the faculty member lacking adequate lab space or the administrator short on operating dollars. Building a case for the upcoming budget battle may be the most pressing reason to examine program errors but in the long run, it is not the most important. Understanding program failure is an essential, if painful, step toward improving the overall quality of service to students and our institutions.

### Identifying Errors: A Practitioner's Model

Many student services programmers assume that errors in program planning will naturally be identified as part of the evaluation process. Ideally, evaluation is an integral part of the program planning process (Lenning, 1980). In practice, however, evaluation tends to be an ex post facto event. Most student services program evaluations are focused on program outcomes rather than the process of program design and implementation. Outcome, or product evaluations, can help identify whether the programs met the goal; however, product evaluations will not identify errors that occurred within the planning process, for student services program evaluations are directed to and limited by a specific evaluation goal.

Brown (1981) lists thirteen diverse purposes for student services program evaluations including clarifying program goals, justifying the existence of ongoing programs, and improving program quality and delivery. It could be argued that evaluations designed to gather information on program quality would also detect errors in program planning, but once again, the error question must be asked before it can be answered. Even the most sophisticated evaluation directed to program improvement may overlook data that could lead to a better understanding of program error. For example, failure to take political considerations into account has led to the demise of countless student services programs. Yet Brown states that "a major purpose of the planning and evaluation models being applied in higher education today is to minimize political considerations in resource allocation by establishing criteria and providing data concerning program merit" (1981, p. 3). Obviously, outcomes emanating from these models are unlikely to provide critical information on political error.

Many evaluations aimed at improving student services programs are quite limited in scope. Goodrich (1978) attributes this tendency to our concern with making evaluations scientific. "We limit ourselves to what we think we can measure well and so often focus on the trivial parts of the program" (p. 632). Such narrow evaluation designs generally provide information on behavioral outcomes (Did participants' behavior change? Did enrollment increase?) or success as judged by users (Did they attend? Did they enjoy themselves?). But errors in program planning are often rooted in factors that Lenning (1980) labels "extrinsic criteria." Evaluations that fail to provide information on questions of program cost-effectiveness, efficiency, or relative worth vis-à-vis institutional or division goals are of limited value in planning future programs or correcting errors in current ones.

The difficulties associated with after-the-fact or single-focus evaluations have led many programmers to use more informal methods of identifying and correcting problems. Stake (1973) defines a systematic form of this approach as "responsive evaluation," in which the practitioner analyzes the program "based on what people do naturally to evaluate things. They observe and react" (p. 5). Unfortunately "responsive evaluation" can easily degenerate into what Burck and Peterson (1975) call the "shot-in-the-dark method," which involves a random search for program impact. This search often occurs in staff discussions and relies heavily on the programmer's intuitive assessment of program success or failure.

Information gleaned from traditional evaluation strategies can provide important indicators of program errors, and the student services professional who is an especially skilled detective uses this information to develop a working list of errors to avoid in future programs. Unfortunately, these lists are the product of an individual's experience and are of limited value to others. Traditional evaluation strategies, whether formal or informal, cannot provide all answers to all questions. Current error identification strategies may point to program errors but do not provide information on error patterns or error types. Discovering errors in program planning is only useful to the extent that the information can be codified in such a way that it can apply in a wide variety of program efforts and settings.

Roberts (1978) suggests that the best way to analyze student services programs is to shift the focus from identifying problems to examining successful programs. This approach has merit, but such efforts may well be hampered by lack of consensus as to what constitutes program success. Does success occur when program participants change their behavior according to measurable criteria? Does the program fail because it was not cost-effective? Does the failed program serve the student but alienate significant staff or faculty? Can a student services program succeed on one level and fail on another?

In an earlier chapter, program success was defined as occurring when the three major elements of student services programs (goal, context, and plan) are congruent. A detailed explanation of these elements is provided in the Introduction. All three elements—goal, context, and plan—exist in every student services program and each element is linked with every other. Therefore, it follows that programs fail when there is a problem *within* one or more of the major elements, or when some kind of mismatch exists *between* program elements.

This view of programming enables the practitioner to classify program errors (and successes) into types or categories that are always linked to the three major elements of a program. Too often, failed programs are analyzed, failures noted, and errors later repeated. The repetition often occurs because the practitioner has not developed the diagnostic skill to link problems in program A with problems in program B. For example, the residence hall staff member who has trouble defining program goals may repeat the goal-setting error on transfer to the admissions office. Because admissions and residence hall programs look different on the surface, it may not be immediately apparent that the program failures result from the same basic error in goal setting. Classifying programming errors by linking them to the major elements of a program can help this professional to generalize his or her experience.

### "Within" Errors

"Within" errors generally occur when the planner lacks adequate knowledge or skill in a particular aspect of the planning process. Those with limited administrative experience may develop an inadequate program budget; the politically naive practitioner may underestimate the importance of the context; those unfamiliar with student development or organizational theory may develop inappropriate program goals. Once detected, a "within" error can usually be corrected through staff training directed to the deficit skill or knowledge.

*"Within" Error: Goal.* For many student affairs professionals, determining program goals is the single most difficult aspect of the program planning process. Many practitioners are more experienced and more comfortable implementing programs; others confuse the mission, the overarching purpose, program goals, and the agency objectives. Chapter Seven in this volume clarifies terminology and details a systematic procedure for determining program goals. Failure to follow a logical and theoretically sound goal-setting strategy can lead to a variety of "within" goal-setting errors.

The first step in examining a program idea should always be to ask a basic question: *"Does this program idea support one of our overarching purposes?"* This question may appear simplistic, but clarifying the link between a program idea and student services' overarching purposes is not always a straightforward process. For example, on many campuses student health centers are viewed as essential institutional services. Thus, programs directed to increasing the quality and availability of medical care support the purpose of providing essential services. In recent years, however, students and some staff have pressed for health education programs directed at increasing students' knowledge about nutrition, birth control, and so on. These programs do not provide essential institutional services; rather, they support the purpose of teaching life management skills. Once the link of the program idea to our larger mission is clarified, the planner can begin to narrow and shape the program goal. At this stage of goal definition, several errors can occur, generally defined as errors of specificity.

- *Too many goals.* The charge of facilitating student development yields hundreds of program ideas, and goal setting in student affairs can be an exciting, creative process. But some planners get stuck in the creative process; like the graduate student searching for a dissertation topic, they get lost in the possibilities. Research reports, staff meetings, the president's latest speech, or conversations with students may provide what Moore and Delworth term a "germinal idea" (1976). How does the planner select among good ideas in planning program goals? Some programmers, unwilling to give up good ideas, identify several program goals and try to make them fit into one program. For example, a peer advising program may be established to provide personalized attention to students in distress, to provide basic academic advising for freshmen, and to provide educational programming on career choice. Each one of these goals is appropriate for a peer program; however, no single program can reasonably be expected to effectively accomplish all three goals. Similarly, some staff try to utilize a single student needs assessment to gather information on student satisfaction with current services, their developmental needs, and their extracurricular interests. The program with too many goals may initially appear to represent an efficient use of resources; in reality, this error decreases the likelihood of achieving any one of the goals.

- *The goal is too vague.* The vague goal has a nice ring to it (to facilitate moral development, to encourage good citizenship) but is so generally stated as to be virtually meaningless. There are two basic types of vague goals. In the first, an adjective or two is added to one of the overarching purposes. Thus, planning a dance translates to "facilitating students' social development"; providing cardiopulmonary resuscitation (CPR) training for university police translates to "providing essential security service." Vague goals provide convenient umbrellas for most student affairs activities and often appear at annual report time or when the boss asks for yearly objectives. The second vague goal is the mother/flag/apple pie goal. These program goals are worthy, well-intentioned, and hard to be against. Who could argue with efforts to eliminate racism on campus or plans to improve academic advising? The rhetoric may be uplifting, but, like the political promise, the goal can seldom if ever be achieved.

    Consistent use of vague program goals may further confuse faculty and other administrators who don't know what we do anyway. Harvey (1976) suggests that the descriptions of many developmental programs are "phrased in either fluffy or jargonic or third-force psychological terms. As such, they hold little appeal to many traditional academicians" (p. 92). More importantly, from the planner's perspective, the vague program goal can easily become something we talk about but can never design programs to address.

- *The goal is too specific.* Some program planners go to the opposite extreme and define program goals too narrowly. Although the goal that is too specific usually can be achieved, it just may not be worth the time, energy, and investment of resources. A common error of specificity occurs when the program planner focuses on a narrowly defined target group. Computer technology now enables programmers in even the largest institutions to quickly generate information on a wide variety of student subgroups; lists and mailing labels are at our fingertips. If the vice-president is worried about transportation on an urban campus, his staff can easily develop a research report or program for commuter students living with their parents who do not live on shuttle bus routes. While it may be important to assess this group's transportation problems, this program goal may not represent a worthwhile investment of time and dollars. Another specificity error occurs when the program goal addresses a minor aspect of a larger issue. Parking is a perennial problem on many campuses, and campus police departments are often directed to develop elaborate procedures to control student access to campus. This goal, which narrows in on one aspect of the facilities and transportation problem, may treat symptoms but never addresses the overall problem. In the example of the parking problem, if the police effectively control student access to campus, the administration may never consider instituting a shuttle bus system. Specific program goals are attractive to many in student affairs because our role is often ambiguous, and the narrowly defined program enables us to feel a sense of achievement. In the long run, however, programs geared to narrow goals can slow or even subvert our larger purposes.

*"Within" Error: Context.* Context errors occur when the program planner ignores or misinterprets one or more aspects of the institutional environment. Student services programs do not exist in a vacuum; they are influenced by the institution's politics and history, its role in the state, and its financial climate. Key student organizations and the student newspaper react to our programs, and faculty and staff have a stake in the student affairs enterprise as well. Correct identification of and response to these context "cues" are critical to establishment of successful student services programs.

Even experienced practitioners can misread the institutional context. Maintaining objectivity about our programs is difficult, for job responsibilities or professional experience naturally bias one's interpretation of institutional norms or expectations. These contextual "blind spots" often become apparent when a staff member changes job responsibilities, transfers to a different office, or moves to a new institution. Unless blessed with excellent supervision, new staff are likely to make major blunders based on assumptions brought from other settings. The first step in assessing context is generally directed to the following question: *"Does this program idea fit this institution at this point in time?"* Failure to adequately answer this question can lead to a variety of context errors.

- *Checking only limited aspects of the context.* Student services programs are affected by a variety of institutional and community influences. Experienced student affairs professionals are quite skilled at assessing student issues or other aspects of the environment that directly affect student services programs, but they are often unaware of the institution's budget process, of institutional or state governing boards, or of community attitudes toward the institution. Failure to take these "external" factors into account can cause multiple program problems. Lacking familiarity with budget processes, program planners may submit proposals that are unrealistic or ill-timed. Failure to adequately assess community resources may lead to development of a campus-based childcare program when a contract with an existing community agency would have been sufficient.

  This error is often a function of the tunnel vision inherent in our role. Those in positions of high student contact may know student issues, and agency directors are usually attuned to division concerns. It is neither reasonable nor appropriate to expect program planners to develop expertise in all areas of the context. But successful program planners must be cognizant of the multiple influences on program planning and develop methods of gaining information about those influences.

- *Misinterpreting context cues.* Programs often fail when information correctly identified as important to the program is misinterpreted. For example, the assistant director of recreational sports hears that a powerful faculty member is very interested in students' recreational sports offerings. After months spent trying to convince the administration that the hours available for recreational sports should be increased, the staff member approaches the faculty member to discuss the problem. Hoping to build support for the hours extension, the staff person vents his frustration and presents an eloquent argument for expanding services. Later, he learns that the faculty member opposed expanding student hours; his real concern was expanding staff access to facilities. The recreational sports staff member was correct to speak to the faculty member; his error was in assuming that faculty interest meant support.

Another misinterpretation error is grounded in the assumption of negatives where, in fact, none may exist (Barr and Keating, 1979). The fact that the agency director does not quickly offer support for a program idea does not necessarily mean she's against it or thinks that the idea is bad. It could mean that she is essentially neutral and that the planner needs to sell the idea in a different way. The wise programmer will take the time to discover the real reason behind this apparent lack of support.

- *Overreacting to context.* In the overreaction error, goal setting and context assessment are reversed. Rather than developing a program idea and then checking the institutional response to the goal, the program planner assesses the institutional climate in search of an idea. The operant question becomes "will this program offend anyone?" rather than "is the program important?" The planner who overreacts to context may be politically astute, and programs solely directed to a reading of the context may indeed be viewed in a positive light. In the long run, however, programs ruled primarily by contextual concerns often lack integrity and may be difficult to carry through.

Overreacting to context may be a response to previous underestimating or misreading of context cues. Smarting from an earlier failure, the program planner spends inordinate time checking with everyone who might possibly have an interest in the program. While the planner carefully touches every base, the program may lose momentum, but at least the planner has not made a big mistake. The program context is important, but program development is not solely a political process. Student affairs staff must occasionally take unpopular stands and identifying potential obstacles in the setting does not negate our responsibility to press for programs we believe to be important. Obviously, a program's allies and critics cannot be ignored, but the planner who concentrates too much on the context risks slighting the important issues of plan and goal.

*"Within" Error: Plan.* Many student affairs professionals claim expertise in program design. This is the easy part, the fun part of the job. Once the goal is established, these programmers proceed on automatic, checklist in hand. After all, putting a program together, marketing it, and delivering the service or presenting the activity is routine. However, approaching program design as routine can cause the program planner to skip the basic design question: *"What is the best method for achieving the program goal within this context?"* Ignoring this question or answering it too quickly can lead to major errors embedded within the program plan.

• *The plan fits the planner.* In this error, the program design is biased toward the interests, skills, or expertise of the program planner or the planner's supervisor. For example, the research-oriented administrator is convinced that we must assess, assess, assess—and that each new program and all current ones should be exhaustively analyzed, documented, and evaluated. Decision makers who withhold program resources until the planner can prove a need encourage this kind of error. One example of this kind of error centers on the problem of alcohol abuse among college students. With the possible exception of students at some church-related institutions, there is no question that many college students abuse alcohol. Many studies exist verifying that fact, yet the research-oriented administrator may demand another study before an alcohol help center will even be considered.

Another example of programming based on staff interest

and expertise occurs in counseling centers or among other "people-oriented" professionals who enjoy small-group activities such as workshops. It's easy to forget that many people are not comfortable in workshop settings. More formal seminars or even a booklet may be a more effective method of communicating with those students. Staff comfort with the workshop or small-group discussions may also blind the planner to the fact that workshops are not particularly cost-effective, especially on a large campus. Program plans can also be biased when the practitioner lacks relevant skills or expertise and thus avoids certain program designs. For example, student affairs professionals who are afraid of computers or who believe we must personalize academic advising may gear their advising program plan to increasing advisers' counseling skills. But today's students who are comfortable with current technology might well prefer a self-advising system using interactive computer programs.

Fitting the plan to the planner may be necessary at times; it is appropriate to take advantage of staff skills and expertise when possible. However, doing so because it is the comfortable or easy way results in ineffective program plans that are less likely to achieve the program goal.

• *The plan is too intricate.* Program designs often become more complicated than necessary when the planners attempt to present information in the most unique, clever, or entertaining manner. Peer adviser training programs provide many examples of the intricacy error. Residence hall staff, who want resident assistants (RAs) to become resourceful in using and locating referral information, spend hours designing a clever simulation activity in which students experience typical student referral questions. The activity is entertaining, and the students learn a few things about being resourceful. But was all that necessary? Could the same information have been effectively communicated with a reduced investment of staff time? Another example of the intricacy error is the program staff that decides that a procedures manual will save time for next year's staff. After expending considerable effort preparing a detailed guide, they later learn that the guide is never used.

The intricacy error often occurs when the program design grows more elaborate than is necessary to fulfill the program goal. A student group may approach the adviser with the general idea of increasing informal contact with faculty. The adviser engineers an elaborate seminar series involving faculty from all over campus, when a simple faculty fireside may well have been sufficient. A slightly different version of the intricacy error occurs when the agency director prepares a thirty-page proposal documenting the need for an increase in program staff. The vice-president neither wants nor needs such detail and asks for a three-page summary.

Labeling some program plans as "too intricate" should not imply that student affairs professionals should take short-cuts in preparation of program plans. Effective plans, however, make effective use of resources, stay focused on the program goal, and, whenever possible, keep it simple.

• *The plan is not effectively administered.* Failure to obtain adequate implementation information or to account for normal problems will result in this error of administration. Purchasing and central duplicating deadlines must be considered when scheduling programs. Similarly, programs that rely on peer advisers to deliver services must provide adequate supervision for the peers, limited-hours services usually need phone coverage during off-hours, and changes from a manual to computerized listing of student organizations must be backed by adequate time for retraining of staff. Errors of administration can usually be prevented by involving the implementators in the planning process. These staff will anticipate problems and ask the nitty-gritty questions about scheduling, mailing labels, and assignment of staff time to the project.

Most "within" errors occur when the programmer lacks sufficient information about goal setting, program design, or the institutional setting. These skill or knowledge deficits can often be predicted, based on the programmer's prior training and experience. Entry-level professionals may be asked to implement preexisting designs; thus, these staff members may need additional information on goal setting and contextual issues. Unfortunately, however, gaining adequate information on the major elements of student services programs does not guarantee program success, for errors of fit can also occur between the goal and plan, the goal and context, or the plan and context.

## "Between" Errors

"Between" errors are more complex than "within" errors and more difficult to isolate. The planner who makes the "between" error usually possesses the requisite information to avoid the obvious "within" error but fails to match program elements. A common example of the "between" error is the program with an appropriate and carefully constructed goal and plan that is blocked politically; thus an excellent seminar on human sexuality that would never work in one context might be readily accepted in another. "Between" errors can be difficult to trace; a mismatch between the program goal and the institutional context will likely lead to problems in the plan as well. However, most "between" errors begin in a mismatch between two of the major program elements.

*Goal-Plan Errors.* Mismatches between the program goal and plan are often difficult to detect. After all, program plans are developed to achieve a specific goal, so the relationship between the two may appear self-evident. Plan-goal errors often occur when the programmer, facing budget or time constraints, takes the easy way and develops a plan that will either be simple to administer or will have some immediate payoff. This error can be prevented by persisting with the basic question: *"Is this plan the best method for achieving the program goal?"*

• *The plan reflects the obvious method of achieving the program goal.* The obvious plan is adopted for a variety of reasons; it is easy to understand, easy to justify, often easy to sell, and clearly related to the goal. This error often occurs in response to key words in the goal statement. For example, one goal of the financial aid program is to personalize service to students. The obvious plan would be to provide more financial aid counselors to talk to students. Increasing the counselor-student ratio may help to personalize service, but so might other actions. Perhaps the office needs to add word processing equipment to reduce time counselors spend on paperwork. A flex-time arrangement could increase the hours that present staff are available to meet with students and reduce the long lines during the day. Perhaps a videotape providing routine information could be developed. All these program plans could lead to greater "personalizing" of services without adding any additional staff. Some supervisors require that each program proposal be accompanied by at least three alternate delivery systems. This or other methods that force staff to look beyond the obvious will help to prevent this error.

• *The piggyback plan.* This error is similar to that of the obvious plan, in that the piggyback plan represents one of the most obvious methods for achieving the program goal. This error is a favorite of the lazy programmer who tries to achieve the goal by piggybacking on an established program. Orientation programs are prime targets for piggybackers. Student organizations or other administrators seeking contact with new students often ask orientation or registration staff to distribute literature to incoming freshman. It's much easier to add to the orientation function rather than develop a new program. Or we piggyback on our own programs. Since the RAs do so well with educational programming, let's have them do some basic academic advising as well. Piggyback programs can dilute the effectiveness of the established program and seldom achieve the piggybackers' goal in as effective a manner as possible.

• *The plan works counter to the goal.* This error often occurs when the plan is designed for maximum efficiency or for administrative convenience. The best examples are found in many programs designed to serve minority and disabled students. It is administratively convenient to locate all such programs in a central location. Minority students will have an easily identifiable place to take their problems, and faculty needing to locate an interpreter for a deaf student can call the office serving disabled students. Unfortunately, these programs can perpetuate the very isolation that the program was designed to overcome. Another example is the campus ombudsman's office that often has a goal "to educate students to make better use of campus resources." The ombudsman then advertises himself as an expert in cutting red tape and wonders why students don't do their own legwork before coming to his office. Ironically, in our efforts to help students, we may design plans that have the opposite effect.

*Goal-Context Errors.* Errors of fit between a program goal and its institutional context are often rooted in a conflict of values. Perfect "matches" of program goal and institutional context are impossible, for American colleges and universities are, by definition, an amalgamation of differing values. Understanding these differences among faculty, students, or other groups' expectations of student services programs is a necessary step in establishing a program goal. There is a basic question that must be asked in a variety of ways throughout the planning process: *"Are the program goal and the institutional context congruent?"* The between error of goal versus context occurs when programs concentrate on facilitating student development without a parallel commitment to institutional development.

- *The program goal works counter to institutional mission or to agency or division goals.* As early as 1971, Halleck argued that the institution defines the limits of counselor practice and uses him as a tool to accomplish specific institutional goals. Halleck's arguments apply to all professionals in student affairs. Like it or not, we are part of a larger organization that maintains clear, if unstated, expectations of the role and function of student services. In an earlier chapter the mission of the student affairs enterprise was outlined in three overarching purposes: to provide essential institutional services, to teach life management skills, and to provide intentional links through which students can integrate knowledge (the student development role). However, the emphasis placed on each of these purposes by individual institutions varies widely. For example, an ongoing debate in academia centers on the role of colleges and universities as educational versus vocational preparation centers. The counselor with a strong interest in career preparation may find his programs consistently blocked at a small liberal arts college; the same counselor would be welcomed in a community college. If institutional or agency goals remained fixed over time, the counselor could simply seek a position where the "values match" was better. But the institutional environment is a dynamic one; the program goal that was a perfect fit one year may work counter to institutional purpose the next year. The liberal arts college that rejected a career program ten years ago may enthusiastically support the concept today if student enrollment in majors is dropping below what can be justified in the budget. The astute programmer monitors these changes and runs a constant "reality check" when developing program goals.

- *The goal supports the institutional mission, division, or agency goal but is at variance with current political reality.* This error is often an error of timing and confuses the new practitioner and experienced professional alike. Events as disparate as an international incident or a staff switch can lead to this error. For years, programs for international students have been routinely funded and generally supported by administrators, faculty, and students. The Iranian hostage crisis of 1980 coupled with increased competition for space in some graduate programs brought tremendous pressure on campus international offices. Proposing an increase in foreign student recruitment at that time would have been a major error; later, the pressure of that period could be used to support an increase in program dollars for the international office. Goal-context errors often accompany a change in administrations. Program staff who have devoted months to developing and researching a program goal may make unwarranted assumptions regarding the new person's understanding of or support for the program goal. Though waiting may be frustrating, the program goal must again be tested against the change in context.
- *The program goal is congruent with institutional, division, and agency goals, is appropriate to the current political climate, but fails to take other important aspects of the environment into account.* This is a catchall category, for there are hundreds of contextual issues to be considered when de-

veloping a program goal. One aspect of the institutional environment that may conflict with worthy program goals is the institution's legal, procedural, or policy constraints. Policies regarding use of facilities provide many examples of this error. The president who is seeking better relationships with the community may encourage student activities staff to develop joint programs with local religious groups. After a year spent developing a brown bag luncheon series on "Religion in America," the student activities office is approached with a request to provide space for a church youth group meeting. Many of the members of the youth group are students and have been active in the brown bag series, and they know that space is available. What they don't know is that institutional policy prohibits use of college facilities by external groups.

*Plan-Context Errors.* The ultimate success of student services programs depends on how good the fit is between the program plan (or delivery system) and the institutional context. Oddly, plans that may, on the face of it, be very inefficient work well in some settings because of tradition, staffing constraints, or even accounting procedures. For example, it would clearly be more efficient to run all health education programs out of the student health center. But if the health center is understaffed and there is a health education expert in the recreational sports division, the best plan for that context might be a jointly sponsored program design. The plan-context error often surfaces in a clash of the real (this institution at this time) versus the ideal (the *best* method for achieving the program goal). The student services professional must be pragmatic in resolving these conflicts, or plan-context errors will occur.

• *The adopted plan.* Administrators in higher education often complain about federal or state agencies who force unworkable plans on colleges and universities. Trying to fit government-mandated funding formulas or affirmative action programs to the realities of college governance and its bureaucracies is indeed frustrating. Yet student affairs professionals are also guilty of trying to force program plans to fit the setting. This error often occurs when staff enter a new setting. The professional who developed an excellent peer advising program and *knows* what works and what doesn't may try to duplicate the program in the new setting. What she doesn't realize is that five years before, the faculty were up in arms because several peer advisers were giving students advice about which professor to avoid. In addition, the secretarial support present in her former setting is not available in her current institution. The list of differences between settings is endless, and the potential for program failure is high.

• *The style misfit.* With experience, most practitioners learn that wholesale transfers of program plans are seldom possible. However, the adoption error can occur at a more subtle level. Many programmers overlook the importance of matching the program plan to institutional "style." One example of this error is provided by the student activities staff member who is committed to the goal of increasing student knowledge of expanded career opportunities for women. In a college where the majority of the women students affiliate with sororities, a seminar on "Women's Choices" conducted by sorority alumnae might be a more effective first step than inviting the president of the National Organization for Women (NOW) to speak. Understanding an institution's tone and style requires creative detective work. Indicators of a college's style include media representations of the college ("a football power," "a tradition of academic excellence"), student assessments ("this is a party school," "this is a tough school"), or the degree of alumni involvement in recruiting and fund raising. Every college and university has a unique culture, and program plans must fit that culture.

Categorizing errors as occurring "within" or "between" the elements of goal, context, or plan does not imply that programming mistakes are always "pure." In reality, most programs fail because of a combination of interrelated errors: The goal was weak, which led to problems in the plan, which led to problems in the setting. The combinations are staggering. However, linking errors to the major elements of plan, context, and goal does provide a framework for interpreting evaluation data and identifying common programming errors and error patterns.

### Diagnostic Errors

The system for identifying program errors presented in this chapter can be used in a number of ways. Student affairs professionals planning new programs can develop lists of questions pertaining to the specific program goal, context, or plan that help them to avoid those more obvious errors. Those charged with maintenance of ongoing programs might use the model as a framework for discussing program modifications. For example, as established programs evolve and change, the fit of the plan and goal will be altered. Each program modification then should include the question: "Does the plan still fit the goal?" The model can also be used as one tool for identifying problem areas in troubled programs. However, when the model is used for this diagnostic purpose on real programs, the programmer may find the errors are still difficult to detect. A word of caution then about possible errors in diagnosis.

*The False Positive.* In this chapter "within" and "between" error types were isolated for purposes of illustration. However, the error model is based on an integrative and interactive definition of student services programs; that is, the elements of program goal, context, and plan are inextricably linked. Therefore, a weakness within any one element will ultimately affect all other elements. If the primary error is a "between" error involving two elements, the potential for problems increases exponentially.

This integrative characteristic of the model can easily lead to faulty diagnosis of the program error. For example, this author spent several years developing and testing an idea for an alcohol program on campus. The goal and plan "fit" and the context had been carefully assessed, but the program never got off the ground. After several frustrating discussions of what went wrong, it was decided that the context was misread and that the institution wasn't "ready" for this kind of alcohol program. When cleaning out files a year later, the plan was un-earthed. With wisdom born of hindsight, it was obvious that the plan was weak and lacked important information required to implement the program. There had been a misreading of the context; but the primary reason the program proposal was re-jected lay in a faulty and incomplete plan.

The same biases that can lead the professional to repeat certain errors of context or plan or goal can also bias the diag-nostic process. Those who are politically astute can still make errors in assessing the context, and a good planner can develop a faulty program design. Therefore it is important when diagnos-ing program errors to analyze all aspects of the program, includ-ing those elements that may generally be considered as program strengths.

*Faulty Transfer.* This diagnostic error is similar to the "within" error of overreacting to context. The same action or decision that is diagnosed as an error in one program could be precisely the right action or decision in another set of circum-stances. For example, failure to pilot new programs will gener-ally result in the "within" plan error of poor program administra-tion, so conscientious professionals generally spend considerable time working out the administrative details of program plans. But when the president wants something in place next week or a student crisis erupts, the wise practitioner responds with a less-than-perfect plan. Demanding adequate preparation time is generally appropriate; asking for such time in this circum-stance might enable the programmer to avoid a minor plan error but would lead to a major error of context. One error does not a maxim make, and error diagnosis must be tied to an individual program.

## Using Errors to Your Advantage

Simple knowledge of error in program planning will not automatically prevent future mistakes or affect program qual-ity. It is important that professional and productive use be made of programming mistakes.

Information on program errors can be used to guide staff

supervision and training efforts. The supervisor who notices that several staff appear to be missing important information about the institutional goal can invite the director or president to speak on his or her vision for the college. The staff members who received feedback that their program plan is incomplete can enroll in informal classes on university procedures.

Some student affairs professionals have made their reputation by "turning around" or "cleaning up" stagnant or failing programs. Experienced administrators expect that errors will occur; their final assessments of staff often turn on the staff member's ability to correct errors. The ability to learn from one's programming errors can be summarized in two words: relax and recycle. The development of successful programs always involves an element of risk; errors can be minimized but unseen problems will always be present. Many professionals, burned by early mistakes, develop an excessively cautious approach to program planning. Identifying and correcting programming errors is appropriate and necessary; obsession about those errors is a waste of time. One error in a program design does not mean that the program goal should be abandoned. Many good program ideas appear to die one year, then resurface later with a new name and a new look. If errors are correctly identified, many failed programs can be retrieved and recycled.

## Summary

The complexity of the task of planning and implementing quality student services programs can lead to a wide variety of programming errors, but identification of common errors and error patterns is essential in order to improve student services programs. The categories of errors presented in this chapter can be used to link those errors to the major programming elements of context, goal, and plan. By examining program errors from the perspective of their relationship to the overall planning process, these errors can provide valuable opportunities for student services professionals to improve their programs.

## References

Barr, M. J., and Keating, L. A. "No Program Is an Island." In M. J. Barr and L. A. Keating (Eds.), *New Directions for Student Services: Establishing Effective Programs,* no. 7. San Francisco: Jossey-Bass, 1979.

Brown, S. "An Evaluation Process for Student Affairs Agencies." *National Association of Student Personnel Administrators (NASPA) Journal,* 1981, *18* (4), 2-13.

Burck, H. D., and Peterson, G. W. "Needed: More Evaluation, Not Research." *Personnel and Guidance Journal,* 1975, *53,* 563-569.

Fenske, R. H. "Historical Foundations." In U. Delworth, G. R. Hanson, and Associates, *Student Services: A Handbook for the Profession.* San Francisco: Jossey-Bass, 1980.

Goodrich, T. J. "Strategies for Dealing with the Issue of Subjectivity in Education." *Evaluation Quarterly,* 1978, *2,* 631-645.

Halleck, S. L. *The Politics of Therapy.* New York: Science House, 1971.

Harvey, T. "Student Development and the Future of Higher Education: A Force Analysis." *Journal of College Student Personnel,* 1976, *17* (2), 90-95.

Lenning, O. T. "Assessment and Evaluation." In U. Delworth, G. R. Hanson, and Associates, *Student Services: A Handbook for the Profession.* San Francisco: Jossey-Bass, 1980.

Moore, M., and Delworth, U. *Training Manual for Student Service Program Development.* Boulder, Colo.: Western Interstate Commission for Higher Education, 1976.

Roberts, B. "Let's Take a Look at What Went Right." *National Association of Student Personnel Administrators (NAPSA) Journal,* 1978, *16* (2), 48-51.

Stake, R. E. "Program Evaluation, Particularly Responsive Evaluation." Paper presented at the New Trends in Evaluation Conference, Göteborg, Sweden, October 1973.

# Part Four

❧ ❧ ❧ ❧ ❧ ❧ ❧ ❧ ❧ ❧ ❧ ❧ ❧

# Trends and Resources for Increasing Professional Effectiveness

An accurate prediction of the future is simply not possible. We can, however, carefully analyze current conditions, identify growing trends, and apply our knowledge to make some fairly accurate predictions of what the future of American higher education, in general, and student services programs, in particular, will be. More importantly, we can use our predictions of the future to prepare today for the decades ahead.

In Chapter Thirteen, James Duncan analyzes the forces at work in American higher education and identifies trends and practices that must be accounted for in developing student services programs. His analysis of changes and emerging priorities for student services provides helpful guidance for all student services programmers as they develop programs today for our shared future.

Program development and implementation are the core of student services units. Chapter Fourteen synthesizes the ideas and information presented in this volume. In addition, it contains a practical guide on how to apply the information and viewpoints presented in this volume to the skill of program development and implementation. Whether the program under consideration is a one-time event, a series of activities and services, or the creation of an entire administrative unit, the skills needed by the professional remain the same. The complexity of the task will, of course, be increased with the level of the program. The core skills will, however, remain the same.

Following Chapter Fourteen is a series of annotated references compiled to help practitioners gain the broad-based knowledge to ensure that effective student services programs are established in institutions of higher education.

13            James P. Duncan

꙳ ꙳ ꙳ ꙳ ꙳ ꙳ ꙳ ꙳ ꙳ ꙳ ꙳ ꙳ ꙳

# Effects
# of Emerging Issues
# on Program Development

Predicting the future for student affairs requires a broad perspective on the issues facing American education, and many
futurists have concerned themselves with such predictions.
However, because of the nature of our shared profession, gaug-
ing the impact of current and projected events on the work of
student services professionals poses a unique challenge.

This challenge was underscored recently during a convention program geared to student services professionals involved
in administering student housing units. I was pontificating on
current and projected stresses in American higher education and
their likely impact on the work lives of housing administrators
over the next few years when a member of the audience asked
how much intuition versus hard data was used in my role as
an administrator. The question served as a reminder of how
much administrative behavior and pronouncements about the
future are tempered by individual style and influenced by one's

301

perceptions and experiences. Although there are obvious changes facing higher education that will affect student services administrators, the ultimate effects of these changes will be influenced to a great extent by the setting in which one works and the personal style of the administrators involved. My crystal ball, or "educated intuition," can hopefully be of some utility in preparing for those changes, but the ultimate responsibility still rests with the one on the "inside," the practicing administrator. Rather than blindly accepting others' pronouncements about administrative practice for the future, working professionals must address the facts of their own individual situations.

One important consideration in projecting future events is a recognition of the impact of past events, that is, a sense of history (see Chapter One by Knock). Without a thorough assessment of the past, any view toward the future is usually found woefully inadequate. To illustrate, the lives and work styles of current and future college and university administrators can never be completely free of the crisis manager style that prevailed in the 1960s. This is not to suggest that the inspirational and philosophical aspects of earlier leadership styles are gone forever or that earlier periods did not have stresses that greatly affected the management of colleges and universities. However, the amount of change associated with earlier crises was nothing compared to what American higher education experienced with the rapid growth beginning in 1946, progressing through the pressures resulting from the 1957 Sputnik flight and the campus disruptions beginning symbolically at Berkeley in 1964. These crises and the resultant administrative behavior have since been influenced by our new affluence as a society, by the civil rights revolution, and by Vietnam. These events and the part played in them by college and university participants brought upon American higher education a public awareness and attention that we are not likely to ever escape (Kerr, 1982).

Even a cursory assessment of future events suggests that administrators in American higher education and student services administrators in particular must prepare for a new period of stress and crisis. If my instincts are correct, the changes to be produced in this crisis period will be much greater than those experienced since the boom in American higher education began in 1946. Higher education in the future reflects a coming together of all that has taken place and must also respond to the changes, largely economic and demographic in nature, that are now occurring in our society.

Responding to this new crisis period is a complex administrative issue, but the general message is clear. All components of an institution, and even the higher education community, must work in concert to respond to the challenges produced by rapid change. This no doubt sounds like a statement of the obvious, but it is important to underscore, particularly for student services professionals, that there is a step beyond "student development." That step is "institutional development."

## Institutional Development

Institutional development is a process that embodies planning based on an analysis of external and internal forces affecting the institution and that identifies both short- and long-term goals. As a process, institutional development has the potential to enhance communication among all constituent groups of an institution. It can be a means to closely interrelate student development programs with the educational process under way in academic departments and with other administrative components within the institution. If this point is adequately recognized and campus administrators work toward that end, there is little need for the paranoia so prevalent among student services professionals about their impact on campus decisions and little validity to the pejorative pronouncements about student services programs often heard from academic and business affairs administrators.

The hard truth is that the challenges of the future provide new opportunities to change for the better, and those challenges are as great for student services professionals as they are for other administrative officers. However, college or university administrators must be in tune with and understand the broader societal picture and its influence on the whole institution if colleges and universities of the future are to succeed in serving students. Similarly, the future in higher education for student services administrators may depend on the extent to which the profession recognizes that the development of students is a function of the *entire* institution. That is, the single factor of student development is only a part of institutional development and the institutional mission. The sooner this is understood and administrators and faculty behave accordingly, the more likely we are to effect change as well as respond to change.

## Future Projections

Many futurists have spent considerable time projecting the impact of changes in American higher education on future administrators. A major reference in the area is *Three Thousand Futures: The Next Twenty Years for Higher Education* (Carnegie Council on Policy Studies in Higher Education, 1980). This book provides important insights into some current and potential challenges to which American higher education must respond. A composite of the changes presented by these authors and others (Mayhew, 1979; Naisbitt, 1982) is discussed here.

- *Uncertainty about enrollments.* The uncertainty is brought on by projections of significant declines in enrollments nationwide, great regional population shifts, and sizable shifts in the public versus private share of student enrollment (Breneman, 1983). Furthermore, short-run enrollment fluctuations are created by changing job opportunities and shifting financial aid policies. Enrollment shifts within institutions and among academic programs and majors are also occurring.
- *An increase in outside controls and constraints with resultant diminished institutional autonomy.* The corrosive competition for students, often without regard for student needs and in part from the enrollment uncertainties just mentioned, is bringing on some loss of public confidence and new demands for institutional accountability (Keller, 1983.) These and other factors will heighten the demand for, and

impact of, external controls such as federal regulations and rules adopted by state coordinating agencies.

- *Increased diversity of student enrollments.* This is already a reality for most colleges and universities. Compared to ten to twenty years ago, more ethnic minorities, more part-time students, and more commuters are currently enrolling (Astin, 1977). These trends will continue, with the white, eighteen- to twenty-two-year-old, full-time, residential student being a decreasing proportion of the total student body. Another well-documented element of diversity that may demand further attention is the increased number of students from single-parent homes. Certainly the implications of this shift in student needs and service programs deserve some attention. Other subtle shifts of this type may also need further study.
- *Shifts in mobility patterns.* Already a substantial number of students earn the initial degree from two or more institutions. The part-time student while full-time employee phenomenon and frequent moves to follow job opportunities add to this change. In contrast, declining enrollments, dual-career marriages, and high moving costs have reduced turnover of faculty and staff. This suggests some real risk that without adequate preparation and staff development, outdated 1960s and 1970s techniques could be applied in the 1980s and 1990s in many of the university's operational and academic units (Keller, 1983; Naisbitt, 1982).
- *Increased appeal of the large, comprehensive universities and decline of the small, single-sex, rural, and religious institutions.* This decline is seen especially in areas or states losing population, or in urban areas where a number of public institutions can effectively compete for students because they offer lower tuitions. Additionally, large, comprehensive institutions generally offer a wide array of student activities and programs that create a traditional university ambience attractive to undergraduates in their early twenties. At the same time, they generally offer graduate students opportunities for study in more disciplines than are found at small, private institutions.

- *Growing tensions between administrators and a faculty resistant to change.* Most college administrations are faced with *mandates* to *implement* change (Keller, 1983). Traditionally, administrators have been stereotyped as being slow to effect change, with faculty identified as change initiators. This "management/labor" adversarial relationship is common in most hierarchical organizations. In the future, however, administrators may increasingly feel the need to respond to external influences on their institution by initiating and controlling long-range planning efforts, in addition to employing crisis management when addressing daily problems. At a time when shared institutional governance is becoming less common, faculty members may grow resistant to administrative control over such planning. Moreover, as enrollment shifts between and among academic programs and as resources are reallocated within the institution, disagreement over the *types* of change needed at an institution is likely. Changing enrollment patterns may also influence the relationship between the academic and nonacademic areas in an institution, especially if the institution is facing a decreasing budget. University administrators must be prepared to adapt to these institutional changes to ensure a continued responsiveness to student needs.

- *Difficulty attracting managerial talent.* Administrative positions in higher education involve management of large entities. The availability of attractive job opportunities in other fields with much better salary and fringe benefit packages will continue to attract some of higher education's best talent (Powers and Powers, 1983). This is likely to be particularly acute in "front-line" student services areas that demand heavy time commitments in relation to the remuneration and other rewards. The success of equal employment practices nationally has also opened doors to women and minorities to professions not previously available, thereby robbing the student services profession in particular of some key administrative talent.

- *Academic standards.* As institutions put more energy and resources into raising admissions requirements and developing more rigorous curricula, a new set of student development programs may emerge: for example, academic support services such as tutoring or preparing for graduate study. New opportunities for cooperative programs between an institution's student affairs area and academic programs may also evolve. Tightening of academic standards is also reflected in the increased competition for research dollars. As the availability of federal and private research support decreases, competition for those dollars intensifies. As administrators search for replacement dollars, they face ethical and legal issues related to increased dependence on industrial and other private sector support; they must also make difficult decisions about commitment to teaching versus research (Breneman, 1983; Fiske, 1983).

• *The computer revolution.* High technology has changed instructional delivery and program delivery systems due to advances in telecommunication and computer technology (Naisbitt, 1982). Properly used, these technological advances have enormous potential to improve the quality of administration, teaching, and research at our colleges and universities. However, faculty and administrative officials must pay particular attention to the intra- and interpersonal needs of students who may develop a sense of isolation, or at least "detachment," as machines become a greater part of their instructional experience.

In enumerating these conditions, existing or potential, the most significant point is how enrollment-driven our system of higher education is. Regardless of the type of institution in which one functions and/or whether one is in student affairs or other administrative areas, there are striking similarities in the problems caused by changing enrollments.

## Implications for Student Services

Some of the more obvious future challenges to face American higher education have been enumerated, and these anticipated stresses do provide new opportunities to change for the better. As the challenge for change is great, student services professionals must consider the implications of this new crisis period.

*Professional Preparation and Training.* I believe that an administrator's understanding of the broader societal picture and its implications for the institution will be the largest determinant in whether he or she successfully meets future challenges. This immediately suggests some shifts in the academic preparation of student services administrators. First is the obvious need for a better grasp of the historical and sociological aspects of American higher education and its development in relation to other social institutions. This in turn suggests more preparation as generalists rather than as student development specialists who expect to move up through on-the-job training (Delworth, Hanson, and Associates, 1980).

The doctorate is already becoming the norm, and organizational shifts in higher education are likely to make such preparation even more critical in the future. Individually, student services professionals will need to weigh issues such as holding academic appointments and earning tenure as faculty members simultaneously with service as an administrator, rendering even more important the doctoral degree decision. Academic appointments and teaching service for student services administrators give a greater degree of identification with the faculty and their perspective, as well as that of the student. Tenure also provides a measure of job security but, more importantly, gives a degree of independence that may be critical in standing up to political and other external or internal pressures.

With student affairs dollars becoming more vulnerable, understanding good business/fiscal principles and directing their application will be as important to a program coordinator or dean of students as to the chief business officer. In fact, business skills will be critical if one is to participate in the "total enterprise" effectively and are especially important in demonstrating fiscal responsibility to a president or trustee from the business world.

The rapid development and dependence upon new technologies suggest the need for technical skills in the areas of computer science, mathematical modeling, and systems and data analysis. These skills were not formerly a part of the preparation of student affairs administrators, but the need for such training now is obvious. Whether one is talking about food management systems, the development of a campus student data base, the computerization of records so that housing assignments and admission decisions can be coordinated, needs assessment as a basis of program design and/or evaluation, or energy management systems, technical tasks and skills are now a part of most student services' day-to-day routine.

An ever-broadening knowledge base is also required of the successful student services practitioner. The previously enumerated challenges strongly suggest a campus change agent role for student affairs administrators. To serve effectively in this role, student affairs administrators will need to be effective at presenting ideas and programs to students, faculty, and other administrators and have an adequate grasp of organizational theory, organizational behavior, and the organizational change process.

*Communications Skills and Management Style.* Volumes could be written on the importance of communications skills, and certainly writing and speaking skills have always been important to student services administrators. The treatise by Peters and Waterman (1982) on American corporations offers much cogent advice for the student services administrator. However, with rapid developments in the use of telecommunications technology, these skills will become even more important. Testing job applicants on effective communications skills must begin with the screening and selection process. Of equal importance is the provision of staff development experiences to help continuing staff improve in these areas and to stay abreast of developing technology.

On another level, but of equal importance, is recognition of the need to attend to communication flow within an organization. This involves translation skills at various levels. Student services program development often involves translating theory to practice; that is, selling a program need to superiors, selling the program to subordinates responsible for implementation, and selling program credibility and utilization to students. Translation skills are important when communicating up, down, and across the organization. They are also needed when interpreting institutional goals to student services staff and students or when clarifying student development goals and purposes to other institutional representatives and constituencies. Translation also implies the opportunity for input from others and an ability to handle input counter to one's own sense of direction without appearing to be defensive or "receiving but never using."

The public interest in higher education suggests a need to give increased attention to external communication. The enumeration of future challenges suggests the likelihood of a broadening of external constituencies due to more diverse interests in and involvement in higher education. Student services administrators, along with other administrators in American higher education, must develop clear strategies to deal with parties of "self-interest" and those with legitimate claim to involvement, while maintaining decision-making prerogatives. (Chapter Three devotes more attention to the political dimensions of program decisions.) Preserving one's prerogatives while facing trustees, state commissioners and their staff, or legislators can only require more, not less, skill and planning in the future (Carson, 1960). Adequate advance communication with various publics to preserve or generate their support, without dishonestly using those publics, is also important. Students and faculty are certainly among such publics.

The communication demands and skills required for the future will also influence management style. The more open and the more complete the communication flow, the more flexible must be the style of the successful manager in order to utilize the information generated. This in turn places heavy stress on conceptual ability and the skills of on-the-spot processing and decision making. Insight and the ability to anticipate needs or changes are closely related to conceptual ability. At the same time, the ability to move a concept to reality, be it a plan of action or program design, or to adequately guide subordinate staff in doing so, will become ever more critical to the successful student services administrator.

Developing, in advance, clearly written and concise policy statements in order to guide administrative practices in student affairs is an art of anticipation that also tests one's effectiveness in written communication. This need will continue to be important with our growing legalistic and consumer orientation.

The need for understanding and utilizing good business/ fiscal principles and directing their application is critical to our survival in a future world of shrinking fiscal resources. The bottom line affects *all* of us—program coordinator, dean of students, or chief business officer. Understanding fiscal issues is also important if one is to participate in the "total enterprise" effectively.

The student services administrator of the future must possess sophisticated management and communication skills in order to balance student needs and institutional needs. An adequate grasp of this delicate balance is the key to helping the student services administrator "walk the tightrope" between student and institutional advocacy.

*Organizational Considerations.* A common organizational trap is that of attempting to fit an ideal organizational structure into an already existent institutional setting without regard to individual organizational needs and specific staff strengths and weaknesses. The challenges of the future suggest the need for considerable creativity in organizing student services administrative structures. Further, if all components of the institution take seriously the challenge for more cooperative efforts, organizational lines will likely be less clear across administrative functions such as academic affairs, student affairs, and business services. In fact, the presence of auxiliary services currently within the student affairs area and the blending of academic support services such as admissions and registration with those of student financial aid and new student orientation programs suggest less organizational distinction between the traditional areas within academic institutions. When this trend is coupled with the future challenges enumerated earlier, it appears that flexible assignment of duties across multiple areas, within and outside student affairs, will be the pattern for the successful student services administrator of the future. This shift suggests that individual staff members should certainly be discouraged from possessing a program or piece of turf. Objective evaluation of one's own turf is likely to be colored by the closeness of the relationship, and it is difficult to give up such possessed turf. Chief student services officers must also be wary of turf issues in deciding organizational structures. Where in the organization student affairs reports or which agency is responsible for particular programs is less important than the act of addressing our role in contributing to the total institutional mission. In some cases, it will be more appropriate to propose that units outside the student services division respond programmatically to a particular student need than to utilize our own resources.

This trend toward "program substitution" dictates that more consistent program evaluation and needs assessment be utilized as the basis for program development. Anticipating or discovering institutional needs and effectively translating these needs into viable program designs spells a sure road to success, or at least survival, for a student affairs unit. Staff or units directing needs assessment or research must be properly located within an institution, have sufficient commitment from the top to have legitimacy, and involve decision makers to ensure credibility. If not located within the student affairs area, student services staff must be involved participants in the needs assessment process. However, it is dangerous to assume that all identified needs must be met by traditional student services units. In other words, student services personnel must recognize the distinction between the role of influencing an institution's student programs versus being "saddled" with all student program maintenance responsibilities.

The changes of the next twenty years make obvious the necessity for both long- and short-range planning. Future student affairs administrators must understand the process and participate in institutional planning alongside other campus administrators. Familiarity with planning strategies can free us from a reactive mode and will better enable the programmer to effectively argue the academic and administrative merits of student services program proposals.

## Summary

There is a key role for the student affairs administrator to play in both effecting and responding to the numerous changes which will characterize American higher education of the future. Control of higher education's future rests on many variables and the combined convictions and orchestration of many institutional players. That orchestration, or working together toward a common institutional purpose, is the key to the future of student services. The key to interrelation of purpose and function is both the justification for and the assurance of a future for student affairs. Working toward institutional development is the vehicle for moving student services from a "second-class" status into the institutional mainstream.

Student services administrators of the future must be secure enough to take the risks typical of the profession's past. However, those risks can be taken with a degree of security if the messages suggested by the future challenges are adhered to and student services administrators take the lead in selling their need and viability. The need does exist—a need largely for an institutional sage, or "conscience" if you will, with an "ear to the ground," a wealth of data about student and institutional needs, and an ability to lead the program development process necessary to address ever-changing institutional needs. After adequate preparation, only the delivery of a quality product remains.

## References

Astin, A. W. *Four Critical Years: Effects of College on Beliefs, Attitudes, and Knowledge.* San Francisco: Jossey-Bass, 1977.

Breneman, D. W. "The Coming Enrollment Crisis: Focusing on the Figures." *Change,* 1983, March, pp. 14-15.

Carnegie Council on Policy Studies in Higher Education. *Three Thousand Futures: The Next Twenty Years for Higher Education.* San Francisco: Jossey-Bass, 1980.

Carson, J. J. *Governance of Colleges and Universities.* New York: McGraw-Hill, 1960.

Delworth, U., Hanson, G. R., and Associates. *Student Services: A Handbook for the Profession.* San Francisco: Jossey-Bass, 1980.

Fiske, E. B. "Higher Education's New Economics." *New York Times Magazine,* 1 May 1983, pp. 46-58.

Keller, G. *Academic Strategy: The Management Revolution in American Higher Education.* Baltimore, Md.: Johns Hopkins University Press, 1983.

Kerr, C. "The Uses of the University Two Decades Later: Post-1982." *Change,* 1982, October, pp. 23-31.

Mayhew, L. B. *Surviving the Eighties: Strategies and Procedures for Solving Fiscal and Enrollment Problems.* San Francisco: Jossey-Bass, 1979.

Naisbitt, J. *Megatrends: Ten New Directions Transforming Our Lives.* New York: Warner Books, 1982.

Peters, T. J., and Waterman, R. H., Jr. *In Search of Excellence— Lessons from American's Best-Run Companies.* New York: Harper & Row, 1982.

Powers, D. R., and Powers, M. F. *Making Participatory Management Work: Leadership of Consultive Decision Making in Academic Administration.* San Francisco: Jossey-Bass, 1983.

Margaret J. Barr
Lou A. Keating

14

❧ ❧ ❧ ❧ ❧ ❧ ❧ ❧ ❧ ❧ ❧ ❧ ❧

# Integrating Context, Goals, and Plans

This volume has defined the three necessary elements for successful program design and implementation in student services: the context, the goal, and the plan. Each of the elements is independently important and each element is interdependent on the other two elements. No matter what the programming task, the level of complexity involved in that task, or the context of the program involved, the three elements remain constant. Successful student services programmers must understand each element and master the skills and competencies associated with each element in order to design successful programs. Programs in student services fail for a variety of reasons; however, most often program failures are directly associated with lack of understanding regarding one of the program elements *or* the relationship of the elements to each other.

This volume was designed as a broad-based approach to student services programming. We deliberately chose not to provide a descriptive or "how-to" approach to the functional areas in student services. With this broad view of programming, each of our coauthors provided examples and information designed to increase the reader's understanding of each program element and the complex task of programming.

## Core Knowledge Base

Successful program development in student services requires the practitioner to master a body of knowledge of both a practical and theoretical nature. Core knowledge areas to be mastered include the following:

- *Organizational theory.* Institutions of higher education are complex organizations. Understanding of organizational theory provides a foundation to explain and predict the dynamics of the institution and each student services unit. As practitioners acquire responsibility for more complex programming and management tasks, mastery of the principles of organizational theory becomes increasingly important.
- *Student and human development theory.* Student services professionals who participate in academic preparation programs in college student personnel, counseling, and higher education administration usually have developed a strong foundation in human and student development theory, while professionals who come to student services programs from other disciplines need to work actively to acquire that foundation. Engaging in student services program development without the requisite theoretical foundation can lead to unsuccessful programs; in addition, professional biases, institutional political pressures, and tradition have a much greater chance to affect the development of programs. Senior student services administrators also carry the additional responsibility of translating human and student development theory into constructs and concepts that can readily be understood and supported by others in the institution.
- *Management theory.* Management and programming cannot be separated. Successful program development requires the

application of sound management principles in the use of human and fiscal resources. Professionals with responsibility for supervision and budget have the greatest need to acquire this foundation.

- *History of higher education.* The prepared practitioner will have a thorough knowledge of the history of American higher education in general and of the institution of current employment in particular. At a minimum, new staff members should understand the history of the institution prior to engaging in new program development. Mid-level managers and senior student services administrators must also be able to relate the unique institutional history to the historical development of American higher education.

- *Educational philosophy.* The history and philosophy of American higher education are inextricably intertwined. In both the chapter on politics (Chapter Three) and the chapter on the institutional view of student services (Chapter Two), the importance of understanding the institutional mission and philosophy was highlighted. All student services programmers must understand the educational philosophy of their institution, and senior programmers must be able to effectively link that philosophy to program ideas in order to assure institutional support.

- *Institutional governance.* Colleges and universities have complex administrative structures. Decisions are governed by rules, regulations, committee prerogatives, and approval procedures. Each institutional governance structure is unique and must be accounted for in program plans. Experienced professionals have a responsibility to instruct new and less experienced staff with regard to governance prerogatives and to provide standard information to all staff with regard to governance. New staff members should actively seek information in this area.

- *Policies and procedures.* Each student services programmer must acquire knowledge of basic policies and procedures that may influence program planning. These include but are not limited to purchasing, affirmative action, fiscal policies, accounting, and use of student records. The variation in administrative procedures among institutions is enormous. Ignorance in this core knowledge area is *not* bliss, for lack of knowledge or inattention to appropriate procedures can cause irreparable damage to program plans.

- *Fiscal management.* Senior-level programmers must have a broad-based understanding of institutional budgets, accounting reports, and revenue stream projections. Student services programs require investment of resources, and sound program development requires both understanding and the ability to apply basic budgeting and cost-projection techniques. Each programmer must be able to outline and justify the expenditures associated with the program effort. At a minimum, mid-management professionals need to develop fiscal management knowledge that permits weighing alternatives in fiscal expenditures.
- *Application of new technology.* Advances in computer technology, information processing, and video capabilities are proceeding at a rapid rate. Student services professionals must remain current with regard to technological advances and their potential application to program development and maintenance.
- *Current issues.* Institutions of higher education and their many constituencies are dynamic and changing entities. The astute programmer makes a conscious attempt to remain current on issues both on and off the campus. Programmers can then use this knowledge to monitor current program activities and assess methods to adjust for changing conditions in program efforts.

We believe that each of these ten core knowledge areas represents a necessary knowledge base for the establishment of successful student services programs. Sophistication in each of these core knowledge areas will be enhanced and developed through experience and practice and will be required in varying degrees according to the programmer's level of responsibility. However, basic knowledge in each of these ten areas is essential for all programmers. Knowledge alone is not enough; the ability to translate that knowledge into practice is essential for successful programming. Therefore, in the next section the core skills necessary for student services program development will be addressed.

## Core Skills and Competencies

Core skills necessary for the successful development and implementation of effective student services programs are by definition wide in range and scope. For purposes of this discussion, it is assumed that student services professionals are committed to the ideals of the academy and have the qualities to be effective contributors to the academy. All professionals in higher education, whatever their specific role and function, should possess qualities related to intellectual curiosity, academic inquiry, critical thinking, and knowledge of an academic discipline. In addition to these broad qualities of commitment to and support of the intellectual life, there are additional core skills and competencies that are necessary for successful program development in student services.

Delworth and Yarris (1978) define skills as the ability to "do what we now think or feel we should do" (p. 3) and competence "as a combination of 'cognitions,' 'affect,' and 'skills' " (p. 3). Knowledge of both what should be done and how to do it are equally important components of effective programming. The set of core skills and competencies, grouped here into three broad areas, should be a standard against which programmers can assess their own professional skills and abilities.

*Broad Professional Competencies.* Delworth, Hanson, and Associates (1980) identified seven professional competency areas for student services professionals. Four (assessment and evaluation, consultation, counseling, and instruction) were evaluated as major competency areas for all professionals. Three additional, more complex professional competencies (program development, environmental assessment and redesign, and the training of paraprofessionals) were also cited. Our focus here is on the complex competency of program development and the specific competencies required to engage in that task. We believe that, in order to acquire mastery over program development, specific attention must be paid to the acquisition of skills in the following areas:

- *Interpersonal communication skills.* Program development requires working with people who must understand and support each other. The successful programmer has highly developed skills in both the content and process of interpersonal communication.
- *Group facilitation skills.* Because much of the work of program development occurs in a group setting, these skills are essential to the program development process.
- *Supervision skills.* Student services programs require the work of professional staff, support staff, student paraprofessionals, volunteers, and students to be organized and productive. Supervision skills assist the programmer in accomplishing that goal.
- *Assessment and evaluation skills.* Throughout this volume, implicit and explicit reference was made to this set of essential skills, particularly when dealing with the critical program element of the context.

*Specific Programming Skills.* The development of programs in student services requires an amalgamation of skills from the four basic areas previously defined by Delworth and Hanson (1980). These include the following:

- *Budgeting.* All programs use resources, and the skilled programmer must be able to develop a budget and use that budget as a tool to meet programming goals.
- *Professional writing.* Very often plans need to be communicated in writing. The programmer needs to work to develop skills in cogent, effective written presentation of program plans.
- *Goal setting.* The development of specific, measurable goals and objectives for student services programs is essential. Lack of skill in this area can cause diffuse and ineffective program efforts.
- *Work organization.* One of the essential skills in effective

program development is the ability of the programmer to design a series of incremental tasks toward a program goal. Tasks do interrelate and organization of those tasks in a logical plan goes a long way toward assuring program success.

- *Idea generation.* The skill required here, although program directed, is based on the broad professional competency of group facilitation and interpersonal communication. The skilled programmer is able to assist others in exercising their creativity in developing new approaches to old problems.
- *Conflict resolution.* Again, this skill is derived from a broad professional competency in interpersonal communication. It is essential in programming, however, that specific attention be paid to the ability of the programmer to identify potential sources of conflict and assist in the resolution of these conflicts.
- *Resource allocation.* A skilled programmer is able to appropriately allocate human, fiscal, and space resources in support of the program effort. This skill is related to the skill of budgeting but is more broad based in that it requires the programmer to assess the use of *all* resources.
- *Public speaking.* In both the development stage of a program and the actual implementation of the program plan, presentations before groups are often required. Programmers need to intentionally devote attention to their ability to effectively present concepts in such settings.

These specific programming skills are certainly not exhaustive. Our intent has been to highlight the intradisciplinary nature of programs and the broad range of competencies necessary for successful programming efforts.

*Personal/Professional Skills and Perspectives.* In addition to the specific skills and the broad professional competencies, successful programmers need to attend to their individual skill development and keep an appropriate perspective on their work. Some areas to contemplate and assess on a personal level include the following:

- *Time management.* For all of us who are excited about our work, the risk of overcommitment is great. Acquisition of skills in time management assists in organizing the work at hand and assuring time for personal activities.

- *Patience.* Program development takes time, and it is essential that patience be exercised during the process. We may want to get it done now, but now may not be the most opportune time.
- *A sense of humor.* Being able to gain perspective through judicious exercise of a sense of humor may be the most important skill of all for the student services programmer.
- *Developing support.* Personal and professional support systems can help each of us retain our perspective, solve problems, and gain ideas. Professional support networks both on and off the campus are essential elements in one's personal/professional life.
- *Continued growth.* Investment in yourself as a professional is also essential. Successful programmers read the literature, participate in professional development activities, and continually strive to become more skilled and knowledgeable in their approach to professional work.

These major areas of skill development were derived from the chapters in this volume. Additional skills can and probably should be identified. However, if attention is paid to the initial acquisition of core knowledge and skills in these specified areas, then the development of programs in student services will be greatly enhanced.

### Program Planning Guide

Each professional will approach the task of program planning from a unique perspective. However, there are basic questions that need to be answered by the programmer at each stage of the program planning process.

- *Preplanning.* This stage of program development provides essential background for any program effort. The questions to be answered at this point focus on the elements of context and goal.

1. What is the history, philosophy, and mission of the institution?
2. What demographic data are available about the student body?
3. What are the governance structures of the campus?
4. What do we know about student/human development that may be applicable to students in this setting?
5. What are the perceived and real areas of responsibility, territory, and authority on the campus?
6. What are potential sources for critical information on the campus?

The programmer will not get definitive answers to all these questions. These questions, however, provide guidance with regard to areas of concern that may emerge later in the program development process.

• *Idea generation.* At this stage, program planners have acquired baseline information with regard to the context of program development and general goals that may be appropriate in that context. Questions now focus on the process of development of program ideas.

1. Who should be involved in generating program ideas?
2. What information do we have about current efforts?
3. What needs/priorities are currently not being addressed on the campus?
4. What potential and current resources are available to support program efforts?
5. What dreams do significant constituency groups hold for the campus?

• *Idea focusing.* This stage takes the broad range of ideas and begins the process of narrowing the proposed scope of activities.

1. Is the idea congruent with the context?
2. Is the idea based on sound, theoretically based principles?
3. Will the idea make a significant difference on the campus? Or for students?

4. Who needs to review and have input into further development of the idea?
5. Which idea is *most* important to concentrate on at this point in time?

• *Goal setting.* After the idea is chosen and focused, attention needs to be paid to the goals of the program intervention.

1. What are the overarching purposes of the intervention?
2. What specific outcomes can be attributed to the planned program?
3. What makes this program intervention qualitatively unique from current program efforts?
4. Can the proposed goals be met through current programs or modification of current efforts?

• *Initial design.* After the goals are established, increasingly specific questions need to be asked.

1. What methods are appropriate for the program?
2. What is the specific target of the program intervention?
3. What resources are available (human, fiscal, and space) to support the program?
4. What organizational problems may arise as a result of the planned program?
5. What strategies can be employed to maximize support for the program?

• *Planning.* After the initial design questions are broadly answered, then again more specific questions need to be answered.

1. Do we have the skills and competencies available to develop the program?
2. If we are missing skills and competencies, where can they be acquired?
3. What is the target date for program implementation?

4.  What specific tasks need to be accomplished at what time to meet the specified target date?
5.  What institutional procedures may support or detract from the program implementation plan?
6.  Are resources committed to the program and are they sufficient to accomplish the task?
7.  How will the program effort be judged?
8.  What people need to be involved at this stage?
9.  What approvals are necessary to proceed?
10. What details need to be attended to prior to implementation?

• *Implementation.* Questions with regard to implementation focus on who, what, when, and where.

1.  Who is responsible for specific tasks?
2.  What detailed tasks need to be accomplished?
3.  When will the program or programs be implemented?
4.  Where will the program be located?
5.  Who will take responsibility for ongoing program maintenance?

• *Evaluation.* Each and every student services program needs to be monitored and evaluated. A number of criteria are useful and appropriate to determine whether the program is of value to the campus community. Answers to the following questions will aid in that process.

1.  Does the program meet the stated goals?
2.  Is the program making the most efficient and effective use of resources?
3.  Are there elements of the program that need to be modified to enhance program effectiveness?
4.  Should the commitment to the program be reevaluated in order to meet other pressing needs or priorities within the institution?

Often these evaluation questions are answered in other

stages of the program development process. However, specific attention must and should be given to such questions in order to enhance student services programs on the campus.

## Summary

Program development is not a static process and the task of successful program development is complex and difficult. We believe, however, that the process of program development remains constant across functional units of student affairs and only the content and the complexity of the task varies.

For all programs, the three program elements must be accounted for and the process of program development must be theory-based, intentional, and goal-directed.

The guided questions to program development presented in this chapter will not always flow logically from one step to another. New data become available, new contextual issues arise, and student and institutional needs can and will change. Thus, the program planning guide provides direction and a check on program development. Each practitioner can use the guide as a tool to assure that the three elements of programs are accounted for in all phases of the program, and programmers must acquire and use a range of core knowledge and skills to assure program success. The skills and competencies and the knowledge base necessary for successful program development will by necessity become more sophisticated over time.

## References

Delworth, U., Hanson, G. R., and Associates. *Student Services: A Handbook for the Profession.* San Francisco: Jossey-Bass, 1980.

Delworth, U., and Yarris, E. "Concepts and Processes for the New Training Role." In U. Delworth (Ed.), *New Directions for Student Services: Training Competent Staff,* no. 2. San Francisco: Jossey-Bass, 1978.

❦ ❦ ❦ ❦ ❦ ❦ ❦ ❦ ❦ ❦ ❦ ❦ ❦

# Annotated Bibliography

John L. Baier, Margaret J. Barr
Gary R. Hanson, Bernard D. Yancey
Lou A. Keating, Gary H. Knock

American College Personnel Association, Tomorrow's Higher
Education Project. (T. K. Miller, Chair) "A Student Develop-
ment Model for Student Affairs in Tomorrow's Education."
*Journal of College Student Personnel,* 1975, *16,* 334–341.
This report of a conference called to advance Phase II of the
American College Personnel Association's Tomorrow's Higher
Education Project outlines a process model for student devel-
opment.

American Council on Education. *The Student Personnel Point
of View.* American Council on Education Studies, Series 1,
Vol. 1, No. 3. Washington, D.C.: American Council on Education, 1937. This definitive statement on the nature of student personnel work in higher education imposes on colleges
and universities an obligation to consider each student as a
whole and to conceive of education as more than intellectual
development.

American Council on Education, Committee on Student Personnel Work. (E. G. Williamson, Chair) *The Student Personnel*

*Point of View.* (Rev. ed.) American Council on Education Studies, Series 6, No. 13. Washington, D.C.: American Council on Education, 1949. This revised edition of the student personnel point of view provided a definitive basis for professional practice for more than twenty years.

Appleton, J. R., Briggs, C. M., and Rhatigan, J. J. "A Corrective Look Backward." In H. F. Owens, C. H. Witten, and W. R. Bailey (Eds.), *College Student Personnel Administration.* Springfield, Ill.: Thomas, 1982. Believing that few student affairs administrators view historical forces and issues as relevant or important to the present state of student personnel administration and that this perspective is a grievous miscalculation, the authors demonstrate that current practice is tied to the past. Understanding gained from historical examination should help current student affairs administrators to function with greater confidence and perspective.

Baldridge, J. V. *Power and Conflict in the University.* New York: Wiley, 1971. This volume brings the politics of higher education out of the closet. Cogent analysis of internal institutional political issues is offered and methods are presented to help the practitioner not only survive but flourish within a politicized environment.

Barr, M. J., and Keating, L. A. (Eds.). *New Directions for Student Services: Establishing Effective Programs,* no. 7. San Francisco: Jossey-Bass, 1979. This sourcebook discusses the procedures and processes involved in all phases of student services program development. Chapters on political and staff issues and on creating, maintaining, and terminating quality programs for students are written by practitioners for practitioners and will be especially useful to the new professional.

Berdie, R. F. "Student Personnel Work: Definition and Redefinition." *Journal of College Student Personnel,* 1966, 7, 131–136. The address by a former president of the American College Personnel Association focuses on student personnel work as the application of knowledge and principles derived from the social and behavioral sciences. The student personnel worker is regarded as a behavioral scientist whose subject matter is the student and whose sociopsychological sphere is the college.

Brouwer, P. J. *Student Personnel Services in General Education.* Washington, D.C.: American Council on Education, 1949. This report of a five-year study in general education provides analyses of ways to identify and satisfy needs of college students. Practices in student personnel work are related to principles of a personnel philosophy of education. The emphasis of the report is on a unified program of student personnel work as an integral part of general education.

Brown, R. D. *Student Development in Tomorrow's Higher Education—A Return to the Academy.* Washington, D.C.: American College Personnel Association, 1972. This review and reconceptualization of the basic assumptions of college student services provides a discussion of the philosophical bases for implementing model student services. This monograph represents Phase I of the American College Personnel Association's Tomorrow's Higher Education Project.

Brown, S. "An Evaluation Process for Student Affairs Agencies." *NASPA Journal,* 1981, *18* (4), 2-13. This article outlines the various purposes of student services program evaluation and considerations affecting evaluation design. The author then describes the development of a specific program evaluation process (including constitution of an evaluation team) and analyzes the strengths and weaknesses of the process.

Brubacher, J. S., and Rudy, W. *Higher Education in Transition, An American History, 1936-1976.* (3d ed.). New York: Harper & Row, 1976. This third edition of an educational history published first in 1958 provides in-depth considerations of developments that have shaped and fashioned higher education in the United States since the founding of Harvard College to the mid-1970s.

Canon, H. J. "Developing Staff Potential." In U. Delworth, G. R. Hanson, and Associates (Eds.), *Student Services: A Handbook for the Profession*. San Francisco: Jossey-Bass, 1980. The author provides an excellent summary of the rationale and components for division-wide staff development programs. Staff development programs are necessary for at least three reasons: to provide remediation, to provide enhanced accountability, and to fulfill professional duty. Successful staff development programs utilize a staff committee to design, implement, and evaluate the various programs, require the active support and participation of the chief student affairs officers, and include a variety of programs presented at various times and in various formats. Canon offers examples of selected staff development programs and identifies and discusses the problems and pitfalls to establishing effective division-wide staff development programs.

Creamer, D. G. (Ed.). *Student Development in Higher Education: Theories, Practices, and Future Directions*. Washington, D.C.: American College Personnel Association, 1980. Issues in student development, unresolved questions, and controversial matters in the broad field of student services are presented and analyzed by eighteen authors. Major themes considered are theories, concepts, and issues; environmental considerations; practices and future directions; and professional and institutional constraints.

Crookston, B. B. "Student Personnel—All Hail and Farewell." *Personnel and Guidance Journal*, 1976, *55*, 26-29. On the basis of educational philosophy and research in organizational development, the author concludes that the term *student personnel work* should be given its due and retired into history; *student affairs* should be used to describe the administrative subdivision of a college or university concerned with student development; and *student development* is the term that should be used to describe the concept, philosophy, underlying theories, and methodologies used in settings in which student development occurs.

Deegan, W. L. *Managing Student Affairs Programs: Methods, Models, Muddles.* Palm Springs, Calif.: ETC Publications, 1981. Consideration of the management issues facing the student affairs profession is provided by the author in order to stimulate reflection and action in improving the quality of the theory and practice of management of student affairs programs in colleges and universities.

Delworth, U., and Hanson, G. R., and Associates (Eds.). *Student Services: A Handbook for the Profession.* San Francisco: Jossey-Bass, 1980. This comprehensive book provides perspectives on the identification, assessment, and evaluation of ideas and competencies that can influence students. The book is intended for both the experienced professional and the beginning graduate student. Five major topics are considered: growth and status of student services, theoretical bases of the profession, models for practice, essential competencies and techniques, and organization and management.

Fried, J. (Ed.). *New Directions for Student Services: Education for Student Development,* no. 15. San Francisco: Jossey-Bass, 1981. For this volume, a broad definition of developmental instruction has been chosen that aligns developmental education with humanistic education. The contributors reflect a recognition that much developmental instruction in colleges and universities is conducted by members of the student affairs staff.

Hanson, G. R. (Ed.). *New Directions for Student Services: Measuring Student Development,* no. 20. San Francisco: Jossey-Bass, 1982. This volume examines what is known about measurement of student development. Also provided is a review of available assessment instruments and a case study of how a student development program used assessment results for programming purposes.

Harrington, T. F. *Student Personnel Work in Urban Colleges.* New York: Intext Educational Publishers, 1974. This book is directed primarily to individuals involved in college student personnel work on an urban campus. However, the ideas presented by the author and the contributing authors are valuable to those concerned with higher education in general. A unique feature of the book is presentation of a framework for college student personnel work in urban settings.

Harvey, T. "Student Development and the Future of Higher Education: A Force Analysis." *Journal of College Student Personnel,* 1976, *17* (2), 90-95. Harvey identifies nine variables that act as driving or restraining forces to the full integration of student development in higher education. The author believes that in the interplay of these variables, the driving force of the future will be toward student development and toward a greater faculty involvement in student personnel functions.

Henry, D. D. *Challenges Past, Challenges Present: An Analysis of American Higher Education Since 1980.* San Francisco: Jossey-Bass, 1975. In this report for the Carnegie Council on Policy Studies in Higher Education, the author examines higher education from the Depression to the so-called new depression of higher education in the 1970s.

Huebner, L. A. (Ed.). *New Directions for Student Services: Redesigning Campus Environments,* no. 8. San Francisco: Jossey-Bass, 1979. After a review of emergent issues of ecosystems theory and practice, this sourcebook describes four applications of the "ecosystems perspective" to program planning (in residence halls, dean of students office, a medi-

cal school, and a small college). The final chapter critiques
the four projects and outlines advantages and difficulties inherent in the "ecological" approach to program development.

Kantor, R. M., and Stein, B. A. *Life in Organizations.* New
York: Basic Books, 1979. This volume provides insight on
what really goes on inside organizations. Underlying themes
of organizational life are identified and principles of organizational behavior are articulated. Kantor and Stein use extensive examples from higher education, government, and business to illustrate their points. The volume is particularly useful to the student services practitioner seeking to understand
just how a college or university operates.

Keller, G. *Academic Strategy: The Management Revolution in
American Higher Education.* Baltimore, Md.: Johns Hopkins
University Press, 1983. Keller's extensive study of current
problems and trends in American higher education pinpoints
changes that must occur if the enterprise is to continue to
flourish. His conclusions with regard to the efforts of high
technology, accountability, and new student populations
have great significance for student services programs.

Knock, G. H. (Ed.). *Perspectives on the Preparation of Student
Affairs Professionals.* Washington, D.C.: American College
Personnel Association, 1977. This book provides a series of
six position papers regarding professional preparation for the
field of student affairs. Each paper is followed by a statement
of reaction. No attempt has been made to provide a consensus view, and differences in philosophical and pedagogical
orientations are evident.

Levine, A. *When Dreams and Heroes Died: A Portrait of Today's College Student.* San Francisco: Jossey-Bass, 1980. A
documented description of today's college students, this re-

port for the Carnegie Council on Policy Studies in Higher Education points out the dangers of stereotyping and cautions educators against formation of policies and practices based on misconceptions about college students.

Lloyd-Jones, E. McD., and Smith, M. R. *A Student Personnel Program for Higher Education.* New York: McGraw-Hill, 1938. This book outlines the scope of a total student personnel program as defined and interpreted at the time of publication. The book is a very useful reference to the person seeking an understanding of the philosophical and organizational roots of student personnel services in higher education.

Martin, J. *Applications Development Without Programmers.* Englewood Cliffs, N.J.: Prentice-Hall, 1982. This volume is a nontechnical discussion of strategies and approaches for effectively using computers, or how to be one of the survivors of the computer revolution. The book is filled with case study examples of actual applications. Some topics discussed include people costs versus computer costs, the changing DP environment, application development without conventional programming, languages for end users, data base user languages, and application generators, to mention a few. This book should be required reading for any administrator considering an application using computers and for all data processing administrators.

Martin, J. *Strategic Data-Planning Methodologies.* Englewood Cliffs, N.J.: Prentice-Hall, 1982. This book provides a nontechnical discussion of how to design, implement, and use data bases. Some of the topics covered are the need for top management involvement, developing models, top-down planning, and planning for data distribution, to mention a few. This book is particularly suited to any administrator who must rely on data stored in data bases or analysis of such data in his decision making.

Merkle, H. B., and Artman, R. B. "Staff Development: A Systematic Process for Student Affairs Leaders." *NASPA Jour-*

*nal,* 1983, *21,* 55-63. This article briefly outlines the steps for planning staff development programs. It discusses the importance of staff development and the role of the chief student affairs officer, presents a systematic process for designing and implementing staff development programs, and identifies some of the obstacles to successful staff development efforts. The article also includes an excellent summary of recent literature on the subject and includes a useful bibliography.

Miller, T. K., and Prince, J. S. *The Future of Student Affairs: A Guide to Student Development for Tomorrow's Higher Education.* San Francisco: Jossey-Bass, 1976. The authors provide a process model for helping college students learn developmental skills as a guide to implementation of the student development philosophy. Specific examples of existing student development projects and programs are cited.

Morrill, W. H., and Hurst, J. C. (Eds.). *Dimensions of Intervention for Student Development.* New York: Wiley, 1980. This book proposes a two-part conceptual foundation for student affairs (student development and environmental development), and then outlines the target, purpose, method, and evaluation of student services program interventions (the "cube" model) in light of the student-environment development concept. In the section on intervention programs, practitioners from eight student services program areas (orientation, unions, unique populations, and so on) describe specific applications of the student-environment model.

Mueller, K. H. *Student Personnel Work in Higher Education.* Boston: Houghton Mifflin, 1961. This book offers a comprehensive analysis and overview of student personnel work with respect to historical and philosophical development and modes of professional practice.

Owens, J. F., Witten, C. H., and Bailey, W. R. (Eds.). *College Student Personnel Administration—An Anthology.* Springfield, Ill.: Thomas, 1982. This volume is a collection of particularized writings that have been thoughtfully assembled for study and comparison. The topical divisions of the book include student personnel administration: an introduction; philosophical foundations; the modern college student; organization, administration, and program effectiveness; legal issues; professionalism and the student affairs administrator; and the future of student affairs.

Parker, C. A. "Student Development: What Does It Mean?" *Journal of College Student Personnel,* 1974, *15,* 248-256. Three uses of the term *student development*—humanism, complexity, and developmental stage theory—are considered, with a case made for the latter as most useful to student personnel work. Two examples of the use of developmental stage theory in changing student personnel structures are described.

Parker, C. A. (Ed.). *Encouraging Development in College Students.* Minneapolis: University of Minnesota Press, 1978. Following an introductory chapter that provides a discussion of the current state of development theory, student development programs, and the origins of college student personnel work, a series of theory and practice presentations are offered. Some of these presentations focus on international programs of student development while others consider theoretical perspectives of human development.

Penny, J. F. "Student Personnel Work: A Profession Stillborn." *Personnel and Guidance Journal,* 1969, *47,* 968-972. This critical analysis of the professional status of college student personnel work reflects the author's belief that status as a profession has not been achieved by the field nor has recognition and acceptance as a vital aspect of the academic world been achieved.

Portman, D. N. (Ed.). *Early Reform in American Higher Education.* Chicago: Nelson-Hall, 1972. The essays in this collection represent the educational convictions of some of the early reformers of the post-Civil War period on such topics as liberal education, academic freedom, the idea of a university, the state university in America, higher education for women, and the values of a classical education.

Rhatigan, J. J. "Student Services versus Student Development: Is There a Difference?" *Journal of the National Association of Women Deans, Administrators, and Counselors,* 1975, 38 (2), 51-59. While challenging certain assumptions and positions of student development theory and student development devotees, the author offers four suggestions in regard to professional practice in the future. In addition, the author examines the notion that a services perspective is inappropriate for student affairs professionals. He intimates that if there is a difference between concepts of student services and student development, there need not be.

Rudolph, F. *The American College and University—A History.* New York: Vintage Books, 1962. This readable yet scholarly book gives the reader historical understanding of how and why and with what consequences higher education in the United States has developed.

Rudolph, F. *Curriculum: A History of the American Undergraduate Course of Study Since 1636.* San Francisco: Jossey-Bass, 1978. The author provides an in-depth perspective on the development of the American undergraduate curriculum over the past three and a half centuries.

Russel, J. D. (Ed.). *Student Personnel Services in Colleges and Universities.* Chicago: University of Chicago Press, 1941. This volume is the Proceedings of the Institute for Administrative Officers of Higher Institutions (1940) held at the University of Chicago. The six half-day sessions considered: the obligation of the institution to its students, administrative organization for student personnel services, institutional provisions for understanding students, interpretations and use of data in counseling students, the extra-classroom life of the student, and evaluations of student personnel services.

Saddlemire, G. L., and Rentz, A. L. (Eds.). *Student Affairs: A Profession's Heritage.* Washington, D.C.: American College Personnel Association, 1984. Fifty-five directors of professional preparation programs assisted the editors in the selection of materials that reflect the basic assumptions, concepts, and rationales of the student affairs profession. The book makes available articles authored by early writers who contributed to the initial stages of professional development, as well as significant documents and statements by professional associations, commissions, and committees. Understanding of the evolution of the student affairs profession is enhanced by direct exposure to the literature of the profession's heritage.

Sanford, N. *Where Colleges Fail: A Study of the Student as a Person.* San Francisco: Jossey-Bass, 1967. The thesis developed by the author is that institutions of higher education should have as their primary goal the individual development of each student enrolled. The author advocates creation of a developmental community in which forces that challenge an individual's present capabilities are balanced by those that provide personal support.

Shaffler, R. H., and Martinson, W. D. *Student Personnel Services in Higher Education.* New York: Center for Applied Research in Education, 1966. The focus of this book is on defining ways in which institutional resources and student energies may be directed so that the greatest possible educational gain may result. This book is valuable historically in that it depicts models of student services based on the student personnel point of view.

Stamatakos, L. C. "Student Affairs Progress Toward Professionalism: Recommendations for Action—Part 1." *Journal of College Student Personnel,* 1981, *22,* 105-113. Stamatakos, L. C. "Student Affairs Progress Toward Professionalism: Recommendations for Action—Part 2." *Journal of College Student Personnel,* 1981, *22* (3), 197-207. In this two-part treatise, the author examines the progress of student affairs toward becoming a profession on eight traditional criteria used originally by Wrenn and Darley in 1949. Recommendations follow analysis on each criterion.

Thomas, L. E., and Good-Benson, P. "Supervision: A Key Element in Training." In U. Delworth (Ed.), *New Directions for Student Services: Training Competent Staff,* no. 2. San Francisco: Jossey-Bass, 1978. In order to effectively provide student services, proper supervision of staff is necessary. This article briefly describes several innovative approaches to assessing training needs, establishing training schedules, and developing supervision agreements. It also provides an excellent checklist for supervisors and supervisees and an example of a typical supervisory session.

Tollefson, A. L. *New Approaches to College Student Development.* New York: Behavioral Publications, 1975. Consideration of new ways of creating closer relationships between student services and the efforts of faculty are presented in this book. The author also calls for development of courses with nontraditional content that have promise of contributing to students' personal growth.

Walker, D. E. *The Effective Administrator: A Practical Approach to Problem Solving, Decision Making, and Campus Leadership.* San Francisco: Jossey-Bass, 1979. This volume, although by no means a scholarly approach to managing higher education, provides practical insight and wisdom from a presidential perspective. The book is both entertaining and insightful.

Williamson, E. G. (Ed.). *Trends in Student Personnel Work.* Minneapolis: University of Minnesota Press, 1949. This collection of papers read at a conference at the University of Minnesota provides an overview of developments in American higher education during the past quarter century. The intent of the conference was to celebrate a quarter century of student personnel work at the University of Minnesota and to honor Professor Donald G. Patterson.

Wrenn, C. G., and Darley, J. G. "An Appraisal of the Professional Status of Personnel Work." In E. G. Williamson (Ed.), *Trends in Student Personnel Work.* Minneapolis: University of Minnesota Press, 1949. This paper provides an appraisal of the professional status of college student personnel work on criteria of a profession originally advanced by B. J. Horton in *Scientific Monthly* of February, 1944.

# Index

341